T0224413

IFIP Advances in Information and Communication Technology 421

IFIP – The International Federation for Information Processing

IFIP was founded in 1960 under the auspices of UNESCO, following the First World Computer Congress held in Paris the previous year. An umbrella organization for societies working in information processing, IFIP's aim is two-fold: to support information processing within its member countries and to encourage technology transfer to developing nations. As its mission statement clearly states,

> *IFIP's mission is to be the leading, truly international, apolitical organization which encourages and assists in the development, exploitation and application of information technology for the bene t of all people.*

IFIP is a non-profitmaking organization, run almost solely by 2500 volunteers. It operates through a number of technical committees, which organize events and publications. IFIP's events range from an international congress to local seminars, but the most important are:

- The IFIP World Computer Congress, held every second year;
- Open conferences;
- Working conferences.

The flagship event is the IFIP World Computer Congress, at which both invited and contributed papers are presented. Contributed papers are rigorously refereed and the rejection rate is high.

As with the Congress, participation in the open conferences is open to all and papers may be invited or submitted. Again, submitted papers are stringently refereed.

The working conferences are structured differently. They are usually run by a working group and attendance is small and by invitation only. Their purpose is to create an atmosphere conducive to innovation and development. Refereeing is also rigorous and papers are subjected to extensive group discussion.

Publications arising from IFIP events vary. The papers presented at the IFIP World Computer Congress and at open conferences are published as conference proceedings, while the results of the working conferences are often published as collections of selected and edited papers.

Any national society whose primary activity is about information processing may apply to become a full member of IFIP, although full membership is restricted to one society per country. Full members are entitled to vote at the annual General Assembly, National societies preferring a less committed involvement may apply for associate or corresponding membership. Associate members enjoy the same benefits as full members, but without voting rights. Corresponding members are not represented in IFIP bodies. Affiliated membership is open to non-national societies, and individual and honorary membership schemes are also offered.

Marit Hansen   Jaap-Henk Hoepman
Ronald Leenes   Diane Whitehouse (Eds.)

Privacy and Identity Management for Emerging Services and Technologies

8th IFIP WG 9.2, 9.5, 9.6/11.7, 11.4, 11.6
International Summer School
Nijmegen, The Netherlands, June 17-21, 2013
Revised Selected Papers

 Springer

Volume Editors

Marit Hansen
Unabhängiges Landeszentrum für Datenschutz Schleswig-Holstein
Holstenstr. 98, 24103 Kiel, Germany
E-mail: marit.hansen@privacyresearch.eu

Jaap-Henk Hoepman
Radboud University Nijmegen, Digital Security / Privacy and Identity Lab
P.O. Box 9010, 6500 GL Nijmegen, The Netherlands
E-mail: jhh@cs.ru.nl

Ronald Leenes
Tilburg University, Tilburg Institute for Law, Technology, and Society (TILT)
P.O. Box 90153, 5000 LE Tilburg, The Netherlands
E-mail: r.e.leenes@tilburguniversity.edu

Diane Whitehouse
The Castlegate Consultancy
27, Castlegate, Malton, YO17 7DP, UK
E-mail: diane.whitehouse@thecastlegateconsultancy.com

ISSN 1868-4238   e-ISSN 1868-422X
ISBN 978-3-662-52572-2   e-ISBN 978-3-642-55137-6
DOI 10.1007/978-3-642-55137-6
Springer Heidelberg New York Dordrecht London

Typesetting: Camera-ready by author, data conversion by Scientific Publishing Services, Chennai, India

Printed on acid-free paper

Springer is part of Springer Science+Business Media (www.springer.com)

Preface

Current technological trends such as Web 2.0, mobile applications, cloud computing, big data analysis, and sensor technologies lead to the gathering and processing of more and more personal information. In such a situation, the privacy of individuals is at stake. In 2012, several legislative initiatives that may foster better privacy protection were introduced or proposed, among them the United States' Consumer Privacy Bill of Rights, Australia's Privacy Amendment (Enhancing Privacy Protection) Bill, and the European Data Protection Regulation that promotes "data protection by design" and "data protection by default." In addition, the European Commission proclaimed 2013 as the European Year of Citizens and encouraged public debate about the rights associated with European citizenship. In this context, how can individuals' rights to privacy be achieved in an effective way considering the rapid and far-reaching changes stemming from emerging information and communication technologies and services? What frameworks and tools are needed to gain, regain, and maintain self-determination of the dissemination and use of information, and of lifelong privacy? These were the crucial questions raised at the 8th International Summer School on Privacy and Identity Management for Emerging Services and Technologies.

During June 17–21, 2013, the International Federation for Information Processing (IFIP) working groups 9.2 (Social Accountability and Computing), 9.5 (Virtuality and Society), 9.6/11.7 (IT Misuse and the Law), 11.4 (Network Security), and 11.6 (Identity Management) held a summer school in Berg en Dal in The Netherlands. Its focus was on privacy and identity management for emerging services and technologies.

The 2013 summer school was again a successful event. Some 70 people attended, of whom the vast majority were young researchers. While the youngest had recently graduated with a bachelor's degree, another had been awarded his PhD just one month before the school took place. The school hosted student participants from 14 countries: Belgium, Denmark, Estonia, France, Germany, Greece, The Netherlands, Norway, Slovenia, Sweden, Switzerland, the UK, as well as Canada and India.

The aim of this series of eight IFIP summer schools has been to encourage young academic and industry participants to share their own ideas about privacy and identity management and related issues in a rigorous and academic manner, and to build up collegial relationships with others. Over the years, the schools have been introducing participants to the various legal, organizational, and social implications of information technology through a continuing process of informed discussion.

Following the school's holistic approach, contributions that combined technical, social, ethical, or legal perspectives were especially solicited. As in previous years, a diverse group of participants – ranging from young doctoral students to leading researchers in the field from academia, industry, and government – responded and engaged in discussions, dialogues, and debates in an informal and supportive setting. The interdisciplinary, and international, emphasis of the summer school enabled a broad understanding of the issues in both social and technical spheres.

Each day of the school started with morning introductory lectures by invited speakers, followed by parallel workshops and seminars in the afternoons. The workshops were targeted at optimizing student involvement and giving the most effective feedback possible to the contributors. Intensive discussions were initiated between PhD students and established researchers from different disciplines. The workshops consisted of short presentations based on the contributions submitted by the participating students, followed by active discussions.

Thirty student presentations were given. Prize winner of the best student submission was Paulan Korenhof of Tilburg University's law school in The Netherlands, who received the award for both her paper and her presentation. She explored the notions of erasure and "the right to be forgotten" in her paper entitled "Forgetting Bits and Pieces", which is included in this volume.

Eleven thought-provoking and challenging keynote talks were given. On the social science and economics side, Alessandro Acquisti (CMU), Colin Bennett (University of Victoria), and David Lyon (Queen's University) paid visits from North America. From a more technical perspective, talks were given by Jan Camenisch (IBM Zürich), Simone Fischer-Hübner (Karlstad University), Yannis Stamatiou (University of Patras), and Rodica Tirtea (ENISA). Further presentations on wider, provocative, topics were given by Eleni Kosta (TILT), Bart Jacobs (RU Nijmegen), Siani Pearson (HP Labs), and Caspar Bowden (independent advocate for privacy rights).

These proceedings include a range of both keynote papers and submitted papers, accepted by the Program Committee and presented at the Summer School. However, not all of the papers presented at the summer school have been included in this volume. The volume's 19 papers are grouped into several sections. Six keynote papers are in a section that covers the global dramatic changes, including legislative developments, that society is facing today. Privacy and identity management are explored in specific settings, such as the corporate context, civic society, and education, and using particular technologies such as cloud computing. Thirteen other papers examine the challenges to privacy, security, and identity; ways of preserving privacy; identity and identity management; and the particular challenges presented by social media: they are laid out in four separate sections.

The papers in this volume were subject to a two-step review process. In the first step, contributions for presentation at the summer school were selected based on reviews by the Summer School Program Committee of submitted short papers. The second step took place after the summer school, when the authors all had the opportunity to revise their papers in light of the discussions held at the school itself and to resubmit them. These were again evaluated, each by three reviewers according to a common set of quality criteria.

Several projects, including European co-financed projects, contributed to the summer school on which this book of proceedings is based. Among them, ABC4Trust, the Cloud Accountability project (A4Cloud), DigIDeas, FutureID, and PRISMS.

We would like to thank all the members of the Program Committee, the additional reviewers, the members of the Organizing Committee, and the school's speakers, especially the keynote speakers, for their input. Without their dedication and contributions, this summer school would not have been possible. Last but by no means least, we owe a particular vote of thanks to the school's kind hosts from the Privacy & Identity Lab (PI.lab), which is a collaboration between Radboud University, Tilburg University, TNO, and SIDN.nl, and to IFIP for its support.

January 2014

Marit Hansen
Jaap-Henk Hoepman
Ronald Leenes
Diane Whitehouse

IFIP Summer School 2013

General Chair

Ronald Leenes   TITL, Tilburg University, The Netherlands

Program Chairs

Marit Hansen	Unabhängiges Landeszentrum für Datenschutz Schleswig-Holstein, Germany
Jaap-Henk Hoepman	Radboud University Nijmegen, The Netherlands
Diane Whitehouse	The Castlegate Consultancy, UK

Program Committee

Michele Bezzi	SAP, Germany
Katrin Borcea-Pfitzmann	Technische Universität Dresden, Germany
Caspar Bowden	Independent Privacy Advocate, UK
Sonja Buchegger	KTH, Sweden
Bruno Crispo	DISI, University of Trento, Italy
Colette Cuijpers	TILT, Tilburg University, The Netherlands
Bart De Decker	KU Leuven, Belgium
Claudia Diaz	KU Leuven, Belgium
Penny Duquenoy	Middlesex University, UK
Simone Fischer-Huebner	Karlstad University, Sweden
Michael Friedewald	Fraunhofer Institute for Systems and Innovation Research ISI, Germany
Carlisle George	Middlesex University, UK
Thomas Gross	University of Newcastle upon Tyne, UK
Seda Gurses	KU Leuven, Belgium
Serge Gutwirth	Vrije Universiteit Brussel, Belgium
Martin Gilje Jaatun	SINTEF ICT, Norway
Audun Josang	University of Oslo, Norway
Thomas Keenan	University of Calgary, Canada
Kai Kimppa	University of Turku, Finland
Markulf Kohlweiss	Microsoft Research Cambridge, UK
Bert-Jaap Koops	TILT, Tilburg University, The Netherlands
Eleni Kosta	TILT, Tilburg University, The Netherlands
Ioannis Krontiris	Goethe University Frankfurt, Germany
Louise Leenen	Council for Scientific and Industrial Research, Pretoria, South Africa

Table of Contents

Preserving Privacy

Social Networks

Identity and Identity Management

Two of the Grand Changes through Computer and Network Technology

Bart Jacobs

Institute for Computing and Information Sciences, Radboud University Nijmegen
P.O. Box 9010, 6500 GL Nijmegen, The Netherlands
bart@cs.ru.nl
http://www.cs.ru.nl/~bart

Abstract. This essay identifies and discusses two grand changes that are part of the widespread use of computer and network technology, namely (1) the separation of content and carrier, and (2) the transition from broadcast to point-to-point communication.

Although it is all too easy to think that we are living in revolutionary times, it is fair to say that computer and network technology has had a profound influence on our individual lives and on society as a whole. This influence is of a global scale. My aim in this essay is to elicit some essential features of these changes. I'm not content to just observe that computer chips and systems have become smaller, faster, and more connected, but I wish to explore some of the more fundamental "grand" changes that come with the widespread use of computer technology. Thus, I'm looking for big, possibly even paradigmatic, changes instead of incremental ones.

Two such grand changes are identified, namely:

1. The separation of content and carrier;
2. The change from broadcast to point-to-point communication.

This essay contains a discussion of these two changes and their consequences.

The work presented here is not based on empirical research. Instead, it is based on my own analysis of the developments, on discussions with colleagues, and on the literature. In the end it is difficult to say whether the analysis presented here is "true" or "false". But hopefully it does help to clarify and see some structure in the developments of the past few decades. My aim is to present the developments neutrally, in a non-judgemental manner, but I am well aware of the difficulty, or even impossibility, of doing so, since many issues are highly political. Therefore, in the end, it is better to see this article as a personal essay, and not as a solid scientific study.

This essay consists of two parts, each of which first describes the relevant grand change, and then discusses some of its consequences.

1   The Separation of Content and Carrier

When you buy a book, you get at the same time both the *carrier*, namely the book's paper pages bound together, and the *content*, namely the book's

M. Hansen et al. (Eds.): Privacy and Identity 2014, IFIP AICT 421, pp. 1–11, 2014.

text. This unity of content and carrier has been the norm for centuries, also in other fields: a painting consists both of a carrier, namely the painted cloth, and content, namely the image; an LP record consists of a vinyl disc, as carrier, in which music, as content, is encoded in its grooves.

The emergence of digital media formats has separated content and carrier. This separation has many consequences, as are discussed below. It happened roughly in the 1980s and 1990s. For the generations that grew up after 1980 it is strange that you have to pay for the pages of a book, or for a CD: it is much easier — and cheaper, in principle — to get the content without the carrier. The carrier has almost become an anomaly.

True, content still needs some form of carrier, like a hard disk, a USB stick, or even a DVD. Content can even be stored somewhere in "the cloud", where the carrier itself is completely invisible to the user. An important aspect of digital content is that it can easily be copied or transferred from one carrier to another, without loss of quality. Also, the direct costs of such a transfer are usually zero, given that most people have flat rate connections. At most, the copying takes some time. In contrast, copying in earlier days, when carrier and content were still united, resulted in small changes of the content, either in form, message, or quality.

Before looking into the consequences of the lost unity of content and carrier, I would like to address three finer points. First, one may argue that the separation of content and carrier started with the introduction of tape recorders and audio cassette players. They involved analogue audio recording. Copying, from one tape to another, meant significant loss of quality, notably through the increase of noise. Hence there was still some bond between the original carrier and the content. These tape recordings are thus not the clearest example of the change that I am trying to identify; they are a precursor.

Second, one may argue that "copying without loss of quality" is the more important change, more fundamental than "separation of content and carrier". The two are of course closely related. Still, copying without any sign of loss seems the more instrumental aspect, whereas the content-carrier separation is of a more conceptual, maybe even paradigmatic, nature.

Third, this discussion about carrier and content bears some resemblance to the discussion about atoms and bits, as initiated in [5]. However, the focus there is more narrow and concentrates on commercial value.

Controlling Information Carriers

A basic consequence of the lost unity of content and carrier is that one can no longer control the spread of information by controlling the spread of the carrier. Since a carrier is a tangible, physical substrate, its movements can be monitored and controlled via traditional searches and confiscation. This is a hard lesson, primarily for oppressive authorities, but also for individuals who wish to keep their information private. As we shall see, the lost physical control has now been replaced by new forms of control in the digital world.

Historically one can find many examples where authorities tried to control the flow of information via the information-carriers. One can think of the right to publish books, explicitly granted only to Cambridge University, in 1534 by Henry VIII of England. In the 17th century Holland became Europe's main book publisher because of its free climate, without much censorship. These examples address (non)interference with the production/sending of information. But also the consumption/receiving of information could be controlled in the past via the information-carriers. The Vatican long used its *Index* for blacklisting unwelcome books, and the book-burnings of the Nazis in the 1930s were public actions against subversive literature. These days such carrier-control mechanisms no longer work and are completely ineffective. For instance, the British Government was ridiculed in July 2013 when it ordered the Guardian newspaper to destroy a few hard drives with information leaked by Edward Snowden. The sensitive information had long been copied to several other carriers, located elsewhere.

Democratic governments have become more relaxed about citizens' access to information, except in cases where their own secrets are involved, like in the Bradley Manning (wikileaks) or Snowden examples, or where the content is clearly illegal, like in child pornography. Modern constitutions have "free press" clauses, guaranteeing the freedom to publish. In the past such publishing involved "physical" aspects, related to the carrier (books, newspapers, radio/TV signals) that required certain investments and physical infrastructure. Today everyone can be a publisher, via blogs, tweets, comments, webpages, *etc.* because information is separate from a fixed carrier and can be copied and spread easily. Thus, freedom to *send* information has become easy and is often take for granted. Freedom to *receive* information is becoming an issue, as is discussed towards the end.

Beyond Controlling Carriers

The reaction to the carrier-content separation is different in the public and private sector. These differences are described briefly.

The private sector has tried various technical copy control measures to restrict the consumption of digital information, under the name 'Digital Rights Management', commonly abbreviated as DRM. These approaches focus on the users' devices, in particular on the way of organising and accessing data at these endpoints. The movie and music industry — often referred to as the content industry — has been a strong proponent of DRM techniques. DRM restrictions may apply to the copying itself, or to the viewing or listening process. The former often involves protective measures at the hardware level, whereas the latter involves some level of auditing on the users' side (which raises privacy concerns). Many of these DRM techniques have been broken and turned out to be less successful than expected. DRM has not disappeared completely, but survives often in lightweight form as part of a set of other control mechanisms, such as listed below.

- Locking customers into a closed hardware-software eco-system, like Apple does.

- Enforcing proprietary data or storage formats, like Microsoft does, or some game producers.
- Seducing users to put all their data in your own cloud, like Google, and many others, do.
- Building cryptographic authenticity checks into your hardware, like for printer cartridges.
- Introducing cryptographically closed domains, as in the Trusted Platform Module (TPM) approach. When added to ordinary computer hardware, TPM can assure the integrity of the platform, and thus keep content within a closed domain that is trusted by the content provider.

All these approaches are controversial because they decrease the possibilities of the users and/or increase the control by external parties, like hardware/software vendors, content owners, law enforcement, intelligence. These copy control measures have been developed almost exclusively in the private sector, in order to protect commercial interests related to exclusive access to information.

In the public sector most democratic regimes have realised by now that it is nearly impossible these days to prevent altogether that citizens receive available information. What can be done technically, *e.g.* by address filtering, is restricting access to certain services, like YouTube or Facebook. This happens from time to time in countries like Pakistan, Turkey or Iran; they do have democratic elections but at the same time rather explicit public interference with what is morally acceptable or not. Actually filtering specific content is technically much more difficult and requires rather draconian measures, like in the 'Great Firewall of China'. Its main role is to prevent destabilisation of the regime.

More democratic regimes concentrate not so much on blocking information but on getting access to the flow of information in order to keep a finger on the pulse. They have thus moved their attention from the information carriers to the channels that carry the information from one place to another. Thus they developed both technical and legal means for intercepting, and retaining data, for instance in:

- lawful interception, such as tapping mobile or landline phones or tapping internet connections. By law, communication service providers are obliged to organise their systems in such a way that they can provide all communications of individual users, upon a lawful request.
- meta-data retention, like via Europe's data retention directive from 2006, which forces telecom/internet providers to retain between 6 and 24 months who communicates with whom, where and when, but not the content of the communication. This is also called traffic analysis and is useful for relationship mapping, or for obtaining location information. Meta-data are very sensitive from a privacy perspective, because they include location information and contacts, and may for instance reveal that you have been in communication with an abortion clinic.

Increasingly this data interception is hindered by the use of advanced forms of encryption that are unbreakable by police and intelligence services. Here one sees three approaches, which may occur in combined form.

1. Making computer intrusion legal for the police, so that users' endpoint devices may be hacked and data can be accessed before (or after) encryption takes place. In many countries the intelligence services already have the legal power to intrude computers of targets. Such "endpoint operations" are currently more effective for the US National Security Agency (NSA) than breaking into the cryptographic protection of intercepted messages, see [1].
2. Obtaining access to users' data at the other endpoint, namely at the internet company, like Google or Facebook, where the data resides. This is the approach of NSA's PRISM programme. Accessing the data at such a company is of course much easier than tapping the data as it travels the internet, often via different routes, and then assembling the various packets.
3. Undermining the cryptographic techniques and implementations that are used to protect the communications going over the channels. According to recent revelations of Snowden, this approach is also actively pursued by the NSA and by the UK Government Communications Headquarters (GCHQ).

All three approaches are highly controversial because they directly affect the balance of power between the state on the one hand and private companies and citizens on the other. These approaches lead to discussions about how far police and intelligence services should go and how much collateral damage is acceptable.

Transparency

The initial hope of internet pioneers was that, once the unity of carrier and content disappeared, information would be free and could no longer be used or abused to support unequal power relations. Through the carrier-content separation it would no longer be possible to keep information locked-up in government or corporate cabinets. Such information would be freely available to all, making decision-making transparent and preventing abuse of power. How naive!

Today we see that it is not the authorities that have become transparent but rather the citizens themselves. Social media have given people the means to be seen and to share their experiences continuously. For many of us the desire to be visible is stronger than the desire to protect one's private information. Commercial companies, including in particular the social media companies, are keen to advocate such "frictionless sharing" as the right way to behave and to exploit the resulting streams of revelations for various forms of profiling and for behavioural targeting of advertisements. Public authorities can expand their own span of surveillance by demanding access to the many electronic trails that people leave behind in databases of commercial organisations.

Between 2009 and 2011 there was a similar level of naivety regarding the role of social media in the various social uprisings in the Arab world. The social media may have played a role initially in organising people to rally, but in many countries the authorities reacted quickly: by shutting off or limiting the transfer of social media messages, or by exploiting them later for their own benefit, to track and round up those that sent subversive messages, see also [3]. Social media are not "freedom tools": they expose people, for commercial reasons, and do not offer any form of protection, especially not against oppressive regimes.

Having all data freely available is not desirable, because governments, companies, and individuals all have a vested interest in keeping certain information secret, at certain stages. This interest should be acknowledged. The German hacker organisation *Chaos Computer Club* (CCC) uses the sensible slogan *öffentliche Daten nützen, private Daten schützen*. Its message can be interpreted as: public data should be used, private data should be protected.

Business Models, Rewards and Quality Control

In economic terms, the production of digital content has high fixed costs, but low marginal costs. For instance, the production of a game or a movie requires substantial investment, but once a single specimen of the digital content exists, the cost of producing more digital copies is almost zero.

In the age when carrier and content were still united, there was an intermediate reproduction and distribution process to get the carrier, together with its content, in the hands of the different consumers. Payment happened with the transfer of carriers, in the other direction. Because these intermediaries had financial interests in the whole physical infrastructure, they tended to interfere in the production of the content, to ensure a level of quality that increased the likelihood of revenues. For instance, book publishers are picky about the authors they contract and often help authors to edit their manuscripts.

In our digital age it is often claimed that these intermediaries are no longer needed. It is true that certain sectors, like for instance the travel agency business, have changed dramatically because their role as intermediary, for instance between a traveller and an airline, is no longer needed. Some travel agencies survive in niche markets — like eco-tourism — where they can help travellers to select, and thus offer added value and quality.

Similarly, publishers of books, movies, music *etc.* need to adapt to this reality. For a long time there was a tendency to hold on to old business models, based on carriers, supported by controversial copyright laws and copy control mechanisms. Instead, the business should be based on fair rewards, primarily for the producer of the original work of art, but also for the remaining intermediaries that can offer true added value, for instance, via quality control, pre-selection, or distribution and payment of digital content. Within the sea of self-produced content without any quality control there is still a valuable role for intermediaries that focus on quality selection, and that understand their new, more modest position in the market. In fact, the value of information increases with selection, and decreases if there is an overload.

Non-tangible Assets

The most profound consequence of the carrier-content separation is possibly also the most obvious one: content/information is no longer tangible. Through the widespread use of computer technology and the ensuing digitisation, information has become very valuable, for public and private organisations, but also for individuals. At the same time these most precious digital assets are invisible and intangible, and thus hard to protect. Some crucial digital (strategy/product/personal/...) document may be stolen from you without you even noticing that the theft took place. The document can be obtained via remote access to your computer, by abusing some security vulnerability. In contrast, if the information exists only in unity with its carrier, one would either have to steal the carrier or photocopy the content. In the first case you may notice the missing carrier quickly, and in the second case you may notice the act of copying, because it requires physical proximity and time.

Our human intuitions regarding safety and security are still very much connected to the physical world. If you ask an arbitrary person in the street for his/her front-door key, you will probably hear: "go away". But if you ask people online for their login credentials, many more people reply. They don't see the value of digital information. In this sense we, as humans, have not really adjusted our values and intuitions to the new reality where content and carrier are no longer united.

2 The Change from Broadcast to Point-to-Point Communication

In the area of computer networks a distinction is made between *broadcast* and *point-to-point* communication. A broadcast message is sent to everyone on the network. A point-to-point message is sent only to a specific party: the message is going from one point, the sender, to a single other point, the receiver. This means that the message should include a destination address[1].

This distinction between broadcast and point-to-point is useful in a broader context. For instance, traditionally, radio and television signals are distributed in a broadcast manner, namely by a transmitter tower that sends the signal into the ether, for everyone to receive. Locally, you select, on your own radio/TV receiver, which channel you wish to tune into. Which choice you make locally is invisible centrally, for the transmitter. But there is now also IP-based radio/television, where the signal is sent over the internet, upon request, to specific users only, identified by their IP-addresses. In that case the local choices are visible at the central server. Similarly, the distribution of news articles in a paper may be understood as 'broadcast', because every subscriber/buyer gets the whole newspaper, and decides locally which article to read. Again, these local choices are invisible in the newspaper's office. But when you read the news online, on the web, you select only those news articles that you are actually interested in, by clicking, and only those are sent to you (or more precisely: to the IP-address of your computer).

---

[1] There is an intermediate form in which an encrypted message is sent to everyone, but where only one or more specific parties can decrypt it. Conceptually, this is still point-to-point communication.

The following table gives a brief summary of the main characteristics, in a media context.

Broadcast	Point-to-point
− used by traditional media: radio, TV, newspaper, ... − everybody gets all the information − selection is performed locally − the sender does not learn about local selection (what, where, when, for how long, ...) − requires synchronisation between sender and receiver	− used by websites, IP-based radio/TV, apps, ... − selection is centrally visible − only the information that you select is sent to you − enables two-way communication − enables personalised services − enables monitoring / profiling / surveillance

Point-to-point communication is much more efficient, in the sense that only the requested information is posted. For instance, I never read the sports pages in my newspaper; they go directly into the bin. In another sense point-to-point is more wasteful, since if many people want to access the same item, it has to be sent many times, to each one individually — instead of just once, like for broadcast. Indeed, news-servers are sometimes overwhelmed by the many requests, and actually stop working.

There is a clear trend away from broadcast towards point-to-point communication. Partly, this change happens automatically, as many new services appear that are only offered via the web or via apps. But existing services that are traditionally offered in broadcast mode are becoming point-to-point, like television. The main advantage for the service provider is that it yields insight in the behaviour of the user and thus enables additional, personalised services. The main advantage for the user is the asynchronous character of point-to-point: the information can be obtained any time, upon request, and not only at the moment when it is broadcast. The main disadvantage for the user is loss of privacy, and possibly also loss of 'objectivity'. This is discussed below.

Personalised Services

All companies want to reach their most likely customers, via advertisements and direct offers. Advertisements in the broadcast model are also broadcast to everyone and may thus reach — and annoy — people who are not interested. With point-to-point communication it is possible to target advertisements, so that only specific users receive them. To appropriately target messages in point-to-point communication you need to know who is on the other side of the line.

Therefore the advertisement sector builds profiles of customers with commercially relevant information (salary, hobbies, age, sex, purchase history, friends, *etc.*). Some companies urge you to always log-in so that it is easier to track your activities, but others link your activities via other means like cookies, IP-addresses, browser-fingerprints, *etc.* This "behavioural targeting" raises serious privacy concerns. But also there are worries about unfair discrimination.

The advertisement sector cunningly portrays this targeting as a valuable, almost altruistic service that is in your own interest: "You only get advertisements of goods that you are really interested in!". But, of course, this is a form of framing. They only send you the advertisements that *they* want you to see. Profiling may well be used against you, to offer you a — truly personal! — higher price. Also, certain products, like mortgages or insurances, may not be shown to you at all, because of the perceived high risk based on your profile.

Loss of Objectivity

An important aspect of point-to-point communication is that service providers can put different versions of the same message on different point-to-point channels, depending on who is on the other end. For instance, some time ago Google started offering personalised search, where the answers to search queries may be different for different people, depending on what Google knows about you — which is quite a lot, typically. Recently, Google started offering personalised maps, where the annotation on a map depends on what Google wants to show you. It is not clear how far this will go or where this leads to. Will Google only show you gay bars on a map if it thinks you are a homosexual?

News sites may learn the preferences of their customers over time and adapt the selection of news articles accordingly. Thus, the topics that are presented to you most prominently are the ones that you often read about. This may be convenient, but also makes life more boring because you will no longer be confronted with the unexpected.

Maybe, at some stage, news articles themselves will be adapted to their readers: very brief for some, longer with more details for other; factual for some, more colourful for others. Such personalisation of content raises lots of concerns. Which criteria are used for showing me this instead of that? Do (or should) I have a possible influence on these criteria, or even be able to choose or refuse them? How transparent are the evident commercial interests involved? Should this approach be regulated? If each of us gets a different version of reality — and thus lives in his/her own "filter bubble" [6] — what is the consequence for social cohesion or equal opportunities?

A Right to Receive Freely

When other, public or private, parties select what you get to see of the world, they are clearly determining what you receive. This may happen for instance via personalised search, or via personalised news selection. This steering of perspective may limit your options and thus affect your autonomy. As already discussed, the right to *send* is historically protected via free press/print clauses in constitutions. But what about the right to *receive*?

In 2010 a constitution reform committee [7] in the Netherlands recommended to update such free print clauses in the constitution, to the two clauses: (1) no advance permission is needed to publish thoughts or opinions, barring everyone's legal responsibility; (2) the receiving of information is free, barring restrictions set by law. These proposals are interesting because they place sending and receiving on equal footage — but they have not been adopted yet.

The question remains: how should such a freedom to receive be interpreted? Does it mean that I have a right to unpersonalised information? The main task of a news-provider is to collect and select information about what is going on. Thus, selection is part of the job. The question is if making these selections personal should be optional, for the receiver. Many democratic governments support or protect pluriformity of the media, so that citizens can have access to a broad spectrum of information. It seems that personalisation of media reports is undermining this pluriformity, at least on a personal level.

Another question is whether 'freedom to receive' means that we have a right to consume the news, read books, *etc.* without being monitored, that is, without the sender recording what we precisely read/watch/hear, when, where, and how long. This applies for instance to news websites, but also to e-bookreaders and mobile devices. Continuous monitoring on point-to-point channels, and updating of profiles, may have a chilling effect, reducing the pluriformity of choices.

3   Conclusions

This essay discusses several new developments that result from advances in computer and network technology. Many of these developments have been described elsewhere, in one form or another (see *e.g.* [4]). What is new here is that they are presented from a simple coherent perspective, namely as consequences of two grand changes: the separation of carrier and content, and the shift from broadcast to point-to-point communication.

Postscriptum

The basis of the text presented here is an article [2] written in Dutch. It was reorganised into an invited presentation at the 8th International IFIP Summer School on Privacy and Identity Management for Emerging Services and Technologies in June 2013. The current version concentrates on the two most prominent changes identified there. I am thankful to all those who provided feedback, including the referees.

References

1. Aid, M.: The NSA's new code breakers. Foreign Policy National Security 21(11) (2013)
2. Jacobs, B.: Bedwelmende zelfontplooiing. In: Kwakkelstein, T., van Dam, A., van Ravenzwaaij, A. (eds.) Van verzorgingsstaat naar waarborgstaat. Nieuwe kansen voor overheid en samenleving, pp. 85–97. Boom (2012)
3. Morozov, E.: The Net Delusion. The Dark Side of Internet Freedom. Public Affairs, New York (2011)
4. Morozov, E.: To Save Everything, Click Here. Allen Lane, New York (2013)
5. Negroponte, N.: Bits and atoms. Wired 3, 1 (1995)
6. Pariser, E.: The Filter Bubble. Viking (2011)
7. Rapport Staatscommissie Grondwet (2010)

The Draft Data Protection Regulation
and the Development of Data Processing Applications

Eleni Kosta and Colette Cuijpers

Tilburg Institute for Law, Technology, and Society (TILT), Tilburg University
PO Box 90153, 5000LE Tilburg, The Netherlands
{e.kosta,cuijpers}@tilburguniversity.edu

Abstract. Nowadays, data processing components are often part of a multitude of products and services. The current review of the European data protection framework, is proposing the replacement of the Data Protection Directive with a Regulation, which will undoubtedly impact the development of such products and services. This chapter analyses some of the critical changes proposed in the Regulation, highlighting the developments with regard to the actual scope of application of the European legal framework, the consent of the users and the particularities of processing pseudonymous data. It also critically assesses the proposed obligations relating to data security, notification of personal data breaches, the principles of data protection by design and by default, as well as data protection impact assessments. The authors conclude that these changes may actually be a step in the direction of more privacy-aware development of products and applications that entail data processing operations, if certain modalities are taken into account before the final adoption of the draft Regulation.

Keywords: consent, data protection impact assessment, General Data Protection Regulation, privacy by design, pseudonymisation.

1   Introduction

In January 2012, the European Commission presented its proposals for the reform of the data protection legal framework of the European Union (EU), proposing the replacement of the Data Protection Directive [1] (hereafter 'DPD') with a Regulation [2], which was the outcome of consultations and debates lasting three intense years.[1] Although the European Commission found that the objectives and the principles of

---

[1] The legal framework on data protection proposed by the European Commission, consists on the aforementioned draft Data Protection Regulation, as well as a proposal for a Directive on data protection in relation to police authorities and criminal justice, which repealed the Framework Decision on data protection in the third pillar (Council of the European Union, Framework Decision 2008/977/JHA of 27 November 2008 on the protection of personal data processed in the framework of police and judicial cooperation in criminal matters [2008] OJ L350/60 (30.12.2008)) [3].

M. Hansen et al. (Eds.): Privacy and Identity 2014, IFIP AICT 421, pp. 12–32, 2014.
© IFIP International Federation for Information Processing 2014

the current legal framework are still valid and sound, it considered that a Regulation will provide more legal certainty compared to a Directive:

> *"a Regulation is necessary to provide legal certainty and transparency for economic operators, including micro, small and medium-sized enterprises, and to provide individuals in all Member States with the same level of legally enforceable rights and obligations and responsibilities for controllers and processors, to ensure consistent monitoring of the processing of personal data, and equivalent sanctions in all Member States as well as effective co-operation by the supervisory authorities of different Member States."[2]*

Almost two years after the Commission Proposal, on 21 October 2013, the Committee on Civil Liberties, Justice and Home Affairs ('LIBE') of the European Parliament adopted amendments to the Commission's proposal (the 'Parliament text') [4]. A number of Opinions were meanwhile published by various Committees of the European Parliament, such as the Legal Affairs Committee, the Employment and Social Affairs Committee, the Industry, Research and Energy Committee, the Internal Market and Consumer Protection Committee[3], which tabled almost 4,000 amendments. The rapporteur to the LIBE Committee on the draft Regulation published on 16 January 2013 a draft report on the Proposal (known as the 'Albrecht report', after the reporting MEP Jan Philipp Albrecht) [5], which was the basis for the discussion in the LIBE Committee. At the same time, the Council was carrying out parallel work on the draft Regulation and on the 31st of May 2013 the Council released a partial draft compromise text amending the first four chapters of the Commission Proposal ('Council Report') [6]. At the moment of writing, there is heated debate among the European legislative bodies on whether the legislative process for the adoption of the Regulation will be completed before the elections for the European Parliament in Spring 2014, or whether the adoption of the Regulation will be postponed until 2015 [7]. Therefore, this chapter will be mainly based on the text of the Commission Proposal, the Albrecht Report where relevant, and the Parliament text.

Nowadays, a lot of products and services are being developed entailing continuous and complex data processing components. The goal of this chapter is to shed light on whether and how the design and development of such products and services can be influenced by the proposed Data Protection Regulation. Without aiming at being exhaustive, a task that would go way beyond the scope of one book chapter, this chapter wishes to take a closer look at concepts and obligations that will have a direct impact on the development of data processing components and will be important for relevant stakeholders. It discusses in particular changes to traditional data processing concepts and requirements, e.g. consent and data security, as well as critically examines several novel concepts and obligations, e.g. pseudonymous data, privacy by design and by default, privacy impact assessments and data breach notifications. To set the scene of

---

[2] Recital 11 Commission Proposal.
[3] A comprehensive list of all the Parliamentary Opinions can be found at http://www.huntonregulationtracker.com/legislativescrutiny/#ScrutinyEUParliament.

application, first the territorial scope of the Regulation is briefly addressed, explaining when and how the rights and obligations of the Regulation become relevant in the development of data processing applications.

2   Territorial Scope of Application

As multiple international parties may be involved in the development of applications entailing data processing operations, it is critical to clarify the territorial scope of applicability of the European data protection legislation. Article 3 of the draft Regulation differs from Article 4 DPD. A major change introduced by the Regulation is that all EU-established controllers and processors fall within the realm of this Regulation, as no national implementation is required. With the explicit mentioning of 'the establishment of a controller *and processor*', the Regulation as opposed to the DPD, creates a basis for independent obligations pertaining processors. While application to EU-based controllers and cases in which EU-law applies by virtue of public international law are quite similar in the Regulation and the DPD, when it comes to non-EU-based companies engaged in the processing of personal data the Regulation has a significantly different approach [8]. With the Regulation, the criterion 'use of equipment on the territory of a Member State' to determine territorial scope is abandoned.[4] The criteria to determine applicability of the Regulation on data controllers that are based outside the EU are modified and the Commission proposed that the Regulation applies when processing of personal data 'relates to the offering of goods or services to such data subjects or to the monitoring of their behaviour'.[5] This is further clarified in Recitals 19 and 20, which stress that processing of personal data in the context of activities of an establishment in the Union must be in accordance with the Regulation, and also that if actual processing does not take place within the Union, data subjects may not be deprived of the Regulation's protection merely because a controller is not established in the Union.

The meaning of 'monitor the behaviour of data subjects' is clarified in Recital 21: 'If individuals are tracked on the Internet with data processing techniques which consist of applying a "profile" to an individual, particularly in order to take decisions concerning the data subject or for analysing or predicting personal preferences, behaviours and attitudes'. This explanation is not without criticism. Schwartz points to the fact that 'many value-added services that draw on the user's information may be "profiling" and hence "monitoring" in this sense of the Regulation' [9]. According to Schwartz this will lead to the application of the Regulation to many situations where

---

[4] Unless such equipment is used only for purposes of transit through the territory of the Community, Art. 4(1)(c) DPD.

[5] Art. 3(2) Commission Proposal. In such case, on the basis of Article 25 of the Commission Proposal, the controller has to designate a representative, unless the controller is established in a third country ensuring an adequate level of protection, or the controller is a small or medium-sized enterprise or a public authority or body or where the controller is only occasionally offering goods or services to such data subjects.

networked intelligence shapes Internet applications and services to accommodate users, without any privacy impact on EU citizens. In this respect Schwarz refers to the system of the DPD, which at least exempted application of the DPD, if equipment was solely used for transit purposes.[6] Therefore, he claims that 'monitoring' should be explained restrictively, including only situations in which an individual's privacy is at risk.

The Council and the Parliament do not support Schwarz's plea [6]. The European Parliament in the Albrecht Report suggests an even broader scope of application relating to 'monitoring data subjects' [10]. According to the Albrecht Report, not only the monitoring of behaviour, but all collection and processing of personal data about Union residents should be covered by the Regulation. In this spirit, the Albrecht Report proposed the amendment of Recital 21 to incorporate reference to data collection other than through Internet tracking. For the rest, the explanation of monitoring remains unchanged: 'particularly in order to take decisions concerning her or him or for analysing or predicting her or his personal preferences, behaviours and attitudes'. The wording 'particularly' leaves open the possibility of application to situations described by Schwarz, in which privacy is not at stake.

In the Albrecht Report Article 3 is restricted in a sense that application depends on whether monitoring or offering goods or services *is aimed at* data subjects in the Union, while the Commission Proposal used the wording *'are related to'* which covers a broader scope of application. The terminology 'related to the offering of goods or services' is not explained by any of the recitals of the Commission Proposal, while reference could have been made to ruling of the European Court of Justice in the joint cases C-585/08 and C-144/09 (*Pammer and Hotel Alpenhof*):

> *The following matters, not exhaustive, are capable of constituting evidence from which it may be concluded that the trader's activity is directed to the Member State of the consumer's domicile: international nature of the activity, mention of itineraries from other Member States for going to the place where the trader is established, use of a language or a currency other than the language or currency generally used in the Member State in which the trader is established with the possibility of making and confirming the reservation in that other language, mention of telephone numbers with an international code, outlay of expenditure on an internet referencing service in order to facilitate access to the trader's site or that of its intermediary by consumers domiciled in other Member States, use of a top-level domain name other than that of the Member State in which the trader is established, and mention of an international clientele composed of customers domiciled in various Member States. It is for the national courts to ascertain whether such evidence exists.*[11]

The Council Report retains the wording 'when processing activities *are related to* the offering of goods or services'. The Council is however of the opinion that the Regulation should only apply if it is apparent that the controller is envisaging doing

---

[6] Art. 4(1)(c) DPD.

business with data subjects residing in one or more Member States in the Union. To ascertain this, the Council explicitly refers to the criteria established by the Court of Justice in the cases *Pammer* and *Hotel Alpenhof.*

Both the Albrecht Report and the Council Report further clarify the concept of 'offering of goods or services' to explain that the Regulation applies to all processing activities irrespective of whether the goods or services require a payment by the data subject [5, 6].

In relation to the territorial scope, the Parliament text expressly states that the Regulation applies to the processing of personal data in the context of the activities of an establishment of a controller or a processor in the Union, whether the processing takes place in the Union or not. If a controller or processor is not established in the Union, the Regulation applies if the processing activities *are related to* the offering of goods or services, irrespective of whether a payment of the data subject is required; or if the processing activity can be considered to monitor data subjects.

Recital 20 is changed accordingly, stressing that application of the Regulation is irrespective of whether data subjects need to pay for goods or services, and also the phrase 'of the behaviour' is deleted from the original Recital text. Some guidance to determine whether a controller is offering goods or services to data subjects in the Union is provided for in Recital 20 of the Parliament text: "it should be ascertained whether it is apparent that the controller is envisaging the offering of services to data subjects residing in one or more Member States in the Union", although reference is made only to services and not goods. Whether a processing activity can be considered to 'monitor' data subjects is clarified in Recital 21: "it should be ascertained whether individuals are tracked, regardless of the origins of the data, or if other data about them is collected, including from public registers and announcements in the Union that are accessible from outside of the Union, including with the intention to use, or potential of subsequent use of data processing techniques which consist of applying a 'profile', particularly in order to take decisions concerning her or him or for analysing or predicting her or his personal preferences, behaviours and attitudes". As opposed to Recital 21 in the Commission Proposal, after 'profile' the words 'to an individual' are deleted in the version of the Parliament, leaving room to apply the Regulation also in case of group profiling.[7]

Even though the clarifications given in the Parliament text are welcome, the above demonstrates that significant uncertainty remains regarding the territorial scope of the Regulation. In this respect, Kuner regrets that the uncertainty regarding the interpretation of both 'offering goods and services' and ' monitoring behaviour' is not solved by giving delegated power to the European Commission to provide further clarification [8]. However, in view of the discussions regarding desirability of, perhaps too much delegated power with the Commission[8], clarifying the territorial scope within

---

[7] More on data protection and group profiling in [12].

[8] E.g. "The plan to establish the European Commission as the institution to define details through delegated and implementing acts, would put the European Commission into a position of power that does not correspond to the European constitutional requirements. All relevant rules therefore need to be embedded within the regulation itself." [13].

the wording of the Regulation would be preferable. Or, as stated by Aldhouse, "the preferable course would be to leave practical decisions to the data protection authorities who will co-ordinate their efforts through the new European Data Protection Board. Unacceptable decisions should be challenged through judicial mechanisms and determined finally by Court" [14].

3 Consent

The consent requirement is one of the grounds of legitimate data processing and is an essential guarantee of individual control over personal data. The Commission Proposal has sharpened the requirement for consent compared to the DPD by changing the definition of consent and the conditions under which consent is obtained. The changes to the definition of consent have been taken over in their entirety by the Parliament text. In addition to freely given, specific and informed – requirements already foreseen in the DPD – consent has to be 'explicit'. The DPD requires that consent is 'explicit' only in relation to sensitive data. According to the explanatory memorandum of the Commission Proposal, that the 'explicit' requirement is added to avoid confusion with 'unambiguous' consent and 'in order to have one single and consistent definition of consent, ensuring the awareness of the data subject that, and to what, he or she gives consent'[9].

The Commission Proposal specifies in what ways consent can be given to signify the data subject's agreement to the processing of his/her personal data: 'either by a statement or by a clear affirmative action'[10]. Consent can be expressed via the ticking of a box, in online environments, and via any other statement or conduct that would clearly indicate that the data subject wishes to consent to the processing of his/her personal data in a specific context.[11] With regard to electronic consent the Commission Proposal has taken the position that '[i]f the data subject's consent is to be given following an electronic request, the request must be clear, concise and not unnecessarily disruptive to the use of the service for which it is provided'[12]. After the publication of the draft Regulation, the Article 29 Working Party welcomed the modification of the definition of consent, which it saw as intending to "clarify and strengthen data subject's rights" [15], while the European Data Protection Supervisor found that the draft Data Protection Regulation "addresses the notion of 'consent' in a comprehensive and suitable manner in order to further specify and reinforce these conditions" [16]. The Commission Proposal recognises that electronic consent should not be 'unnecessarily disruptive'. Kuner cautions that Recital 25 is in fact softening the consent requirements in online environments, i.e. the Commission Proposal 'would also allow actions such as downloading an application or playing an online game to constitute consent.'[8] Whether the consent rules – if adopted – will be applied in this way

---

[9] Commission Proposal, p. 8 (Explanatory Memorandum).

[10] Art. 4(8) Commission Proposal.

[11] Recital 25 Commission Proposal.

[12] Recital 25 Commission Proposal.

remains to be seen. For instance, it will be difficult to claim that consent in these cases is explicit.

The Commission sharpened the consent rule by imposing on the controller the burden of proof that the consent has been provided for specified purposes,[13] as well as that it has been provided in a valid way for a specific data processing operation. To meet the burden of proof, the controllers should obtain the consent by reliable means, taking into account the sensitivity of each specific data processing [16]. Specific methods have to be developed to ensure that consent has been acquired, without at the same time overburdening the users with additional activity.

Under the Commission Proposal, when the consent is provided as part of a written declaration that concerns another matter, the consent requirement has to be presented to the data subject in a way distinguishable in its appearance from the other elements of the written declaration.[14] The European Parliament further provided that any provisions on consent that are partly in violation with the Regulation will be fully void.

The Commission has followed the Article 29 Working Party position [15] and prohibited the use of consent in cases of a significant power imbalance. This caveat raised a discussion on the kind and range of situations that would potentially involve the imbalance of powers. The Parliament did not keep this provision in its text. Instead it introduced additional qualifications: the consent should be given for specific purposes; and the consent for data processing should not be a precondition for execution of a contract or the provision of a service, when such processing is not necessary for the contract or the service.[16]

The Commission Proposal devoted a dedicated Art. 8 to the processing of personal data of children, paying special attention to issues related to consent.[17] When an information society service is offered directly to a child, the Commission Proposal is differentiating between children above and below 13 years of age. In the latter case, the processing of the children's data is lawful only when and to the extent that the child's parent or custodian ('legal guardian' in the Parliament text) has given or authorised their consent. The Parliament extended the scope of application of Art. 8 to all cases when a child is offered goods or services. Although the Commission Proposal reserves for the Commission the power to adopt standard forms to obtain valid consent[18] and specify the criteria and the conditions of the valid consent of a child[19], there are major technical difficulties of obtaining verifiable consent. The Parliament

---

[13] Art. 7(1) Commission Proposal.

[14] Art. 7(2) Commission Proposal.

[15] 'The Article 29 Working group has taken the view that where as a necessary and unavoidable consequence of the employment relationship an employer has to process personal data, it is misleading if it seeks to legitimize this processing through consent. Reliance on consent should be confined to cases where the worker has a genuine free choice and is subsequently able to withdraw the consent without detriment.' [17].

[16] Art. 7(4) Parliament text.

[17] Art. 8 Commission Proposal.

[18] Art. 8(4) and recital 130 Commission Proposal.

[19] Art. 8(3) and recital 129 Commission Proposal.

replaced these Commission powers by the power of the European Data Protection Board to issue guidelines, recommendations and best practices.[20]

4   Pseudonymous Data and the Concept of Profiling

The concept of profiling is not mentioned as such in the DPD, but does occur on several occasions in the Regulation. However, an explicit definition of the concept is not provided for in Article 4 of the Regulation. It appears that Article 15(1) DPD on automated individual decisions is rephrased in the Regulation into the concept of profiling[21,22]. Article 20 grants data subjects the right not to be subject to a measure based on profiling, described as: 'automated processing intended to evaluate certain personal aspects relating to this natural person or to analyse or predict in particular the natural person's performance at work, economic situation, location, health, personal preferences, reliability or behaviour'. The Council Report and the Albrecht Report suggest to include a definition of profiling in Article 4 of the Regulation while retaining rules regarding profiling similar to the proposed Regulation. As explicitly described in the Albrecht Report, a general ban is proposed on profiling, making such activity only permissible when provided for by law.[23] Kuner warns in this respect that the broad definition of profiling includes data processing operations that benefit data subjects and that are merely routine, and that the unclear terminology used is likely to be difficult to implement in practice [8]. One of the proposals in the Albrecht Report might aggravate the situation regarding profiles, as in respect of 'legitimate interest' as processing ground it is suggested to explicitly state that: 'The interests […] of the data subject […] override the legitimate interest of the controller, as a rule, if personal data are processed in the context of profiling'.[24]

While the strict rules on profiles make data processing in a lot of situations difficult, both the Council Report and the Albrecht Report foresee possibilities to ease data processing when use is being made of pseudonyms. This might be a welcome addition to the proposed Regulation that, similar to the DPD, only refers to an exception to process *anonymous data*: 'the principles of data protection do not apply to anonymous information, meaning information which does not relate to an identified or identifiable natural person, or to data rendered anonymous in such a way that the data subject is not or no longer identifiable'.[25] However, researchers like Ohm, but also the Article 29 Working Party, have warned that true anonymisation is increasingly hard to achieve in our current information society where lots of information is

---

[20] Art. 3 Parliament text.

[21] Art. 15 states: "automated processing of data intended to evaluate certain personal aspects relating to him, such as his performance at work, creditworthiness, reliability, conduct, etc.".

[22] In this respect, the Regulation refers to [18].

[23] Albrecht report, 32 and Council report, 40.

[24] Suggested to incorporate in Article 6(1c)(d) of the draft Regulation.

[25] This wording is identical to [6] but corresponds to the meaning of anonymous data in the DPD.

disseminated and a variety of technologies exist to link and combine different data sources [19, 20].

In the Albrecht Report the definition of anonymous data is changed to meet this problem, by clarifying that the Regulation also does not apply when identification 'would require a disproportionate amount of time, expense, and effort, taking into account the state of the art in technology at the time of the processing and the possibilities for development during the period for which the data will be processed'.[26] However, the assessment whether this actually is the case might be difficult in practice.

Contrary to anonymous data, the concept of *pseudonymous data* is not incorporated in either the DPD, or the Regulation. However, both the Albrecht Report and the Council Report suggest to cover this concept and to regulate the processing of such data. Even though the approach of the Council is more detailed then the approach of the Parliament, e.g. not addressing the legal consequences of processing pseudonyms [10], the rationale to offer leniency when processing pseudonyms is to be found in both reports. The Council Report defines pseudonymous data as: 'personal data processed in such a way that the data cannot be attributed to a specific data subject without the use of additional information, as long as such additional information is kept separately and subject to technical and organisational measures to ensure non-attribution'.[27] Moreover, the Council Report explains that pseudonymous data must be seen as a security measure and privacy by design. In case of a data breach, the Council Report states that the obligation to notify does not apply if only pseudonymous data are affected.[28] To support the idea that pseudonymous data should be considered as a solution to protect personal data while enabling the processing thereof, the proposed Recital 39 states in respect of legitimate controller interests to process personal data, that these: 'could include the processing of personal data for the purposes of anonymising or pseudonymising personal data'.[29]

The position that anonymised, pseudonymised and encrypted data should generally not be covered by the data protection regulation has been heavily criticised in the position published by a number of academics, known as the 'academic manifesto' [13]. These data can still be used to re-identify individuals, and thus are personal data. However, the manifesto does acknowledge that such data might be treated in a different manner, as anonymisation, pseudonymisation and encryption are useful instruments to protect personal data. In this respect the manifesto recommends to have (regularly updated) binding rules that define when data is sufficiently pseudonymised or can be considered anonymous. In a response to the manifesto, Aldhouse presents a risk-based approach [21]. According to Aldhouse, the Regulation should retain its wide scope, but the focus should be on people instead of data, 'so that the strictness of regulation can be matched to the invasiveness and harm of the data processing'.[30]

---

[26] Albrecht report, 15.

[27] Council report, 38.

[28] Council report, 70, 77, 80

[29] Council report, 1, 18

[30] This also relates to the previously mentioned opinion of Schwarz in relation to monitoring, which according to Schwarz should only include situations in which an individual's privacy is at risk [9].

The explanation provided for in relation to Articles 6 and 20 in the Parliament Report raised a lot of criticism. The balance struck in the Albrecht Report and the Council Report is deemed to be completely undermined by the proposed Recital 58a: 'Profiling based solely on the processing of pseudonymous data should be presumed not to significantly affect the interests, rights or freedoms of the data subject. Where profiling, whether based on a single source of pseudonymous data or on the aggregation of pseudonymous data from different sources, permits the controller to attribute pseudonymous data to a specific data subject, the processed data should no longer be considered to be pseudonymous'.[31] Privacy advocates like the European Digital Rights (EDRI) have warned that the Parliament text will 'amount to a badly drafted license to profile without consent'.[32] In this respect we favor the approach in the Albrecht report in which the rights of data subjects in relation to profiling and the use of pseudonyms seems to be better safeguarded.

5   Data Security

Both the design and the deployment of technical systems need to be designed in such a way that they will ensure the security of data. The draft Regulation pays special attention to the security of data. It focuses not only on the need for adoption and the implementation of technical and organisational measures for the protection of personal data, something that already existed under the DPD, but also introduces new rules on the notification of the Data Protection Authorities and of the users, when personal data breaches occur.

5.1   Security of Processing of Personal Data

Article 30 of the Commission Proposal is dedicated to the security of processing. Contrary to the DPD that assigned the responsibility for data security to the data controller, the Commission Proposal stipulated that both the controller and the processor are responsible for the security of data that are being processed. The Commission Proposal specifies the steps that need to be taken by the data controllers and processors: First, there needs to be an evaluation of risks, making in this way risk assessments obligatory when personal data are being processed. Based on the outcome of the risk evaluation, then the data controller and the data processor shall take and implement 'appropriate technical and organisational measures to ensure a level of security appropriate to the risks represented by the processing and the nature of the personal data to be protected, having regard to the state of the art and the costs of their implementation'.[33] This strongly relates to the introduced concepts of Data Protection Impact Assessments and privacy by design and default, which will be discussed in the

---

[31] Parliament text, 13

[32] See comments by Joe McNamee on www.edri.org, under the heading 'Data protection vote – one step forward, two big steps backwards'.

[33] Article 30(1) Commission Proposal.

next sections of this chapter. The security threats against which security measures need to be taken have not been modified compared to the DPD. So, the measures taken should protect personal data against 'accidental or unlawful destruction or accidental loss and to prevent any unlawful forms of processing, in particular any unauthorised disclosure, dissemination or access, or alteration of personal data'.[34] The European Parliament enhanced the list of measures that have to be taken, requiring safeguard that only authorised personnel will access the data and that the security policy will be implemented with respect to the processing of personal data.[35]

The Commission has reserved a crucial role in specifying what the aforementioned measures should consist in, by keeping the power to adopt delegated acts on issues such as what constitutes the state of the art, what are the measures that should be adopted in specific sectors or in specific data processing situations.[36] The Commission should establish the aforementioned measures promoting technological neutrality, interoperability and innovation.[37] The European Parliament removed this power of the Commission, providing specific examples on what a security policy should include[38] and entrusting the European Data Protection board with the task of issuing guidelines, recommendations and best practices for the technical and organisational measures.[39]

Moreover, the Commission in its initial proposal was entrusted to adopt implementing acts in various situations and 'in particular to: (a) prevent any unauthorised access to personal data, (b) prevent any unauthorised disclosure, reading, copying, modification, erasure or removal of personal data and (c) ensure the verification of the lawfulness of processing operations'.[40] The European Parliament removed the possibility of the Commission to adopt implementing acts and deleted the relevant paragraph.

The European Commission should involve in this procedure the European Union Network and Information Security Agency (ENISA), which should provide its opinion on the technical and organisational measures for the protection of personal data that should be adopted and on how they should be implemented. This is also in line with the decision of the European regulator to request that the opinion of ENISA should be acquired before the Commission adopted security measures in the area of electronic communications.[41]

5.2   Personal Data Breach Notification

The notification of the competent national regulatory authority of a breach of security or loss of integrity that has had a significant impact on the operation of networks and services has been regulated in Art 13a of the Framework Directive [22].

---

[34] Article 30(2) Commission Proposal.
[35] Article 30(2) Parliament text.
[36] Article 30(3) Commission Proposal.
[37] Recital 66 Commission Proposal.
[38] Article 30(1a) Parliament text.
[39] Article 30(3) Parliament text.
[40] Article 30(4) Commission Proposal.
[41] Article 13(a) Directive 2002/21/EC, as modified by Directive 2009/140/EC.

The Commission Proposal contains for the first time a general provision on the notification of personal data breaches. A personal data breach is defined as 'a breach of security leading to the accidental or unlawful destruction, loss, alteration, unauthorised disclosure of, or access to, personal data transmitted, stored or otherwise processed'[42]. The data controller has to notify both the national supervisory authority and, under conditions, the data subjects concerned that a personal data breach occurred. When the processor becomes aware of a personal data breach, then he has to notify the controller immediately.

The notification to the national supervisory authority has to take place without undue delay, which is specified as within 24 hours from the moment that the data controller becomes aware of the breach. Any delay in notifying the supervisory authority should be justified.[43] The European Parliament removed the time frame of 24 hours, requiring the notification of the national supervisory authority without undue delay. The Commission Proposal specified the information that should be included in the notification[44], while the Commission may adopt delegated acts in order to specify the criteria and the requirements for the establishment of the data breach and for particular circumstances relating to the notification.[45] The European Parliament deleted the power of the Commission to adopt delegated acts and entrusted the European Data Protection Board to issue guidelines, recommendations and best practices for establishing the data breach and determining the undue delay. The European Parliament also deleted the possibility of the Commission to adopt implementing acts on the standard format for the notification to the supervisory authority and the form of the documentation.

After notifying the supervisory authority, the data controller has to notify the data subjects 'without undue delay' and 'when the personal data breach is likely to adversely affect the protection of the personal data or privacy of the data subjects'.[46] The European Parliament extended the obligation to notify the data subject when the data breach is also likely to adversely affect the rights or the legitimate interests of the data subject.[47] Such breaches can result for instance in 'identity theft or fraud, physical harm, significant humiliation or damage reputation'[48]. The concept of undue delay in this case is not specified, neither are the situations that are likely to adversely affect the privacy or the personal data of the data subjects. The Commission is empowered to adopt a delegated act in order to specify the circumstances under which the data subject should be notified of the personal data breach.[49] This power of the Commission was replaced by the Parliament's amendment to entrust the European Data Protection Board with the task of issuing guidelines, recommendation and best practices on when a data breach may adversely affect the data subject. The supervisory authority may even order such notification, taking into account the adverse effects of the

---

[42] Article 4(9) Commission Proposal.

[43] Article 31(1) Commission Proposal.

[44] Article 31(3) Commission Proposal.

[45] Article 31(5) Commission Proposal.

[46] Article 32(1) Commission Proposal.

[47] Article 32(1) Parliament text.

[48] Recital 67 Commission Proposal.

[49] Article 32(5) Commission Proposal.

breach.[50] The notification to the data subject is not necessary if the data controller demonstrates that he has implemented technological protection measures to the data concerned by the personal data breach that will render the data unintelligible to any unauthorised person.[51] Given the increasing number of data breaches in Europe, the Commission wished to give incentive to the industry to implement encryption measures for the protection of personal data.

6   Data Protection by Design and by Default

Even though one could argue that identification of risks precedes questions of how to mitigate such risks in the design of products and services, the Regulation first presents the principles of privacy by design and default, before addressing Data Protection Impact Assessments (Art. 33). Art. 23 concerns the obligations of the controller arising from the principles of data protection by design and by default. Both at the time of the determination of the means for processing and at the time of the processing itself, a controller must implement appropriate technical and organisational measures and procedures in such a way that the processing will meet the requirements of the Regulation and ensure the protection of the rights of data subjects. Cost and state of the art are mentioned as criteria to be taken into account in assessing the standard of such measures. Data protection by default is explained in Art. 23 (2) along the lines of data minimisation and purpose specification:

> *Only those personal data are processed which are necessary for each specific purpose of the processing and are especially not collected or retained beyond the minimum necessary for those purposes, both in terms of the amount of the data and the time of their storage. In particular, those mechanisms shall ensure that by default personal data are not made accessible to an indefinite number of individuals.*

The exact meaning of what privacy by default entails is unclear. Recital 61, regarding privacy by design and default, does not add to the wording of Article 23. Some clarification is to be expected from delegated acts and standards provided for by the Commission, specifying further criteria and requirements for appropriate measures and mechanisms to attain privacy by design and default (Art. 23(3) and (4)). Some further clarification on the concept of privacy by design can be drawn from its origin in Canada. While the concept is rather new in Europe, already in the 1990s the Information and Privacy Commissioner for the Canadian province of Ontario, Ann Cavoukian, developed seven Foundational Principles to provide guidance on privacy by design [23]. The principles aim to: 'proactively make privacy the default setting in all areas of technological plans and business practices and explain how privacy should be embedded into the design of systems, in a positive-sum manner — that does not

---

[50] Article 32(4) Commission Proposal.

[51] Article 32(3) Commission Proposal.

detract from the original purpose of the system' [23]. Cavoukian's second principle is labelled 'Privacy as the Default Setting' and is explained as:

> Privacy by Design seeks to deliver the maximum degree of privacy by ensuring that personal data are automatically protected in any given IT system or business practice. If an individual does nothing, their privacy still remains intact. No action is required on the part of the individual to protect their privacy — it is built into the system, by default.[52]

In contrast to the Commission Proposal, the Albrecht report does provide some explanation to the concept of privacy by default in adding to Recital 61:

> The principle of data protection by design require [sic.] data protection to be embedded within the entire life cycle of the technology, from the very early design stage, right through to its ultimate deployment, use and final disposal. The principle of data protection by default requires privacy settings on services and products which should by default comply with the general principles of data protection, such as data minimisation and purpose limitation.[53]

The Albrecht Report also suggests to amend Article 23 to incorporate a reference to Privacy Impact Assessments: 'Where the controller has carried out a data protection impact assessment pursuant to Article 33, the results shall be taken into account when developing those measures and procedures', referring to the measures to be taken in light of privacy by design and default. The Albrecht Report also claims to further clarify the principle of data protection by default by amending Art. 23 to include: 'Where the data subject is given a choice regarding the processing of personal data, the controller shall ensure that [...] and that data subjects are able to control the distribution of their personal data'.[54] However, this does not provide a lot of guidance regarding the contents of the measures to be taken; the standard to adhere to in a default setting; and the framework to assess the appropriateness of measures taken.

In the Parliament text, the most striking amendment concerns the deletion of sections 3 and 4 of Art. 23, deleting the possibility for the Commission to, by way of delegating acts, specify any further criteria and requirements for data protection by design and default, or to determine technical standards for such requirements. The Parliament text tries to provide clarification regarding the requirements by adding criteria to Art. 23:

> Having regard to the state of the art, current technical knowledge, international best practices and the risks represented by the data processing, the controller and the processor [...] shall [...] implement appropriate and proportionate technical and organisational measures and procedures in such a way that the processing will meet the requirements of this Regulation.

---

[52] http://www.privacybydesign.ca/index.php/about-pbd/7-foundational-principles/
[53] Albrecht report, 34.
[54] Council report, 111.

Several points stand out when comparing the initial Art. 23 of the Commission proposal with the amended Art. 23 in the Parliament text. First of all the Commission Proposal only referred to the criteria 'state of the art and cost of implementation'. While several criteria are added in the Parliament text, the criteria 'cost of implementation' is deleted. Furthermore, as opposed to the initially proposed Art. 23, the obligation is not only directed towards controllers, but also to processors. And besides the required appropriateness of the measures, they should according to the Parliament text also be proportionate.

The Parliament text adds a rather extensive part to Art. 23 explaining the scope and focus of data protection by design: 'Data protection by design shall have particular regard to the entire lifecycle management of personal data from collection to processing to deletion, systematically focusing on comprehensive procedural safeguards regarding the accuracy, confidentiality, integrity, physical security and deletion of personal data'. The Parliament text also establishes a clear link between data protection by design and data protection impact assessments (Art. 33) by explicitly stating in Art. 23 that if a data protection impact assessment has been carried out, the results hereof need to be taken into account in developing the measures and procedures required on the basis of data protection by design. By adding a section 1a to Art. 23, the Parliament text also introduces data protection by design as a prerequisite in public tenders according to the Directive on public procurement [24] and the Utilities Directive [25].

The Parliament text also doubles the length of the text of Recital 61 by adding:

> The principle of data protection by design require (sic) data protection to be embedded within the entire life cycle of the technology, from the very early design stage, right through to its ultimate deployment, use and final disposal. This should also include the responsibility for the products and services used by the controller or processor. The principle of data protection by default requires privacy settings on services and products which should by default comply with the general principles of data protection, such as data minimisation and purpose limitation.

The text regarding privacy by default has not drastically changed in Art. 23 of the Parliament text. It merely clarifies that not only collection and retention of data should be limited to the minimum necessary to achieve the purpose of processing, but that this limitation also extends to dissemination. Moreover it adds a sentence to clarify that data subjects must be able to control the distribution of their personal data.

Within the Council Report, several extra criteria are provided to assess measures to comply with privacy by design and default. Not only the technology and cost of implementation, but also the 'risks for rights and freedoms of individuals posed by the nature, scope and purpose of the processing' should be taken into account to determine technical and organisational measures 'appropriate to the processing activity being carried on and its objectives, including the use of pseudonymous data'.[55] In

---

[55] Council report, 70.

respect to the default, the Council Report complements the proposed Regulation by making a reference to the purpose of processing:

> *if the purpose is not intended to provide the public with information, it must be ensured that by default personal data are not made accessible without human intervention to an indefinite number of individuals.*[56]

There is a rather convincing incentive for data controllers within the Regulation to comply with the principle of privacy by design and default. Article 79 of the Commission Proposal regarding administrative sanctions states: 'The supervisory authority shall impose a fine up to 1,000,000 EUR or, in case of an enterprise up to 2% of its annual worldwide turnover, to anyone who, intentionally or negligently [...] (e) does not adopt internal policies or does not implement appropriate measures for ensuring and demonstrating compliance pursuant to Articles 22, 23 and 30'.[57] As the first section of Art. 79 of the Commission Proposal states 'each supervisory authority' Kuner warns that in theory a company could be sanctioned separately by 27 different data protection authorities for the same violation if it occurred within each jurisdiction, which stands in contradiction to the fact that supervision of a company is limited to the DPA of the company's main establishment[58] [8]. According to Art. 37 of the Commission Proposal it is the task of the Data Protection Officer to 'monitor the implementation and application of this Regulation, in particular as to the requirements related to data protection by design, data protection by default and data security and to the information of data subjects and their requests in exercising their rights under this Regulation'[59].

7   Data Protection Impact Assessment

Privacy Impact Assessments have been carried out in relation to systems and applications that present privacy aspects and interest, but the concept of a Privacy Impact Assessment (PIA) has become broadly known via the discussions regarding the use of Radio-Frequency Identification (RFID) technology. As this technology makes it possible to track and possibly even identify users, the use of RFID poses a number of concerns regarding their privacy. However, given its economic potential, the use of RFID is steadily becoming an integral part of everyday life. Following a long period of consultation and debate, the Article 29 Working Party endorsed the revised PIA framework for RFID applications and called for its implementation [26]. The PIA framework was officially signed on 6 April 2011 [27].

---

[56] Council report, 70.

[57] The Parliament text contains even stricter rules for administrative sanctions, holding on to only the highest fine category, in which 2% of the annual worldwide turnover is amended to 5%. In the Commission Proposal sections 4 and 5 of Art. 79 contained lower fine provisions, 250.000 euro and 0,5% of annual world wide turnover and 500.000 euro and 1 % of annual world wide turnover. These sections are deleted in the Parliament text.

[58] Art. 51(2) Commission Proposal.

[59] Art. 37(3) (c) Commission Proposal.

The Commission Proposal formalises in Art. 33 the requirement for the data controller or the data processor to carry out a Data Protection Impact Assessment in cases when the 'processing operations present specific risks to the rights and freedoms of data subjects', for instance when data subjects are actually excluded from their right or by the use of specific new technologies (Rec. 74). The carrying out of a thorough Data Protection Impact Assessment is expected to limit the likelihood of data breaches (Rec. 71a Parliament text). The Commission Proposal provided some examples of processing operations that present specific risks, such as when sensitive data are being processed, when automated processing leads to profiling of the data subjects, when large-scale video surveillance takes place, or when processing of personal data is carried out in large scale filing systems on children, genetic data or biometric data (Art. 33.2). Recital 71 clarified that Data Protection Impact Assessments should in particular apply to "newly established large scale filing systems, which aim at processing a considerable amount of personal data at regional, national or supranational level and which could affect a large number of data subjects", which aimed at excluding most small and medium-sized enterprises [8]. The European Parliament deleted the section on risks in relation to Data Protection Impact Assessments and created a new Art. 32a, which is dedicated to the respect to risk and is more elaborate compared to the Commission's references to risk.

The Commission Proposal specifies the minimum information that the Data Protection Impact Assessment shall contain, i.e. a description of the data processing operations, an assessment of risks to the rights and freedoms of data subjects, a description of the measures taken to ensure the mitigation of the risks and the measures taken to ensure the protection of the data and to demonstrate compliance (Art. 33.3). The content of the assessment was modified by the European Parliament, which requires also an assessment of the necessity and proportionality of the processing operations in relation to the purposes, an indication for the time limits for erasure and assessment of the context of data processing etc.[60] The provision of the Commission Proposal that the obligation for a Data Protection Impact Assessment does not extend to data controllers that are public authorities that have an obligation to carry out the data processing operation (Art. 33.5 Commission Proposal) was deleted by the European Parliament. The understanding of Data Protection Impact Assessments in the Regulation is that data controllers have to comply with specific points relating to the processing of personal data. In this sense, the Data Protection Impact Assessment as described in the Regulation is narrower in scope, compared to Privacy Impact Assessments [28].

8   Reflections on the Data Protection Reform

Developers of products and services that entail data processing operations offered to European customers, even if the developing entities are established outside the EU, will need to consider the European Data Protection Regulation, if adopted in its current form. The territorial scope of the draft Regulation is meant to extend far beyond the European territory, imposing obligations on data controllers *and* data processors.

---

[60] Art. 33(3) Parliament text.

Besides considering the Regulation from a perspective of possible end-use of products and services, the Regulation might also directly apply to the developers of products and services, even during their test and pilot phases because of the broad interpretation of the notions 'monitoring behaviour' and the 'offering of goods or services', for which no payment by the data subject is required.

Consent has been used often as legitimate ground for data processing especially in online services. The draft Regulation aims at strengthening the rights of the data subjects and ensuring that data subject 'explicitly' consent to the processing of their personal data and imposes the burden to proof that consent has been obtained on the data controller. From this perspective, in the *development* of products and services consent might not be that relevant. However, mechanisms and procedures for end-users of the products being developed to properly provide, register and withdraw consent need to be part of the design of such products. Kuner fears a watering down of the consent requirement because providing consent should not be 'unnecessarily disruptive to the use of the product'. However, based on the rationale and wording of the Regulation as a whole, we expect a rather strict and narrow interpretation of all four consent requirements: freely given, informed, specific and explicit – because of the risks involved – especially in electronic environments.

The specification of the steps that need to be taken by data controllers and processors in view of the requirement of data security closely relate to the introduction of the concepts of Data Protection Impact Assessment and privacy by design and by default. First, there needs to be an evaluation of risks, and based on the outcome of the risk evaluation, data controllers and processors must implement 'appropriate technical and organisational measures to ensure a level of security appropriate to the risks'. As a final step in the security cycle, when a data breach occurred despite the precautions taken, the Regulation introduces a general obligation of notification of personal data breaches. Again, even though data breach notification might not be a primary concern of developers of data processing appliances, the design might benefit from the exception that notification to the data subject is not necessary if proper encryption measures are taken, which thus might be an interesting functionality to incorporate into a product or service with data processing components.

The introduction in the Parliament text of a general ban on profiling, making such activity only permissible when provided for by law, is likely to be an important consideration in the development of data processing appliances. The leeway given when using pseudonyms might spur the development and implementation of pseudonymisation mechanisms and technologies. Even though the Parliament text proposes that the Regulation applies to pseudonyms, it is deemed an important security measure. The trend to keep pseudonymous, anonymous and encrypted data within the scope of the Regulation, but offering these data different treatments, is definitely a trend worthwhile to consider when developing data processing appliances. It is crucial to keep a close eye on the developments regarding the proposed rules on profiling and pseudonyms, as the Parliament text seems to undermine data subjects' rights by offering too much leeway in respect of the use of pseudonyms in profiling. In our opinion, the wording of the Albrecht Report and the Council Report provide a better balance and better safeguards regarding data subjects' rights in relation to profiling and the use of pseudonyms.

The principles of data protection by design and by default lay down a more general obligation to align the development of products and services with the requirements stemming from the Regulation. As explained in the Parliament text, data protection by design shall have particular regard to the entire lifecycle management of personal data, from collection to deletion, where the obligations are not only directed towards controllers, but also to processors. In order to achieve privacy by design and default, these requirements need to be taken into account in the earliest stages of design. The explicit link between data protection by design and data protection impact assessments requires an active investigation of risks, to be followed by factual (technical and organisational) implementation of measures to counteract the identified risks. Because the standard is set at the default level, collection, retention and dissemination of data should be limited to the minimum necessary to achieve the purpose of processing personal data. Combined with the possibility of high administrative sanctions in case of non-compliance with the principles of privacy by design and default, these principles will definitely impact the development of data processing appliances.

When processing operations present specific risks to the rights and freedoms of data subjects, the draft Regulation requires the carrying out of a Data Protection Impact Assessment. Appliances connected to the Internet – providing feedback and feedforward information based on specific and generalised data subject behaviour – most certainly presents specific risks, e.g. relating to the processing of sensitive data and profiling. As with the Parliament text, no exceptions remain regarding small and medium-sized enterprises, Data Protection Impact Assessments will become an important obligation for all developers of data processing appliances, even those not affiliated to large companies. Not only the assessment as such is relevant, but also the documentation regarding Data Protection Impact Assessment and the actual implementation of risk mitigating measures. This follows from the higher standards of accountability to be found in the Regulation, which relate to scope – obligations also pertaining data processors – as well as content – e.g. more strict documentation obligations.[61]

Overall, based on the topics discussed in this chapter, the Regulation sets a hopeful tone regarding increased awareness and incentives to better incorporate privacy and data protection into the design of data processing applications, although there still is room for improvement in specific areas. Whether this will be the case probably depends on the strictness of audit, control and enforcement of the Regulation.

References

1. European Parliament and Council of the European Union: Directive 95/46/EC of 24 October 1995 on the protection of individuals with regard to the processing of personal data and on the free movement of such data [1995] OJ L281/31 (November 23, 1995)

---

[61] E.g. the explicit reference to the principle of accountability in Art. 22 requiring technical and organizational measures to ensure and *demonstrate* – in a transparent manner – that the data processing is consistent with the Regulation, but also e.g. the obligation to appoint a Data Protection Officer when personal data are processed in relation to more than 5,000 data subjects, Art. 35 Parliament text.

2. European Commission: Proposal for a Regulation of the European Parliament and of the Council on the protection of individuals with regard to the processing of personal data and on the free movement of such data (General Data Protection Regulation) COM (2012) 11 final – 2012/0011 (COD) (January 25, 2012)
3. European Commission, Proposal for a Directive of the European Parliament and of the Council on the protection of individuals with regard to the processing of personal data by competent authorities for the purposes of prevention, investigation, detection or prosecution of criminal offences or the execution of criminal penalties, and the free movement of such data, COM (2012) 10 final – 2012/0010 (COD) (January 25, 2012)
4. European Parliament: Report on the proposal for a regulation of the European Parliament and of the Council on the protection of individuals with regard to the processing of personal data and on the free movement of such data (General Data Protection Regulation) (COM(2012)0011 – C7-0025/2012 – 2012/0011(COD)), A7-0402/2013 (November 21, 2013)
5. Albrecht, J.P.: European Parliament, Committee on Civil Liberties, Justice and Home Affairs: Draft report on the proposal for a regulation of the European Parliament and of the Council on the protection of individual with regard to the processing of personal data and on the free movement of such data (General Data Protection Regulation), 2012/0011(COD) (January 16, 2013)
6. Council of the European Union, Proposal for a regulation of the European Parliament and of the Council on the protection of individuals with regard to the processing of personal data and on the free movement of such data (General Data Protection Regulation) - Key issues of Chapters I-IV, 2012/0011(COD) (May 31, 2013)
7. European Council, Cover note 24/25 October 2013 Conclusions, EUCO 169/13 (October 25, 2013)
8. Kuner, C.: The European Commission's Proposed Data Protection Regulation: A Copernican Revolution in European Data Protection Law. PVLR 11, 6 (2012)
9. Schwarz, P.M.: EU Privacy and the Cloud: Consent and Jurisdiction Under the Proposed Regulation. PVLR 12, 718 (2013)
10. Burton, C., Anna, P.: Status of the Proposed EU Data Protection Regulation: Where Do We Stand? PVLR 12, 1470 (2013)
11. Joined Cases C-585/08 and C-144/09, Peter Pammer v. Reederei Karl Schlüter GmbH & Co. KG and Hotel Alpenhof GesmbH v. Oliver Heller [2010] ECR I-12527
12. Schreurs, W., Hildebrandt, M., Els, K., Vanfleteren, M., Cogitas, E.S.: The Role of Data Protection Law and Non-discrimination Law in Group Prolfing in the Private Sector. In: Hildebrandt, M., Gutwirth, S. (eds.) Profiling the European Citizen. Cross-Disciplinary Perspectives, pp. 241–269. Springer, Heidelberg (2008)
13. Data Protection in Europe – Academics are taking a position. CLSR 29, 180–184 (2013)
14. Aldhouse, F.: Data protection in Europe – Some thoughts on reading the academic manifesto. CLSR 29, 289–292 (2013)
15. Article 29 Data Protection Working Party: Opinion 01/2012 on the data protection reform proposals. WP 191 (March 23, 2012)
16. European Data Protection Supervisor: Opinion on the data protection reform package (2012)
17. Article 29 Data Protection Working Party: Opinion 8/2001 on the processing of personal data in the employment context. WP 48 (September 13, 2001)

18. Council of Europe: Recommendation CM/Rec (2010)13 of the Committee of Ministers to member states on the protection of individuals with regard to automatic processing of personal data in the context of profiling (Adopted by the Committee of Ministers on 23 November 2010 at the 1099th meeting of the Ministers' Deputies)

19. Ohm, P.: Broken Promises Of Privacy: Responding to the Surprising Failure of Anonymization. UCLA Law Review 57, 1701–1777 (2010)

20. Article 29 Data Protection Working Party: Opinion 13/2011 on Geolocation services on smart mobile devices. WP 185 (May 16, 2011)

21. Council of the European Union – Press Office: Background – Justice and Home Affairs Council, Brussels 7 and 8 March (March 6, 2013),
http://www.consilium.europa.eu/ueDocs/
cms_Data/docs/pressData/en/jha/135854.pdf (as references in [14])

22. European Parliament and the Council of the European Union, Directive 2002/21/EC of 7 March 2002 on a common regulatory framework for electronic communications networks and services ("Framework Directive") [2002] OJ L108/33 (24.04.2002), as modified by European Parliament and the Council of the European Union, Directive 2009/140/EC amending Directives 2002/21/EC on a common regulatory framework for electronic communications networks and services, 2002/19/EC on access to, and interconnection of, electronic communications networks and associated facilities, and 2002/20/EC on the authorisation of electronic communications networks and services ("Better Regulation Directive") [2009] OJ L337/37 (December 18, 2009)

23. Cavoukian, A.: Privacy by Design in Law, Policy and Practice. A White Paper for Regulators, Decision-makers and Policy-makers (2011),
http://www.ipc.on.ca/images/Resources/pbd-law-policy.pdf

24. European Parliament and Council of the European Union: Directive 2004/17/EC of 31 March 2004 coordinating the procurement procedures of entities operating in the water, energy, transport and postal services sectors, OJ L 134/001 (April 30, 2004)

25. European Parliament and Council of the European Union: Directive 2004/18/EC of 31 March 2004 on the coordination of procedures for the award of public works contracts, public supply contracts and public service contracts, OJ L 134/114 (April 30, 2004)

26. Article 29 Data Protection Working Party: Opinion 9/2011 on the revised Industry Proposal for a Privacy and Data Protection Impact Assessment Framework for RFID Applications. WP 180 (February 11, 2011)

27. Privacy and Data Protection Impact Assessment Framework for RFID Applications (January 12, 2011),
http://cordis.europa.eu/fp7/ict/enet/
documents/rfid-pia-framework-final.pdf

28. Wright, D., de Hert, P. (eds.): Privacy Impact Assessment. Springer, Heidelberg (2012)

Privacy Management and Accountability in Global Organisations

Siani Pearson

Hewlett-Packard, Security and Cloud Lab, Bristol, UK
Siani.Pearson@hp.com

Abstract. Organisations that operate in a global environment can be subject to potentially diverse and complex regulatory requirements. This paper explains some of the key issues that corporate governance faces related to privacy and some mechanisms for addressing these.

Keywords: Accountability, compliance, data protection, privacy, risk, security.

1   Introduction

This paper focuses on 'good willing' organisations that wish to meet, and even exceed, legal privacy and data protection requirements. It considers some of the challenges that they face, best practice today in addressing these challenges and points to examples of cutting edge thinking that may shape future corporate privacy governance.

It is outside the scope of this paper to consider economic incentives for privacy-friendly organisational behaviour and different organisational attitudes towards investment in privacy enhancing mechanisms and privacy-related risk (see for instance [1]), the tension between data minimisation and the value and usage of personal data for organisations (for example, for marketing purposes) and related discussions including issues of market forces leading to erosion of moral standards within an entrepreneurial system (as described for example in [2]) countered to a greater or lesser extent by national regulatory standards, consumer pressure and other mechanisms [3]. Instead, the focus will be on how organisations can satisfy regulatory requirements and provide good data stewardship.

The structure of the paper is as follows: Section 2 considers how privacy requirements are challenging for global organisations, Section 3 describes central aspects and options for privacy governance within organisations, Section 4 shows how accountability forms part of the solutions needed and Section 5 discusses two particular examples of accountability-based privacy management solutions currently being developed or refined by the author. Finally, conclusions are given.

2   How Privacy Requirements can be Challenging

In this section privacy is introduced as a concept and its relationship with security is clarified in order that organisational privacy obligations can be considered and privacy risks and challenges for organisations further elucidated.

M. Hansen et al. (Eds.): Privacy and Identity 2014, IFIP AICT 421, pp. 33–52, 2014.
© IFIP International Federation for Information Processing 2014

2.1   Privacy, Data Protection and Security

At the broadest level (and particularly from a European standpoint), privacy is a fundamental human right, enshrined in the United Nations Universal Declaration of Human Rights (1948) and subsequently in the European Convention on Human Rights and national constitutions and charters of rights. There are various forms of privacy, ranging from 'the right to be let alone' [4], 'control of information about ourselves' [5], 'the rights and obligations of individuals and organisations with respect to the collection, use, disclosure, and retention of personally identifiable information' [6], focus on the harms that arise from privacy violations [7] and contextual integrity [8]. For further discussion about the nature of privacy, see for example [3].

In the commercial, consumer context, privacy entails the protection and appropriate use of the personal information of customers, and the meeting of expectations of customers about its use (which may be reflected as informed consent or within private contracts). What is appropriate will depend on the applicable laws, individuals' expectations about the collection, use and disclosure of their personal information and other contextual information.

Data protection is the management of personal information, and is often used within the European Union (EU) in relation to privacy-related laws and regulations, although in the United States (US) the usage of this term is focussed more on security.

The terms '*personal information*' and '*personal data*' are commonly used within Europe and Asia, whereas in the US the term '*Personally Identifiable Information*' (PII) is normally used, but they are generally used to refer to the same concept. This can be defined as information that can be traced to a particular individual, and include such items as: name, address, phone number, social security or national identity number, credit card number, email address, passwords, date of birth. Some personal data elements are considered more sensitive than others, although the definition of what is considered *sensitive personal information* varies depending upon jurisdiction and even on particular regulations.

Privacy differs from security, in that it relates to handling mechanisms for personal information, although security is one element of that. Security mechanisms, on the other hand, focus on provision of protection mechanisms that include authentication, access controls, availability, confidentiality, integrity, retention, storage, backup, incident response and recovery. Privacy relates to personal information only, whereas security and confidentiality can relate to all information.

2.2   Organisational Privacy Obligations

We have seen that for organisations, privacy entails the application of laws, policies, standards and processes by which personal information is managed. The fair information practices developed in the US in 1970s [11] and later adopted and declared as principles by the Organisation for Economic Co-operation and Development (OECD) and the Council of Europe [12] form the basis for most data protection and privacy laws around the world. These principles are shown in Table 1. This framework can enable sharing of personal information across participating jurisdictions without the need for individual contracts. It imposes requirements on organisations including data collection, subject access rights and data flow restrictions.

Table 1. OECD privacy principles

Principle	Description
Collection limitation	There should be limits to the collection of personal data and any such data should be obtained by lawful and fair means and, where appropriate, with the knowledge or consent of the data subject.
Data quality	Personal data should be relevant to the purposes for which they are to be used, and, to the extent necessary for those purposes, should be accurate, complete and kept up-to-date.
Purpose specification	The purposes for which personal data are collected should be specified not later than at the time of data collection and the subsequent use limited to the fulfilment of those purposes or such others as are not incompatible with those purposes and as are specified on each occasion of change of purpose.
Use limitation	Personal data should not be disclosed, made available or otherwise used for purposes other than those specified in accordance with the above except: a) with the consent of the data subject; or b) by the authority of law.
Security safeguards	Personal data should be protected by reasonable security safeguards against such risks as loss or unauthorised access, destruction, use, modification or disclosure of data.
Openness	There should be a general policy of openness about developments, practices and policies with respect to personal data. Means should be readily available of establishing the existence and nature of personal data, and the main purposes of their use, as well as the identity and usual residence of the data controller.
Individual participation	Individuals should have the right: a) to obtain from a data controller, or otherwise, confirmation of whether or not the data controller has data relating to them; b) to have communicated to them, data relating to them i. within a reasonable time; ii. at a charge, if any, that is not excessive; iii. in a reasonable manner; and iv. in a form that is readily intelligible to them; c) to be given reasons if a request made under (a) and (b) is denied, and to be able to challenge such denial; and d) to challenge data relating to them and, if the challenge is successful to have the data erased, rectified, completed or amended.
Accountability	A data controller should be accountable for complying with measures which give effect to the principles stated above.

The collection and processing of personal information is subject to regulation in many countries across the world. Figure 1 illustrates how many different countries have national data protection legislation in place. The US does not have a comprehensive regime of data protection but instead has a variety of laws targeted at the protection of particularly sensitive types of information that tend to be sector-based or enacted at the state level. This (sometimes inconsistent) matrix of national laws can make it really hard for businesses to ensure full compliance if they are operating in multiple jurisdictions. Hence there is pressure from organisations for greater global interoperability to be achieved via development of a clear and consistent framework of data protection rules that can be applied, in order to reduce unnecessary administrative burdens and risks.

Key
National privacy or data
protection law in place
Other significant privacy laws
in place
Emerging privacy or data
protection laws

Fig. 1. Global data protection laws

Transborder flow of personal information, including access to this information, is restricted by some of these laws. For example, the European Data Protection Directive 95/46/EC [4] (and its supporting country legislation) is an important piece of privacy legislation that restricts the movement of data from EU to non-EU countries that do not meet the EU 'adequacy' standard for privacy protection. Legislation similar to the European Data Protection Directive has been, and continues to be, enacted in many other countries, including Australia, New Zealand, Hong Kong, Japan and Asia-Pacific Economic Cooperation (APEC). In practice contractual mechanisms like Binding Corporate Rules or Model Contracts might need to be put in place in order to allow data access. However, these arrangements typically take several months to set up, and hence are not well suited to dynamic environments. Hence the OECD revised guidelines [13] now recommend the practical implementation of privacy protection through an approach grounded in risk management and stress the need for improved global interoperability.

With regard to security, it is a common requirement under data protection law that if a company outsources the handling of personal data to another company, it has some responsibility to make sure the outsourcer uses "reasonable security" to protect those data. This means that any organisation creating, maintaining, using or disseminating records of personal data must ensure that the records have not been tampered with, and must take precautions to prevent misuse of the information.

Of course, in addition, organisations need to take into account the privacy-related expectations of their customers, which may be specified within private contracts, and this is likely to involve a combination of process-based and access control mechanisms. The legal obligations vary according to the regulatory context and indeed there are likely to be some quite significant changes in the near future. Problems with the 1995 EU Data Protection Directive [4] as a harmonisation measure and in relation to new technologies including cloud computing have led the European Commission (EC) in January 2012 to publish a draft of replacement General Data Protection Regulation [5] that is currently being discussed and revised, in which accountability features and privacy by design take greater precedence. Amongst other things, this imposes new obligations and liabilities for data processors, new requirements on data breach notification and stricter rules on international data transfers. It also empowers National Regulatory authorities to impose significantly higher fines. In addition, a European Cloud Computing Strategy [14] has been launched aiming at more clarity and knowledge about the applicable legal framework and making it easier to verify compliance with the legal framework (e.g. through standards and certification). Furthermore, in February 2013 the European Commission published a cybersecurity strategy [15] alongside a draft directive on network and information security [16]. Once implemented, many service providers will be covered by a range of data security obligations including adopting risk management practices and reporting major security incidents.

2.3   Privacy Risks and Challenges

Privacy challenges for businesses include data breaches, risk of litigation due to country-specific laws, the complexity of managing privacy and negative public attention and loss of brand value if exposures occur. Data breaches can be costly – on average 204 US dollars per record, according to a 2010 Ponemon Institute study. When customers are concerned for the welfare of their privacy, it can affect a company's ability to do business. This concern may arise for example due to worries about unsolicited marketing, identity theft, surveillance or unwanted inferences about behavior.

Privacy issues depend upon the role of the company. For example, an organisation could be a custodian of employee personal data, could collect end-user personal information, or could just be providing outsourcing services for another organisation. Legally, the requirements are quite different depending upon whether the organisation is a data controller or a data processor in that situation (although it might be both).

A *data controller* is an entity which alone or jointly with others determines the purposes for which and the manner in which any item of personal information is processed. It could be a person, public authority, agency or other body and is legally responsible for ensuring compliance requirements are met. Obligations and risks of the data controller include: regulatory fines, criminal liability, civil liability if data subjects enforce their rights, investment risk, business continuity impact and reputational damage. In environments such as cloud computing, a data controller has a responsibility to ensure that the service providers are meeting regulatory obligations and this can be challenging [17].

A *data processor* is an entity which processes personal information on behalf and upon instructions of the data controller. Contractual agreements may add additional responsibilities or constraints with respect to privacy, although data protection laws stipulate that the organisation that is transferring personal information to a third party for processing remains responsible for the personal information. The data processor may also face issues such as lack of training of key personnel and deliberate targeting of sensitive information by criminals.

When considering privacy risks, context is an important aspect, as different information can have different privacy, security and confidentiality requirements and privacy threats differ according to the type of scenario: for example, they would tend to be higher for services that are dynamically personalised, based on people's location, preferences, calendar and social networks, etc. Privacy need be taken into account only if a service handles personal information, in the sense of collecting, transferring, processing, sharing, accessing or storing it. Even if the same information is involved, there may be different data protection requirements in different contexts, due to factors including location and trust in the entities collecting and processing it. There are special laws concerning treatment of sensitive data, and data leakage and loss of privacy are of particular concern to users when sensitive data is processed. In addition, privacy issues vary across different stages of the information lifecycle, e.g. data collection, processing, storage, archival and destruction. Some companies might choose to ignore the issue and pay the penalties if they are found to be in breach, but at the time of writing, regulations, enforcement activities and sanctions are currently increasing the world over.

Privacy risks and concerns are increasing, not least due to the recent revelations about the extent of government surveillance [18] and to the rapid rise in big data analysis [19]. Correspondingly there is a need to push compliance and reduce risks throughout organisations, including to untrained people that might expose hundreds of files by the click of a button, lose a laptop containing unencrypted confidential information or switch sensitive information to the cloud almost instantly using a credit card. However, requirements can be complex to ascertain and a privacy staff is typically small, making effective oversight over hundreds or possibly thousands of projects per year difficult. Hence the role of both process and technology is important. This is considered further in the following section.

3   Corporate Governance for Privacy

In this section it is briefly explained how privacy governance may be achieved within an organisation.

3.1 The Role of Corporate Governance

Companies differ in the resources they have available to deal with privacy. Many larger organisations have a Chief Privacy Officer and privacy staff in order to implement compliance in their organisations. Smaller organisations often do not have the resources for hiring qualified privacy experts and instead the person appointed who is responsible for overseeing the organisation's compliance with applicable privacy legislation could well be the owner or operator. Key elements of privacy management such as defining a corporate privacy policy can often be difficult to achieve in such situations. However, small companies are largely domestically bound, and hence driven by domestic legislation, except in the case for certain small companies in niche areas that might quickly become multinational. For multinational companies, requirements are more diverse and privacy management is more difficult. Nevertheless, data is an asset, so proper privacy management will be valuable for forward-thinking companies, quite apart from being mandatory from a legal point of view.

Privacy management programmes serve as the core operational mechanism through which organisations implement privacy protection. In addition, a related element that needs to be in place within an organisation is data security breach notification, which may require both notice to an authority and notice to an individual affected by a security breach affecting personal data.

Key elements of a successful privacy programme include:

1. Garnering senior management support and establishing a comprehensive organisational privacy policy
2. Establishing clear processes and assign responsibilities to individuals
3. Using proven, existing standard and frameworks for security and IT management
4. Establishing proper monitoring and audit practices, in order to verify and assess what is happening in the organisation against the privacy policies, and take action where required to achieve alignment

More specifically, a privacy management program would ideally include the following measures [20]:

1. Establishing reporting mechanisms and reflecting these within the organisation's privacy management program controls
2. Putting in place privacy management *program controls*, namely:

   – a *Personal Information Inventory* to allow the organisation to identify the personal information in its custody, its sensitivity and the organisation's authority for its collection, usage and disclosure
   – *policies* relating to: collection, use and disclosure of personal information (including requirements for consent and notification); access to and correction of personal information; retention and disposal of personal information; privacy *requirements for third parties* that handle personal information; security controls and role-based access; handling complaints by individuals about the organisation's personal information handling practices

- *risk assessment* mechanisms
- *training and education*
- *breach and incident management*
- procedures for *informing individuals* about their privacy rights and the organisation's program controls

3. Developing an *oversight and review plan* that describes how the organisation's program controls will be monitored and assessed
4. Carrying out *ongoing assessment and revision* of the program controls above

3.2   Privacy by Design

Privacy by Design refers to the philosophy and approach of embedding privacy into design specifications, as first espoused by Ann Cavoukian and others [21, 22]. It applies to products, services and business processes. The main elements are:

1. Recognising that privacy concerns must be addressed
2. Applying basic principles expressing universal spheres of privacy protection
3. Mitigating privacy concerns when developing information technologies and systems, across the entire information life cycle
4. Integration of qualified privacy input
5. Adopting and integrating privacy-enhancing technologies (PETs) [23]

In essence, companies should build in privacy protections at every stage in developing products, and these should include reasonable security for consumer data, limited collection and retention of that data, as well as reasonable procedures to promote data accuracy. Various companies have produced detailed privacy design guidelines (see for example [24]). In addition to the Canadian regulators, there has been strong emphasis and encouragement from Federal Trade Commission (FTC) and EC amongst others on usage of a privacy by design approach [25, 26].

'Privacy by policy' is the standard current means of protecting privacy rights through laws and organisational privacy policies, which must be enforced. Privacy by policy mechanisms focus on provision of notice, choice, security safeguards, access and accountability (via audits and privacy policy management technology). Often, mechanisms are required to obtain and record consent. The 'privacy by policy' approach is central to the current legislative approach, although there is another approach to privacy protection, which is 'privacy by architecture' [27], which relies on technology to provide anonymity. Unfortunately, the latter is often viewed as too expensive or restrictive. Although in privacy by policy the elements can more easily be broken down, it is possible (and preferable) to enhance that approach to cover a hybrid approach with privacy by architecture.

In summary, perfection is not reachable in a complex and moving global context, but companies are expected to think upfront about the impact and the risk they create, and privacy by design has a strong role to play in helping organisations balance innovation with the expectations of individuals. In addition, both regulators and individuals expect organisations to act as a responsible steward of the data which is provided to them, and the way in which companies need to do more to live up to their promises and ensure responsible behaviour is considered in the following section. In particular, corporate governance plays a central role in providing accountability within an organisation, by means of the organisation identifying risks, having appropriate policies that mitigate risks, mechanisms for enforcement internally and for monitoring that these are effective within the enterprise, and for internal and external validation of this. In addition, provision of transparency can help enforce privacy obligations along the service provision chain.

4   Accountability

In this section the role of accountability is explained, in the sense of being an essential aspect of privacy governance. Furthermore, a model of accountability is presented and it is explained how organisations can be accountable. Accountability is a broader notion than just data protection and privacy, but the scope of discussion within this section is largely restricted to that domain as this is the area of interest for this paper.

4.1   What is Accountability?

Accountability is a notion of which there is no universally agreed definition, although it is generally agreed that responsibility, transparency and holding to account are key elements. It is a complex notion that is used in a slightly different sense in different domains. For example, in computer science it is often used to refer to formal verification, compliance and privacy and security policy enforcement; in information security, accountability is meant to generate assurance, transparency and responsibility in support of control and trust; from a corporate governance perspective accountability is an organisational privacy management program and from a social, legal and ethical perspective the emphasis is often on holding organisations and actors accountable for their actions.

In data protection regulation, as we have seen in Section 2, accountability is normally about complying with measures that give effect to practices articulated in given guidelines. For example, a data controller is responsible for complying with particular data protection legislation and, in most cases, is required to establish systems and processes which aim at ensuring such compliance. Indeed, the notion of accountability appears in several international privacy frameworks in addition to the OECD Privacy Guidelines (1980) already considered above, including Canada's PIPEDA (Personal Information Protection and Electronic Documents Act) (2000), APEC Privacy Framework (2005), Article 29 Working Party papers [28] and some elements of the draft European Data Protection Regulation (although in that case not directly associated with the word 'accountability' largely for reasons of translatability) [25]. The usage of this notion by regulators is evolving towards an 'end-to-end' personal data stewardship regime in which the enterprise that collects the data from the data subject is accountable for how the data is shared and used from the time it is collected until when the data is destroyed. This extends to onward transfer to and from third parties.

Building on such analysis, a definition of accountability that is applicable across different domains and that captures a shared multidisciplinary understanding is [29]:

Accountability consists of defining governance to comply in a responsible manner with internal and external criteria, ensuring implementation of appropriate actions, explaining and justifying those actions and remedying any failure to act properly.

Internal criteria are not necessarily visible to stakeholders external to that organisation, as they might for example reflect the risk appetite of that organisation or known security vulnerabilities; external criteria could include best practice on security, data protection and breach notification, as well as privacy regulatory and contractual requirements and societal expectations.

Although it is a complex notion, it could be argued that its core, accountability is a very simple idea. It says that not only should an organisation do everything necessary to exercise good stewardship of the data under its control, it should also be able to demonstrate that it is doing so. Good stewardship is achieved by designing systems appropriately, so that they reflect privacy principles and security expectations from partners, regulators and data subjects, as well as by the organisation living up to its promises and ensuring responsible behaviour. The demonstration – via provision of an account – is an essential aspect, but can be challenging to provide. Furthermore, if events do not work out as planned, organisations need to provide a means of remediation as well as needing to try to prevent such an occurrence happening again. These elements are captured in Figure 2, which shows how accountability should complement the usage of appropriate privacy and security controls in order to support democratically determined principles that reflect societal norms, regulations and stakeholder expectations. Governance and oversight of this process is achieved via a combination of Data Protection Authorities, auditors and Data Protection Officers within organisations, potentially supplemented by private Accountability Agents acting on their behalf.

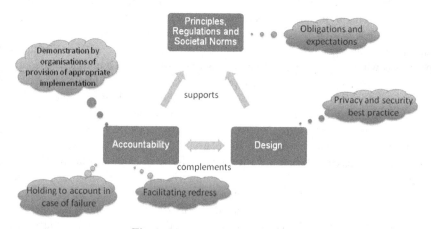

Fig. 2. Accountability context

At its core, in the sense that a data controller should be accountable for complying with measures which give effect to principles that have been set within a democratic context, and that they will be held to account in case of failure, as well as the provision of tools to help organisations to 'do the right thing' (including for better remediation, breach notification, etc.), accountability is obviously a good thing and not very controversial. However, there are a number of different and even conflicting opinions related to additional (or even alternative) potential features of an accountability-based approach. In the main these relate to how accountability can help address the issue of the lack of take up of privacy by design by organisations to date, the role of accountability in moving towards greater regulatory interoperability, the importance of measures that prevent privacy harm and the extent to which punishment for a privacy violation should be lessened by evidence that appropriate privacy and security measures have been taken by an organisation. The former can be done in particular by easing transborder data flow constraints and regulatory complexity in favour of a single set of organisational requirements that need to be adhered to that could apply globally (as is the case with Binding Corporate Rules for instance [30]), allowing differentiation in terms of privacy (so long as legal requirements are met), being less prescriptive in terms of the specification of regulatory requirements, encouraging (or even mandating) usage of privacy impact assessments to guide design and also of course increasing punishment in cases of non-compliance as well as taking into account the controls an organisation has used when determining punishment. Opinions about the relative merits of these approaches differ. In addition, Weitzner views accountability as retrospective (arguing that a shift is needed from hiding information to ensuring that only appropriate uses occur) [31] whereas preventive risk identification and mitigation is viewed as an essential element of accountability by others [32, 20].

It is often regarded as underpinning an accountability-based approach that organisations should be allowed greater control over the practical aspects of compliance with data protection obligations in return for an additional obligation to prove that they have put privacy principles into effect (see for example [32]). Hence, that whole approach relies on the accuracy of the demonstration itself. If that is weakened into a mere tickbox exercise, weak self certification and/or connivance with an accountability agent that is not properly checking what the organisation is actually doing, then the overall affect could in some cases be very harmful in terms of privacy protection. As Bennett points out [33: p45], due to resource issues regulators will need to rely upon surrogates, including private sector agents, to be agents of accountability, and it is important within this process that they are able to have a strong influence over the acceptability of different third party accountability mechanisms. This can be achieved via independent testing of practices, provision of evidence that is taken into account, including auditing against the ISO 27001 series and associated security standards.

Hence, the way in which accountability is achieved is key, which includes the need for adequate resources in checking and enforcing whether organisations are indeed using appropriate measures, involvement of different stakeholders, including the public (or representatives of the public) in data privacy regulation, provision of suitable accountability tools and help for organisations to form appropriate risk assessment mechanisms and policies. In the next two sections the type of measures are elucidated that are needed as part of such an approach.

4.2   A Model of Accountability

In Figure 3 a model of accountability is presented that shows how accountability can be captured at different layers of abstraction. The top layer of the triangle shown in Figure 3 corresponds to the definition of accountability, as given in the previous subsection. Moving down the model in terms of becoming less abstract, the other layers correspond in turn to the following aspects:

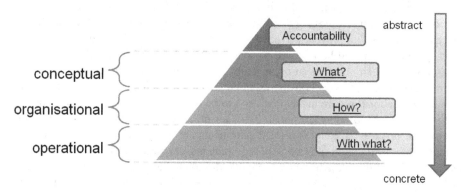

Fig. 3. Conceptual model of accountability

Accountability Attributes. These are the central taxonomic components of accountability, namely: observabililty, verifiability, attributability, transparency, responsibility, liability and remediability. Further details are given in [34].

Accountability Practices. These define the central behavior of an organisation adopting an accountability-based approach. From the definition given above, it can be seen that these are: defining governance, ensuring implementation of appropriate actions, explaining and justifying those actions and remedying any failure to act properly. These map to the Galway project's 'essential elements' of accountability [32]. Further details are given in the following section.

Accountability Mechanisms and Tools. These tools and mechanisms offer enhanced accountability; organisations in addition will need to use privacy and security controls appropriate to the context, as described in the previous subsection. The tools may form a toolbox from which organisations can select as appropriate. They can be (extensions of) existing business processes like auditing, risk assessment and the provision of a trustworthy account, or non-technical mechanisms like formation of appropriate organisational policies, remediation procedures in complex environments, contracts, certification procedures, and so on. Or they can be technical tools, which would include tracking and transparency tools, detection of violation of policy obligations, notification of policy violation, increased transparency without compromising privacy, and so on. The tools are targetted at different stakeholders, and some are designed for usage as a preventive measure (for example, to assess and reduce privacy harm before personal data is collected), some as a detective measure (for example, to assess the degree to which privacy obligations are actually being met) and others as a corrective measure (for example, to facilitate redress).

4.3   How can Organisations be Accountable?

This subsection provides more detail about the third layer of the model above, namely how to be accountable. An accountable organisation must commit to responsible stewardship of other people's data, which in brief entails that it must define what should be done, monitor how it is done, remedy any discrepancies between definition and fact, and explain and justify relevant actions. We now consider these aspects further below.

First and foremost, an accountable organisation must demonstrate willingness and capacity to be responsible and answerable for its data practices with regard to personal data. Analogously, the same applies more broadly with regard to confidential data that may or may not be personal data – for example, business secrets, although that takes us out of the remit of privacy concerns and hence we do not say too much more about that in this paper.

In order to achieve this, senior management support for an accountability-based culture within the organization must be obtained and a reporting structure set up with responsibilities allocated to individuals, as discussed already in Section 3.1. In addition, an accountable organisation must address the following four central aspects:

1. *Define and deploy policies regarding their data practices* that link to relevant external criteria and are supported by senior management. The policies include specification of the entities involved in the processing of data and their responsibilities; the scope and context of processing data; the purposes and means of processing and data handling and data access policies. The policies need to take account of relevant external legal obligations. In addition, policies need to be defined related to risk monitoring and risk mitigation. Mechanisms are also needed in order to put these policies in place, including risk assessment and means to make uses transparent to individuals and to assure that their rights are respected.
2. *Monitor their data practices:* this includes how they process data, evidence that the organisation has acted according to its policies, and a running account that is a record of the monitoring and its results. In particular, periodic internal reviews are needed to provide assurance that the mechanisms are working and improve over time.
3. *Correct policy violations:* this includes both the effects of the violation that need to be addressed, as well as causes of the violation that need to be addressed, and the informing of appropriate stakeholders, who include authorities, customers and affected data subjects. The effects of the violation could involve errors that need to be corrected and damages that need to be compensated, financially or otherwise.

4. *Demonstrate policy compliance:* policy violations need to be reported and compliance with policies needs to be demonstrated in a timely fashion, reactively and where possible, proactively. The organisation must demonstrate that the controls selected and used within the service provision chain are appropriate for the context and should provide evidence that the operational environment is indeed satisfying the policies. There must be openness to oversigh by enforcement agencies, together with remediation if the goals of data protection have been abused in a harmful fashion.

So far, this analysis corresponds in a general way to that given within the Accountability Project [32] and other opinions influenced by that [20]. But in addition, two other important aspects need to be emphasised.

First, accountable organisations must ensure that accountability extends through across their service supply chains, in other words ensuring that the services and partners they use are accountable too, which involves amonst other things proper allocation of responsibilities and provision of evidence about satisfaction of obligations along the service provision chain.

Second, there are implications in terms of the way that the enforcement and verification mechanisms for accountability will operate, the scope of risk assessment and the ways in which other stakeholders are able to hold an organisation to account.

5   Two Example Solutions

Solutions to the above issues could take a number of forms. As considered above, there is a wealth of different privacy and security controls that an organisation could choose to use.

Risk assessment (a core security process) is particularly important for accountability because it is a central part of the process used to determine and demonstrate that the policies (whether reflected in corporate privacy and security policies or in contractual obligations) that are signed up to and implemented by the organisation (that is taking an accountability-based approach) are appropriate to the context. The type of procedures and mechanisms vary according to the risks represented by the processing and the nature of the data [17].

We now consider further two particular solutions for privacy management and accountability within global organisations, namely HP Privacy Advisor, which is a type of privacy risk assessment system, and a range of solutions being developed within the EU Cloud Accountability project. The latter includes further research to provide risk assessment mechanisms in relation to cloud service provision.

5.1   HP Privacy Advisor

Existing organisational risk assessment processes need to be enhanced to meet the requirements above, or else supplemented with separate privacy-specific risk assessment [35]. Privacy impact assessments are already being rolled out as part of a process to encourage privacy by design [35]: in November 2007 the UK Information

Commissioners Office (ICO) (an organisation responsible for regulating and enforcing access to and use of personal information), launched a Privacy Impact Assessment (PIA) [35] process (incorporating privacy by design) to help organisations assess the impact of their operations on personal privacy. This process assesses the privacy requirements of new and existing systems; it is primarily intended for use in public sector risk management, but is increasingly seen to be of value to private sector businesses that process personal data. Similar methodologies exist and can have legal status in Australia, Canada and the US [35]. The methodology aims to combat the slow take-up to design in privacy protections from first principles at the enterprise level. Usage is increasingly being encouraged and even mandated in certain circumstances by regulators [35]. Data impact assessment may also become an obligation for some high risk contexts within the forthcoming EU regulation [cf. Article 33: 25].

As we have considered in Section 4, accountability, as articulated by the Article 29 Working Party [28], begins to shift our thinking from only having an obligation to comply with a principle, to an obligation to prove that you can put those principles into effect. Technology can assist organisations in ensuring proper implementation. New laws and regulations are increasingly having explicit requirements that an organisation not only comply, but that they have programs that put the principles into effect. Hence companies will need to do more to ensure that privacy is indeed considered in their products and services.

HP Privacy Advisor (HP PA) is an intelligent online rule-driven system that assesses activities that handle personal data within HP and provides privacy by design guidance. It is a web-based decision support system used internally within HP to assess risk and degree of compliance for projects that handle personal data and to guide individual employees in their decisions on how to handle different types of data. HP PA elicits privacy-relevant information about a project via a customised sequence of questions. It uses a dynamic interface to minimise unnecessary questions and maintains a record of activities.

As shown in Figure 4, based on the answers given, HP PA:

- Assesses a project's degree of compliance with corporate privacy policy, ethics and global legislation, and the privacy promises the company makes
- Integrates privacy risk assessment, education, and guidance into the process
- Scores projects for a list of ten privacy compliance indicators including transborder data flows, compliance, business controls, security, transparency, and so forth
- Generates tailored privacy design guidance or a tailored compliance report for each project and, if appropriate, notifies an appropriate member of the corporate privacy team for further guidance/intervention
- Provides checklists, reminders, customised help and warnings to users
- Maintains a record of activities for audit purposes.

HP PA is a standard three tier web application using Java Enterprise Technology, where the client is a standard web browser, the application tier is a standard Java application server, and the persistence layer is a standard relational database.

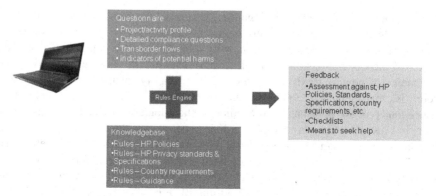

Fig. 4. Functional overview of HP Privacy Advisor

An accurate representation of organisational privacy policies is provided that encodes HP's 300 plus page privacy policies. HP PA uses JBoss Drools 5, a forward chaining rules engine both for validating the users' responses against a set of privacy rules, and to dynamically tailor the user experience using a questionnaire generated by a set of questionnaire rules. Desirable system properties are ensured such as deterministic behaviour of questionnaire and report generation, tailoring, and completeness of the questionnaire generation. For further information about this system, see [37].

5.2 EU Cloud Accountability Project

As data moves to the cloud, new risks and vulnerabilities arise and in addition there are concerns over data security, integrity and privacy due in particular to reduced transparency and less control. As a result, organisations are reluctant to let data flow outside the organisations' boundaries into the cloud, and in addition individuals have concerns over privacy and their relative lack of control.

Cloud computing creates new dynamics in that there is an additional role of cloud provider, and indeed there could be several such parties. This not only can cause legal uncertainty in certain cases, but there is more general a need for clarification of distributed privacy and security responsibilities and control. Privacy is a difficult issue to tackle, because of the underlying complexity across multiple dimensions and the interdisciplinary nature of the problem. For example, location matters from a legal point of view and there are restrictions about how information can be sent and accessed across boundaries as briefly discussed in Section 2 above, but in cloud computing data can flow along chains of service providers both horizontally between software-as-a-service providers and vertically, down to infrastructure providers, where the information can be fragmented and duplicated across databases in different jurisdictions. Furthermore, the cloud model can magnify existing issues (such as transborder flow, data deletion, loss of control and transparency) and new vulnerabilities are also possible (such as security attacks exploiting the vulnerabilities of virtualisation mechanisms). The risks, as well as responsibilities, will vary according to the combination of cloud service and deployment models. Correspondingly, security and privacy requirements will vary widely from one use case to the next. Within a cloud ecosystem, issues from one cloud service provider (CSP) may have ramifications further up the chain, for example in terms of loss of governance. Loss of governance may arise in cloud computing for example as the client cedes control to the CSP, but service level agreements may not offer commitment to provide such services on the part of the CSP, thus giving a gap in security. For further discussion of privacy risks in the cloud, see [17].

The overall goal of the EU Cloud Accountability project [38] is to develop and validate techniques for implementing accountable cloud ecosystems. This includes development of techniques that can enable improved trustworthiness of cloud service provision networks, and to prevent breaches of trust by using audited policy enforcement techniques, assessing the potential impact of policy violations, detecting violations, managing incidents and obtaining redress. The outputs of the project include an accountability framework (including recommendations, guidance, models of data governance, accountability metrics and a reference architecture) as well as a range of accountability tools and mechanisms. These are being developed for organisations using cloud services as well as cloud service providers, regulators and data subjects.

The focus of the project is on personal data, but in addition certain types of confidential information that may not involve personal data, such as business secrets, are being considered. The focus is particularly on the accountability of organisations using and providing cloud services to data subjects and regulators. Government surveillance, including government acquisition of data from cloud service providers, is outside the scope of this project, except where it relates specifically to a data protection law accountability mechanism: no accountability controls of the types considered in the project (which are based upon assisting compliance with domestic data protection legislation and private contracts) are likely to provide effective protection against such activities.

The overall approach is as follows. The legal and contractual context defines obligations, responsibilities and liabilities of actors in a given cloud ecosystem. Businesses need to meet these obligations and mitigate risk and uncertainty in dynamic and global environments. This is a challenging problem especially where service provision chains are complex. Actors within cloud ecosystems may select mechanisms and tools to support accountability practices, and thereby help them to comply with relevant regulatory regimes within specific application domains. Overall, the project aims to move beyond a tick-box culture by providing organisations with the appropriate support to take an accountability-based ethical approach and make that a business advantage.

6   Conclusions

Privacy for companies is about managing privacy requirements end-to-end. Technical point solutions, such as encryption and auditing tools, are vitally important, but often address only a small part of overall privacy concerns. Although a number of different privacy-enhancing technologies are available, privacy requirements for global organisations can still be challenging to properly address.

The way that business environments are changing means that more automation (including much greater adoption of anonymisation techniques and encryption governed by consumers where possible) is needed in order to protect privacy online [39]. The challenge is how to move towards this model, including extension of that beyond the 'good willing' enterprises to others who are not necessarily willing to invest in governance practice that lessens privacy risks. Transparency, responsibility, privacy impact assessment and assurance – key aspects of accountability – are an important part of such a solution.

New technologies and business models can bring a higher risk to data privacy and security. For example, there can be rapid scaling (through subcontracting), remote data storage, and the sharing of services in a dynamic environment. This is a key user concern, especially for sensitive information like financial and health data. In global and dynamic environments especially, the associated lack of consumer trust – whether from individuals or Chief Information Officers in large organisations – can act as a barrier to business, and lack of regulator trust is resulting in increased penalties for non-compliance right across the world at present. The necessary increased trust can come from improved transparency and sound stewardship of information by service providers for which they are held accountable. Ongoing development of complementary solutions in the area of privacy by design and accountability is needed. Some examples of such an approach have been given in this paper.

Acknowledgements. The research leading to these results has received funding from the European Union Seventh Framework Programme (FP7/2007-2013) under grant agreement no: 317550 (A4Cloud). In particular, acknowledgement is given to Daniel Pradelles for assistance in creating Figure 1 (which gives a rough indication of the situation in 2012 and should not be regarded as completely accurate for all countries) and input from other members of Work Package C2 within the Cloud Accountability Project in collectively forming the accountability model discussed in Section 4.

References

1. Information Commissioner's Office (ICO), The Privacy Dividend: The Business Case for Investing in Proactive Privacy Protection (March 2010),
   http://www.ico.org.uk/~/media/documents/library/Data_Protect
   ion/Detailed_specialist_guides/PRIVACY_DIVIDEND.ashx
2. Tressell, R.: The Ragged Trousered Philanthropists. Wordsworth Classics (2012)
3. Bennett, C.J., Raab, C.D.: The Governance of Privacy: Policy Instruments in Global Perspective. MIT Press, Cambridge (2006)
4. Warren, S., Brandeis, L.: The Right to Privacy. 4 Harvard Law Review 193 (1890)
5. Westin, A.: Privacy and Freedom, New York, US, Atheneum (1967)
6. American Institute of Certified Public Accountants (AICPA) and CICA: Generally Accepted Privacy Principles (August 2009)
7. Solove, D.J.: A Taxonomy of Privacy. University of Pennyslavania Law Review 154(3), 477 (2006)

8. Nissenbaum, H.: Privacy as Contextual Integrity. Washington Law Review, 101–139 (2004)
9. Swire, P., Bermann, S.: Information Privacy. Official Reference for the Certified Information Privacy Professional, CIPP (2007)
10. European Commission (EC): Directive 95/46/EC of the European Parliament and of the Council of 24 October 1995 on the protection of individuals with regard to the processing of personal data and on the free movement of such data (1995)
11. Privacy Protection Study Commission: Personal Privacy in an Information Society, United Statues Privacy Protection Study Commission Fair Information Practices (1977)
12. Organisation for Economic Co-operation and Development (OECD): Guidelines for the Protection of Personal Data and Transborder Data Flows (1980)
13. OECD: Guidelines Concerning the Protection of Privacy and Transborder Flows of Personal Data (2013), http://www.oecd.org/sti/ieconomy/2013-oecd-privacy-guidelines.pdf
14. European Commission, Unleashing the Potential of Cloud Computing in Europe (2012), http://eur-lex.europa.eu/LexUriServ/LexUriServ.do?uri=COM:2012:0529:FIN:EN:PDF
15. European Commission, Cybersecurity Strategy of the European Union: An Open, Safe and Secure Cyberspace (2013), http://ec.europa.eu/information_society/newsroom/cf//document.cfm?doc_id=1667
16. European Commission, Directive on Network and Information Security (2013), http://ec.europa.eu/digital-agenda/en/news/eu-cybersecurity-plan-protect-open-internet-and-online-freedom-and-opportunity-cyber-security
17. Pearson, S.: Privacy, Security and Trust in Cloud Computing. In: Pearson, S., Yee, G. (eds.) Privacy and Security for Cloud Computing, Computer Communications and Networks, pp. 3–42. Springer (2012)
18. The Guardian: NSA Prism program taps in to user data of Apple, Google and others (June 7, 2013), http://www.guardian.co.uk/world/2013/jun/06/us-tech-giants-nsa-data
19. Barabási, A.-L.: Scientists must spearhead ethical use of big data (2013), http://www.politico.com/story/2013/09/scientists-must-spearhead-ethical-use-of-big-data-97578.html
20. Office of the Information and Privacy Commissioner of Alberta, Office of the Privacy Commissioner of Canada, Office of the Information and Privacy Commissioner for British Colombia: Getting Accountability Right with a Privacy Management Program (April 2012)
21. Cavoukian, A.: Privacy by Design: Origins, Meaning, and Prospects for Assuring Privacy and Trust in the Information Era. In: Yee, G. (ed.) Privacy Protection Measures and Technologies in Business Organisations: Aspects and Standards, pp. 170–208. IGI Global (2012)
22. Information Commissioners Office (ICO): Privacy by Design. Report (2008), http://www.ico.gov.uk
23. Privacy Enhancing Technologies: A Review. HPL-2011-113, http://www.hpl.hp.com/techreports/2011/HPL-2011-113.html
24. Microsoft Corporation: Privacy Guidelines for Developing Software Products and Services, Version 2.1a (2007)

25. European Commission: Proposal for a Directive of the European Parliament and of the Council on the protection of individuals with regard to the processing of personal data by competent authorities for the purposes of prevention, investigation, detection or prosecution of criminal offences or the execution of criminal penalties, and the free movement of such data (January 2012)
26. Federal Trade Commission (FTC): Protecting Consumer Privacy in an Age of Rapid Change: Recommendations for Business and PolicyMakers. FTC Report (March 2012)
27. Spiekermann, S., Cranor, L.F.: Engineering privacy. IEEE Transactions on Software Engineering, 1–42 (2008)
28. European DG of Justice: Article 29 Working Party. 'Opinion 3/2010 on the principle of accountability (WP 173)' (July 2010)
29. Felici, Pearson: MS:C-2.2, Internal Project Report, A4Cloud project (March 2013)
30. Information Commissioner's Office (ICO): Binding Corporate Rules., http://www.ico.gov.uk/for_organisations/data_protection/overseas/binding_corporate_rules.aspx
31. Weitzner, D.J., Abelson, H., Berners-Lee, T., Feigenbaum, J., Hendler, J., Sussman, G.J.: Information accountability. Communications of ACM 51(6), 87 (2008)
32. Center for Information Policy Leadership (CIPL): Data protection accountability: the essential elements (2009), http://www.huntonfiles.com/files/webupload/CIPL_Galway_Accountability_Paper.pdf
33. Bennett, C.J.: The Accountability Approach to Privacy and Data Protection: Assumptions and Caveats. In: Guagnin, D., et al. (eds.) Managing Privacy through Accountability, pp. 33–48. MacMillan (2012)
34. Catteddu, D., et al.: Towards a Model of Accountability for Cloud Computing Services. In: Proceedings of the DIMACS/BIC/A4Cloud/CSA International Workshop on Trustworthiness, Accountability and Forensics in the Cloud (TAFC) (May 2013)
35. Trilateral Research and Consulting, Privacy Impact Assessment and Risk Management, ICO report (May 2013), http://www.ico.org.uk/~/media/documents/library/Corporate/Research_and_reports/pia-and-risk-management-full-report-for-the-ico.pdf
36. Information Commissioner's Office UK (ICO): Data protection guidance note: Privacy enhancing technologies (2007)
37. Pearson, S., Sander, T.: A Decision Support System for Privacy Compliance. In: Gupta, M., Walp, J., Sharman, R. (eds.) Threats, Countermeasures, and Advances in Applied Information Security. Information Science Reference, pp. 158–180. IGI Global, New York (2012)
38. EU Cloud Accountability project, http://www.a4cloud.eu
39. Mowbray, M., Pearson, S.: Protecting Personal Information in Cloud Computing. In: Meersman, R., Panetto, H., Dillon, T., Rinderle-Ma, S., Dadam, P., Zhou, X., Pearson, S., Ferscha, A., Bergamaschi, S., Cruz, I.F. (eds.) OTM 2012, Part II. LNCS, vol. 7566, pp. 475–491. Springer, Heidelberg (2012)

Concepts Around Privacy-Preserving Attribute-Based Credentials

Making Authentication with Anonymous Credentials Practical

Jan Camenisch

IBM Research, Zurich, Säumerstrasse 4, 8803 Rüschlikon, Switzerland

Abstract. This article provides a short overview of the concepts around privacy-preserving attribute-based authentication. It then briefly discusses the cryptographic realisation of these concepts and describes an architecture implementing them.

1 Introduction

The Internet has transformed our environment and how we interact with each other dramatically. Soon all things surrounding us will be part of the Internet, producing, processing, providing, and consuming enormous amounts of data. It seems impossible to protect all devices and systems, virtually or physically. Therefore secure authorisation and communication and protecting stored data are of vital importance. To this end, it is necessary to authenticate and encrypt every single bit as well as explicitly define who is allowed to do what with the bit, i.e., to attach a data-usage policy to each bit. However, authenticating every bit communicated will most probably decrease users' privacy substantially and, more generally, the security of the overall system.

To alleviate this, privacy-preserving authentication mechanisms, in particular attribute-based authentication together with anonymous credentials, should be applied. Unfortunately, today they are not employed in practice. One reason for this might be the complexity of privacy-preserving authentication mechanisms due to the large numbers of features they provide. Also, the security properties, such as unlinkability, of privacy-preserving authentication mechanisms are often counterintuitive. To address this, the ABC4Trust project [1] has put forth a number of concepts that capture, simplify, and unify the properties of privacy-preserving authentication technologies. These concepts aim to make these authentication technologies easier to understand, deploy, and use. The ABC4Trust project also runs two pilots to show the applicability of these technologies in real-world scenarios [1,15].

In this article we summarise and explain these concepts. To this end, we first discuss the basic authentication scenario and the entities involved. Then we discuss each of the concepts. Next, we describe the realisation of these concept in the ABC4Trust architecture and the reference implementation. Finally, we

M. Hansen et al. (Eds.): Privacy and Identity 2014, IFIP AICT 421, pp. 53–63, 2014.

conclude with a discussion on obstacles that need to be overcome in order for privacy-preserving authentication to be used practice.

2   Authentication Scenario and Entities

The basic entities of a privacy-protecting authentication system with attribute-based credentials (privacy-ABC system) include a user, an issuer (often called identity provider), and a verifier (often called relying party). These entities essentially occur in any authentication scenario, in particular also if authentication is performed with X.509 certificates or the OpenID protocol. The remaining two entities are the revocation authority and the inspector. The former also occurs in traditional certificate-based authentication systems, whereas the latter is a specialty of privacy-preserving authentication. All these entities are depicted in Figure 1. In a real deployment, there are further entities involved, for instance the providers of the computing platforms, different software components, and a public key infrastructure, etc. In this article, however, we do not consider such entities as they are not particular to privacy-ABC systems.

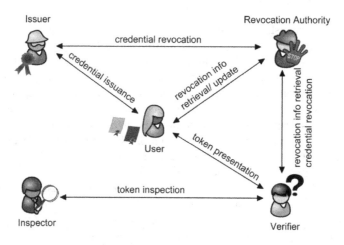

Fig. 1. Entities and the interactions between them [4]

These parties each perform a number of tasks and interact with each other to make the authentication system work. First, to initiate the overall system, each issuer generates a secret issuance key and publishes the *issuer parameters* that include the corresponding public verification key. Similarly, each inspector generates a private decryption key and a corresponding public encryption key, and each revocation authority generates and publishes its revocation authority parameters. It is assumed that all entities have a means to retrieve the public keys of the issuers, revocation authorities, inspectors, and verifiers, e.g., by using some form of public key infrastructure.

Most parties interact with each other, as can be seen from Figure 1, where these interactions are depicted and named according to their purpose. Now, depending on which (privacy-preserving) authentication technology is used, these interactions might be realised differently and consist of only a single flow or an interactive protocol. Also the time at which they occur depends on the technology used.

The first interaction, the *credential issuance* protocol, allows a user to obtain credentials from an issuer. A credential contains attributes that its issuer vouches for with respect to the user. A credential can also specify one or more revocation authorities who are able to revoke the credential if necessary for some reason. To issue a credential that is revocable, the user and/or the issuer might need to interact with the revocation authority prior to or during the issuance protocol. Using her credentials, a user can form a presentation token that contains a subset of the certified attributes, provided that the corresponding credentials have not been revoked. This process does not require the user to interact with the issuer! However, the user might need to retrieve information from the revocation authority, depending on the specific revocation scheme used. Additionally, some of the attributes can be encoded in the presentation token so that they can only be retrieved by an inspector. The user can attach inspection grounds specifying under which conditions the inspector should reveal these attributes. Upon receipt of a presentation token from a user, a verifier checks whether the presentation token is valid with respect to the relevant issuers' public keys, the inspectors' public keys, and the latest revocation information (thus, the verifier will interact with the revocation authority). If the verification succeeds, the verifier will be convinced that the attributes contained in the presentation token are vouched for by the corresponding issuers. Finally, if a presentation token contains attributes that can only be retrieved by an inspector and the inspection grounds are met, the verifier can forward the token to the inspector who will then follows the instructions defined in the inspection grounds, e.g., to reveal the attribute to a designated party.

Informally, a secure realisation of a privacy-ABC system guarantees (1) that users can only generate a valid presentation token if they were indeed issued the corresponding credentials that have not been revoked, (2) that attributes encoded in the presentation token for an inspector can indeed be retrieved by that inspector, and (3) that the presentation tokens do not reveal any further information about the users other than the attributes contained in them.

3   Concepts

In this section we provide a brief explanation of the main features of privacy-ABCs. We start by explaining what we mean by an identity as all the concepts are based on this view of identity. We then discuss the concepts underlying the authentication and authorisation with a privacy-ABC system.

3.1 Attributes and Identities

For the purpose of this exposition, we consider an *identity* to consist of the *attributes* that another party knows linkable a user, say Alice. Figure 2 shows some identities that Alice has with some parties. For instance, she has an identity with her employer comprising her full name, salary, address, education, and the languages she speaks. Her identity with an on-line shop may comprise her name, address, credit card number, and purchase history. Her identity with an on-line forum may comprise a nickname and her hobbies. There might of course be many other people who have a similar or the same identity as Alice with some party, i.e., the set of attributes that the party knows about Alice is the same as the set of attributes the party knows of another person, say Jim. Thus, the party can per se not distinguish whether it is communicating with Jim or Alice. Often parties ensure that this does not happen by requiring some attributes to be unique, e.g., by requiring users to provide different nick names. Nevertheless, we do not want to rule out that different users can have the same identity with the same party or with different parties.

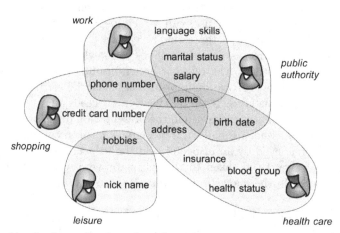

Fig. 2. An identity is a collection of attributes someone knows about. Shown here are some of Alice's identities [7,14]

Now, for this concept of identities is to be useful, we require two basic mechanisms: one that allows a user to authenticate as the owner of an identity and one that allows a user to transfer an attribute from one identity to another identity, i.e., to let the latter learn an attribute that the former entity knows and vouches for.

These mechanisms shall protect the privacy of the user, i.e., the parties with which the user has established these identities shall not be able to link them – unless this is implied by the uniqueness of an attribute value or a set of attribute values.

While we consider an identity to be a set of attributes that someone knows about a user, the same set of attributes can be different identities. That is, a party might know the same set of attribute values about two different users and indeed should consider these to be different entities. Similarly, two parties who know a single or two users by the same set of attribute values, should consider these as different identities. Here the concept of the authentication mechanism becomes especially useful. If the specific authentication parameters (e.g., public key or pseudonym value) associated with different sets of attribute values are identical, then the identity should considered to be the same. Also, a user can link different identities of hers together using the authentication mechanism by either using the same authentication parameters with the different identities or, preferably, by using specific properties of the authentication mechanism to prove that she is the holder of both identities. We discuss such mechanisms next.

3.2 Pseudonyms

To authenticate as the owner of an identity, a user can establish a (cryptographic) *pseudonym* with a party. Technically, a pseudonyms is essentially a public key of a cryptographic identification scheme. However, different from a traditional cryptographic identification scheme where there is a single secret key and public key pair, here an unlimited number of pseudonyms (public keys) can be derived from the same secret key. Pseudonyms are unlinkable, i.e., a party cannot tell whether two given pseudonyms correspond to different secret keys. While technically, a user can also have different secret keys, it is instructive to consider each secret key to define a separate user – very much like a real-world passport defines a person's identity.

In some situations, however, the possibility to generate an unlimited number of unlinkable pseudonyms is undesirable. For instance, a verifier might want to allow only one account per user. To still support privacy in such cases, ABC technologies allow *scope-exclusive* pseudonyms. Such pseudonyms are generate from the secret key and a scope identifier (string) and are unique per scope for a given user secret key. Nevertheless, scope-exclusive pseudonyms for different scopes remain unlinkable.

3.3 Credentials

A credential is a set of attributes that is (digitally) signed by an issuer. While in principle an issuer could first generate a credential and then send it to the user, e.g., by email, privacy-ABCs typically require an interactive issuance protocols to realise the enhanced privacy properties to ensure that the issuer does not learn the secret key of the user and, for some special applications, to allow the user to keep some of the attributes hidden from the issuer. An example of such a special application is one-show credential: here the user encodes a random attribute in the credential that is hidden during issuance but is require to be revealed during presentation.

The validity of a credential can be verified with regard to the issuer parameters published by the issuer and a credential specification. The latter defines the semantic of a credential such as what attribute types the credential contains.

While the issuer parameters are specific for each issuer, a credential specification can be shared by many issuers. The credential specification further defines whether a credential is revocable and/or bound to a key of the user. We discuss these two features next.

3.4   Binding Credentials to Keys

When a credential specification requires that a credential be key bound, the issuance protocol will require the user to input a secret key to which the credential will be issued without the issuer learning any information about the secret key. A key-bound credential can only be presented with knowledge of the secret key. Per se, the secret key can be any secret of the user's choice. However, for some applications, it might make sense to restrict the user in this choice. To this end, the issuer can specify in the *issuance policy* that the credential be bound to the same key as some other credential(s) or to the secret key underlying some particular pseudonym that the user has sent to the issuer earlier. For instance, to enforce that all of a user's credentials be bound to the same secret key, one could require each user to register with some root authority from which a user would get a key-bound (root) credential. Later, whenever some issuer issues a credential to a user, he would specify that the credentials issued be key-bound to the same key as a root credential.

3.5   Revocation of Credentials

There might be many reasons why a credential should be revoked. A user might have lost the right that the credential attested to her or her secret key and all her credentials were compromised. In this case, the issuer(s) of the credential(s) concerned must be able to invalidate them. For ordinary credentials, this is typically done by some whitelist or blacklist containing the serial numbers to the valid or invalid credentials, respectively, or by letting credentials be valid for only a short time. The latter works for privacy-ABC as well, whereas the former does not as it would require users to reveal the serial number of their credential and thus all privacy would be lost again. Fortunately, the cryptographic literature provides several mechanisms that allow users to convince a verifier that the serial number of their credential is on a whitelist or not on a blacklist. These mechanisms all have in common that the issuer publishes some public revocation information which both users and verifiers should consult. Some mechanisms further require that users be able to retrieve specific information related to their credential so that they will be able to perform the proof of validity of their credential. We refer to this as issuer-driven revocation.

Sometimes, however, a credential might not need to be revoked globally but rather some verifier might want to stop accepting a credential from a specific user. For example, a hooligan may see his digital identity card revoked for accessing sport stadiums, but may still use it for all other purposes. The specification therefore also allows for verifier-driven revocation Here, verifiers can specify their own lists and have users prove to them whether or not they figure on such a list.

The ABC4Trust specifications define revocation very generically and just define a revocation authority who manages and publishes the revocation information. The only difference between issuer-driven and verifier-driven revocation is that the former is performed based on the revocation handle (which is treated as a dedicated attribute), whereas the latter can be performed based on any attribute value or even a combination of values, possibly even from different credentials.

3.6   Presentation Policy and Presentation Token

The probably most important difference between privacy-ABCs and ordinary credentials is how a user authenticates to a verifier with them. In an ordinary PKI, the user sends her credentials (thereby revealing all attribute values!) to the verifier and authenticates as the holder of the credentials. The verifier then verifies the validity of the credentials and whether or not the attributes contained therein match his access control requirements.

A privacy-ABC system is much more privacy friendly than such traditional approaches. It first requires the verifier to specify which attributes certified by whom it requires from the user. We call this statement the *presentation policy*. In fact, the policy allows an even more privacy-friendly option. Instead of requiring a user to reveal an attribute, the verifier could request only a predicate over an attribute such as "over 18" instead of "reveal birthdate" or just ask that the last name in one credential be the same as in another credential without having to reveal the value of the last name. It can further be specified that a user also send a pseudonym and authenticate with regard to it. A presentation policy further allows one to restrict verifiers in what attributes they learn, e.g., by requiring that policies be signed by a data protection authority.

In a second step, once the user has received the presentation policy from the verifier, the user can decide whether she wants to reveal this information to the verifier, and if so, which credentials she wants to use (in case multiple credentials apply) provided she possesses all necessary credentials. If not, the user will have to somehow get the missing credentials issued. To support the user in these tasks, ABC4Trust provides a graphical user interface (identity selector) showing the user the different choices. Once the user has made her choices, she creates a *presentation token* from the credentials she selected. A presentation token can be seen as a transformed (set of) credential(s) that contains only the attributes from the original credential(s) that the user wishes to reveal. Cryptographically, a presentation token verifies with regard to the signature verification keys of original credentials' issuers, just like the original credentials themselves.

3.7   Inspectable Presentation Tokens

In some situation, the information required from a user changes depending on the behaviour of the user. So, while it might be fine that a user can access some service by convincing the service provider that she has obtained a subscription credential, it might be necessary that additional information be available in case of abuse. To address such scenarios, a presentation policy can state that certain attributes need to be provided in encrypted form, encrypted under the public key of a designated party – the inspector. That is, the verifier will not be privy to inspectable attributes unless he forwards the presentation token to the designated inspector and the *inspection grounds* stated in the presentation policy are met. An inspection ground is a free format text that cannot be modified and that the inspector is expected read and comply with before handing the decrypted attributes to the verifier.

3.8   Issuance of Credentials

As mentioned, a credential is issued in a protocol between the user and the issuer. Issuing a credential is in some sense just a special case of providing a service and so an issuer might require a user to present a number of credentials issued by other parties or to authenticate with regard to a pseudonym beforehand. While in many cases, the issuer might know all the attributes values of the issued credential, that is not always necessary and sometimes even undesirable. Therefore, ABC4Trust provides an advanced issuance protocol that allows the issuer to "carry over" attribute values from credentials that a user already possesses into the credential that gets issued without the values getting revealed. To enable this technically, the presentation policy is extended into an *issuance policy*, and accordingly the user will generate an *issuance token*.

4   Realisation

The concepts discussed in the preceding section can be implemented with a number of cryptographic schemes and algorithms, such as credential systems, group signatures, blind signatures, and verifiable encryption. More precisely, a full-fledged privacy-ABC system that realises all the concepts can be built from signature schemes with special properties (e.g., Camenisch-Lyskanskaya signatures [8,9,10] and Brands signatures [3]), commitment schemes, verifiable encryption schemes [11], and generalised Schnorr proofs [5].

As the combined cryptographic protocols get quite complex and therefore hard to use, the ABC4Trust project developed a policy language to deal with these concepts and to orchestrate the cryptographic protocols. The ABC4Trust privacy-ABC system thus can be used merely by understanding the concepts and not having to worry about the underlying cryptography. More precisely, the architecture provides XML schemas for all artefacts, including issuer parameters, revocation authority parameters, inspector parameters, credential specification, issuance policies and tokens, presentation policies and tokens, and pseudonyms [6]. The architecture further defines the components of a privacy-ABC system and their interfaces. The (main) components of the user and the verifier are depicted in Figure 3.

The architecture has three layers: an application layer, a policy layer and a crypto engine layer.

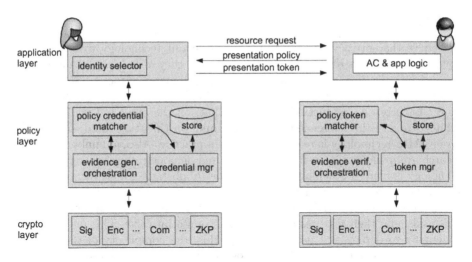

Fig. 3. ABC4Trust architecture, partial view on user and verifier [4,6]

The application layer is the consumer of the privacy-ABC system, it could be a browser on the user's side and a web service on the verifier's side. The application layer interacts with the policy layer by means of the APIs provided and is responsible for exchanging policies and tokens between the parties. How this is done is outside of the scope of the ABC4Trust architecture. On the user's side the application layer is also responsible for the presenting the presentation (and issuance) policy to the user and for allowing her to make her choices.

The policy layer processes presentation and issuance policies, matches credentials against policies and tokens against polices (policy credential matcher and policy token matcher), and orchestrates the generation and verification of presentation and issuance tokens (evidence generation orchestration and evidence verification orchestration). The policy layer is also responsible for storing a user's credential and tokens that a verifier receives (store) and for managing the credentials and tokens (credential manager and token manager). The latter includes dealing with revocation information and updating the credentials accordingly.

The crypto engine layer implements the cryptographic operation of privacy-ABCs. It contains the u-Prove and the IBM identity mixer (idemix) signature schemes (Sig), the idemix verifiable encryption (Enc) and revocation schemes, pseudonyms, commitment schemes (Com), and various cryptographic mechanisms to prove and verify attribute predicates, including zero-knowledge proof protocols (ZKP). The forthcoming ABC4Trust crypto architecture will describe this in detail. In the mean time, the reader is referred to the identity mixer specifications [2,13], which can be seen as a preliminary versions of this architecture.

The reference implementation of ABC4Trust encompasses all components of the policy and crypto layer, the identity selector, as well as an example application. The reference implementation is available from the GitHub repository [12] (and the sites linked from there).

5   Conclusion

We believe that privacy-ABCs should be the default technology to be used to implement any form of access control and that they will be as essential for a secure Internet just as there would be no e-commerce without SSL (Secure Socket Layer). The technology per se is ready for this. Indeed, the ABC4Trust project is currently conducting two pilots that, on the one hand, validate the architecture and the reference implantation and, on the other hand, show that privacy-ABC technology is ready to be used in practice. Also, a number of other research groups have successfully run pilots and demonstrator showing that the technology is ready for deployment. A number of obstacles, however, remain to be overcome before the privacy-ABCs will be in widespread use.

First of all, privacy-ABCs are more complex than ordinary attribute-based credentials, and their features are somewhat counterintuitive. This makes them challenging to deploy and use. To address this, the complexity of these technologies needs to be reduced and their possibilities communicated to the various stakeholders.

Furthermore, to enable the use of privacy-ABCs, the different cryptographic mechanisms and the policy languages need to be standardised. The architecture of ABC4Trust is a step towards this goal.

The obstacle that is probably the most difficult to overcome is the design of intuitive user interfaces for privacy-ABCs. A few approaches have been proposed, but for all of them it seems that users were not able to clearly understand what information they will reveal to verifiers (see, e.g., [16]).

Finally, the speed with which the Internet evolves and new applications are introduced and embraced makes it very challenging to address the emerging security and privacy problem, in particular because privacy and security too often are not taken into consideration by design. Thus, without privacy becoming a mandatory design principle, privacy technology will not be used as it is always easier to build applications without addressing security and privacy. Fortunately, the general public is becoming increasingly aware of the need of proper security and privacy protection and we have reason hope that future applications will only succeed when taking this into account.

Acknowledgements. The author enjoyed many discussions with his IBM colleagues and the people participating in the ABC4Trust project. The paper benefitted a lot from the comments by the reviewers. Thank you! This work was supported by the EC-funded project ABC4Trust.

References

1. ABC4Trust – Attribute-based Credentials for Trust, http://www.abc4trust.eu
2. Bichsel, P., Camenisch, J.: Mixing Identities with Ease. In: de Leeuw, E., Fischer-Hübner, S., Fritsch, L. (eds.) IDMAN 2010. IFIP AICT, vol. 343, pp. 1–17. Springer, Heidelberg (2010)

3. Brands, S.: Rethinking Public Key Infrastructure and Digital Certificates – Building in Privacy. PhD thesis, Eindhoven Institute of Technology, Eindhoven, The Netherlands (1999)
4. Camenisch, J., Dubovitskaya, M., Lehmann, A., Neven, G., Paquin, C., Preiss, F.-S.: Concepts and Languages for Privacy-Preserving Attribute-Based Authentication. In: Fischer-Hübner, S., de Leeuw, E., Mitchell, C. (eds.) IDMAN 2013. IFIP AICT, vol. 396, pp. 34–52. Springer, Heidelberg (2013)
5. Camenisch, J., Kiayias, A., Yung, M.: On the Portability of Generalized Schnorr Proofs. In: Joux, A. (ed.) EUROCRYPT 2009. LNCS, vol. 5479, pp. 425–442. Springer, Heidelberg (2009)
6. Camenisch, J., Krontiris, I., Lehmann, A., Neven, G., Paquin, C., Rannenberg, K., Zwingelberg, H.: D2.1 Architecture for Attribute-based Credential Technologies – Version 1, http://abc4trust.eu/download/ABC4Trust-D2.1-Architecture-V1.2.pdf
7. Camenisch, J., Lehmann, A., Neven, G.: Electronic Identities need Private Credentials. IEEE Security & Privacy 10(1), 80–83 (2012)
8. Camenisch, J.L., Lysyanskaya, A.: An Efficient System for Non-transferable Anonymous Credentials with Optional Anonymity Revocation. In: Pfitzmann, B. (ed.) EUROCRYPT 2001. LNCS, vol. 2045, pp. 93–118. Springer, Heidelberg (2001)
9. Camenisch, J.L., Lysyanskaya, A.: A Signature Scheme with Efficient Protocols. In: Cimato, S., Galdi, C., Persiano, G. (eds.) SCN 2002. LNCS, vol. 2576, pp. 268–289. Springer, Heidelberg (2003)
10. Camenisch, J.L., Lysyanskaya, A.: Signature Schemes and Anonymous Credentials from Bilinear Maps. In: Franklin, M. (ed.) CRYPTO 2004. LNCS, vol. 3152, pp. 56–72. Springer, Heidelberg (2004)
11. Camenisch, J.L., Shoup, V.: Practical Verifiable Encryption and Decryption of Discrete Logarithms. In: Boneh, D. (ed.) CRYPTO 2003. LNCS, vol. 2729, pp. 126–144. Springer, Heidelberg (2003)
12. Github Repository. Privacy-preserving attribute-based credential engine (p2abcengine), https://github.com/p2abcengine/p2abcengine/.
13. IBM Research. Specification of the Identity Mixer Cryptographic Library – Version 2.3.0. IBM Technical Report RZ3730
14. Leenes, R., Schallaböck, J., Hansen, M.: PRIME White Paper – third and final version (2008), https://www.prime-project.eu/prime_products/whitepaper/
15. Stamatiou, Y.: Privacy Respecting ICT Innovation in Education: Electronic Course Evaluation in Higher Education and Beyond. In: IFIP Summer School 2013 on Privacy and Identity Management for Emerging Services and Technologies. IFIP AICT. Springer (2014)
16. Wästlund, E., Fischer-Hübner, S.: The Users' Mental Models' Effect on their Comprehension of Anonymous Credentials. In: Privacy and Identity Management for Life. Springer (2011)

Privacy Respecting ICT Innovations in Education: Electronic Course Evaluations in Higher Education and Beyond

Yannis C. Stamatiou[1,2]

[1] Dept. of Business Administration, University of Patras, Patras, Greece
`stamatiu@ceid.upatras.gr`
[2] Computer Technology Institute and Press ("Diophantus"), Patras, 26504, Greece

Abstract. In this paper we present our institute's vision towards the introduction of privacy respecting innovative ICT services in the Greek educational sector and, gradually, to other sectors of public interest as well. This vision was shaped during our work within the scope of the EU funded research project ABC4Trust in which our institute implemented a pilot system, based on Privacy-ABCs (Attribute Based Credentials) for the support of anonymous course evaluations in Universities. Privacy-ABCs support cryptographic primitives and tools for eIdentity management that allow users to take full control of what personal information they reveal towards the services they use, providing only the information required to satisfy the service policy. We, first, discuss the set-up of the ABC4Trust pliot and then we explain how we plan to extend the pilot scenarios and characteristics in order to boost eParticipation of members of the educational community of Greece, through the Greek School Network (GSN), in a privacy respecting manner. In particular, we discuss a number of scenarios in which Privacy-ABCs play an important role in ascertaining that users of the GSN only reveal their identity elements which are necessary in order to use a school service. Finally, based on the experiences gathered from our pilot, we present our views with respect to the factors that can inhibit or advance the widespread use of innovations, such as the Privacy-ABCs and the systems based on them, in society. We argue that there are two key factors that affect widespread adoption of innovations: (i) initial introduction of the innovation within groups whose members are linked, somehow, with each other and (ii) gradual introduction to more user groups, of progressively increasing size. This was the model the ABC4Trust project actually adopted in the case of the pilot we discuss in this paper.

1 Introduction

The widespread use of *personalized services*, i.e. services that ask for personal information about users and then process this information or tailor themselves according to users' characteristics has increased, considerably, over the past few years. Such services are, most often, e-Commerce services that address individuals' needs for products based on their buying history as well as the personal information that they voluntarily provide in web forms. Beyond e-Commerce, *social media* applications, where revealing personal (even sensitive) information is exactly what they all are about, are gaining increasing popularity, especially among young people.

M. Hansen et al. (Eds.): Privacy and Identity 2014, IFIP AICT 421, pp. 64–76, 2014.

As a consequence, personalized services, along with their corresponding security and privacy issues, have attracted much attention from researchers in the ICT security domain. Numerous research and survey papers have appeared over the last few years studying various aspects of privacy and privacy preserving authentication mechanisms (see, especially, the publications and work programme of the *Digital Enlightenment Forum*). The discussed aspects include the design of privacy preserving authentication cryptographic primitives, methodologies for verifying, formally, security properties of systems, legislation related to privacy and personal information handling by services as well as the development of new, attractive services whose behavior is determined by personal information items provided by users. Two seminal works (among other similar ones) that, in our opinion, provide an excellent, condensed perspective on the Personal Data Ecosystem and its facets are [10] and [11]. Ann Cavoukian in [10] stresses the role of the individual in handling own personal information and builds the framework for empowering people to handle their own electronic identities in the Web. In [11] Mireille Hildebrandt considers the role of the (digital) environment of the individuals in profiling their habits and actions in order to offer them better personalized services and adjust itself according to their needs. The author discusses the privacy issues arising from this profiling as well as the pros and cons. On the lower level of the PDE, that of cryptographic primitives on which one may build the services and functionalities as described in [10,11], Florian Kerschbaum in [12] discusses the main cryptographic tools that need to be considered for future privacy preserving and secure Web services.

Privacy Attribute-Based Credentials or Privacy-ABCs, which are described briefly in Section 3, is a technology that enables *privacy preserving*, partial authentication of users. Privacy-ABCs are issued just like normal electronic credentials from a PKI using a secret signature key owned by the credential issuer. However, the distinguishing feature of this technology is that the user can transform his/her credentials into a special *presentation token* that reveals only the personal information which is required by the service policy and nothing else. The verification of this token is performed with the issuer's public key. The *ABC4Trust project* aims at eliminating the gap between theory and practice in Privacy-ABCs technologies in order to pave the way towards their deployment in applications requiring partial user authentication. In particular, the project's two main goals are the following: (i) to propose an architectural framework for Privacy-ABC technologies that allows their co-existence and interchangeability, and (ii) to provide a *reference implementation* of those ABC components for potential adopters who wish to incorporate them into their own systems and services. One of the key features of the project is the provision for two pilots, as proofs of concept for Privacy-ABCs: one pilot that involves pupils of a primary school in Sweden and one pilot than involves students of a University in Greece.

In Section 4 we will present, in some detail, the key elements of the pilot, after giving a brief profile of our institute in 2, and will discuss how it served the ABC4Trust project's goals. However, our paper is not limited to only this discussion. Our aim is to present our plans about future extensions of the pilot scenarios and system in order to support safe and privacy preserving services in the educational community in Greece, through the *Greek School Network* that CTI operates and controls, which we describe in 5. Then, taking as a starting point our experiences from running the pilot with a focus on maximizing acceptance of Privacy-ABCs among the pilot participants and beyond, we make an attempt towards generalization: we propose in 6 a generic strategy for introducing Privacy ABCs as well as similar innovation to large user targets by implementing, in a step-wise manner, pilots that involve increasingly larger number of users and provides increasingly complex services. We believe that his *innovation diffusion* strategy may be more effective and efficient in convincing potential users of the usefulness and privacy properties of a service than an abrupt, maybe even by law-enforcement, attempt to introduce the service within large and unrelated user groups right from the start, as it was attempted before by other innovations such as eVoting, with the well-known negative consequences for the innovations. Finally, we conclude in Section 7 with a summary of our findings and pointers to issues for further investigation.

2   The Computer Technology Institute and Press-"Diophantus"

The Computer Technology Institute and Press-"Diophantus" is a research and technology organization focusing on research and development in Information and Communication Technologies (ICT). Particular emphasis is placed on education, by developing and deploying conventional and digital media in education and lifelong learning; publishing printed and electronic educational materials; administrating and managing the Greek School Network; and supporting the organization and operation of the electronic infrastructure of the Greek Ministry of Education, Lifelong Learning and Religious Affairs and all educational units. Since its establishment in 1985, and in the past decades of rapid technological development, CTI has actively contributed to many of the advances that today are taken for granted. The Information Society Sectors are the organization's conveying mechanisms of know-how, in turn supporting the Hellenic State's devolvement into the Information Society.

The principal activity sectors of CTI are the following:

- Educational Technology Sector.
- Networking Technologies Sector.
- E-Government Sector.
- Center of Telematics & Applications for regional development.
- Further Education & Training Sector.
- Strategic & Development Policy Sector.
- Computing & Networking Systems Security Sector.

CTI is, today, in the strong position of combining two important elements which are of great importance in realizing the proposed pilot activities: (i) it administers the Greek School Network, and (ii) it participates in a prominent European project, called ABC4Trust, whose aim is to provide a technical and legal framework for privacy preserving, eIdentity management. The Greek School Network (GSN) is the educational intranet of the Greek Ministry of Education, Life Long Learning and Religious Affairs (abbreviated MoE) that interconnects all schools and a large number of educational administrative units and organizations. It is the biggest public network in the country, having the largest number of users, and has been recognized internationally as a remarkable educational network that promotes the introduction and exploitation of Information and Communication Technologies (ICT) in the Greek educational system. Because of its sensitive educational character and the need to protect pupils while accessing the Internet, GSN needs to adopt strong, privacy preserving authentication mechanisms for its users as well as enhance its services towards the educational community based on these mechanisms.

3   Basic Concepts of Privacy-ABCs

Commonly used user authentication methods (e.g. PKI-based) that are employed today for controlling access to Internet services most often fall short, with regard to respecting users' privacy. In general this situation arises in services in which only a subset of a user's full identity profile is necessary to allow access to a service. Such services range from accessing online libraries, where there is no need to give full identity profile to access books but only a proof that you are subscribed to the library, to online borrowing of movies, where you may have to prove that you are of appropriate age (e.g. older than 18) in order to watch particular films. In such types of applications there is, clearly, a need for a partial, and not complete, revelation of the user's identity. Privacy Attribute-Based Credentials or Privacy-ABCs, for short, is a technology that enables privacy preserving, partial authentication of users. Privacy-ABCs are issued just like normal electronic credentials (e.g. those based on currently employed PKIs) using a secret signature key owned by the credential issuer. However, and this is a key feature of this technology, the user is in position to transform the credentials into a new form, called presentation token, that reveals only the information about him which is really necessary in order to access a service. This new token can be verified with the issuer's public key.

Research has resulted in a number of different proposals of how to realize anonymous credentials [3,5,7] which are based on different number-theoretic problems and also differ somewhat in the functionality that they offer. There are two leading anonymous credentials systems: Idemix (see, e.g., [8,6,9]) of IBM and U-prove of Microsoft (see, e.g., [4]). These two systems provide nearly the same functionality, using different cryptographic primitives. With regard to Idemix, it relies, mostly, on the hardness of the strong RSA problem while U-prove relies, mostly, on the difficulty of discrete logarithms. Also, credentials are represented in different formats. The ABC4Trust project is an attempt to unify these two credential formats into one, focusing on interoperability and operation efficiency. Some of the outcomes of this project may be found in [2] (reference architecture and implementation) and [13] (the University pilot system and scenarios).

4   The Course Evaluation Pilot within the ABC4Trust Project

The purpose of the course evaluation pilot was to demonstrate some of the basic functionalities of Privacy-ABCs, to prove their applicability in a real-life scenario and to provide early feedback to the project.

According to the scenarios what where defined within the context of the ABC4Trust project, a number of volunteer students attending a class of the Computer Engineering and Informatics Department of the University of Patras had, first, to collect on the smart cards that were given to them credentials in the form of Privacy-ABCs. These credentials were capable of proving, *anonymously*, that they are indeed students of the University of Patras and that they were registered to the course under evaluation. In some sense, the students obtained a *certificate*, but one whose presentation does not reveal *identifying information*, that could prove their studentship as well as enrollment in the course that will be evaluated in the end of the semester.

During the semester, the students attended the course lectures normally. The additional element (as dictated by the pilot scenarios) was that upon entering the lecture room, they received one attendance credit or certificate of their attendance at that day. This unit was recorded, securely, in their smart cards.

In the end of the semester, they had to anonymously evaluate the course using an online, Privacy-ABCs based, course evaluation system. The entities that were involved in the first round of the pilot and their corresponding ABC roles were the following: (i) University Registration System (ABC Issuer & Verifier), (ii) Class Attendance System (No ABC role), (iii) Course Evaluation System (ABC Verifier), and (iv) Students (ABC User).

The students accessed the University Registration System in order to obtain their credentials, proving their studentship and their registration to the course. The Class Attendance System is the system operated in the lecture room through which the students obtained attendance credits on their smart cards. The Course Evaluation System was the system which the students used in order to evaluate, anonymously, the course they had attended. Also, the students had to install an ABC User Client (User Service + GUI) on their computers in order to be able to interact with the pilot system components. As soon as the pilot started, we provided the students with an envelope containing a properly initialized smart card and the card's PIN and PUK values. We also gave to each of them a contact smart card reader and a slip of paper containing a one-time-password for the initial logging in the University Registration System. The first step for the students was to log in the University Registration System using their matriculation numbers as usernames and their one-time passwords. Then, they were able to register their smart cards so that the University System could link their smart cards with the students' information residing in the system database. After a student had registered his smart card, he was able to obtain the University and Course credentials from the University Registration System. The University credential proves the studentship of the participants and includes, as attributes, his first and last names, the name of the University (Patras University), the Department name (Computer Engineering & Informatics Department) and finally his matriculation number. The Course credential proves that the student is registered to the course under evaluation. In order to be able to evaluate the course in the end of the semester, the students had to collect a minimum amount of attendance credits at the lecture room during the semester. This was accomplished through their interaction with the Class Attendance System. This system, which was operated and supervised by senior personnel of CTI, was located on desk, near the entrance of the lecture room. The students, upon entering the lecture room, had to wave their smart card in front of the contactless SC reader of the Class Attendance System. This action would trigger the execution of a secure protocol between the smart card and the Class Attendance System at the end of which the attendance credit counter residing in the SC was increased by 1. If the student attempted to obtain, illegally, one more attendance credit by waving the SC once more, during the lecture (or, in general, during the same day), then the SC software would block the increase operation. In the end of the semester, the students could access the Course Evaluation System in order to evaluate, anonymously, the course they had attended. The presentation policy of the Course Evaluation System asked from the users to prove the possession of a Course credential as well as present a scope-exclusive pseudonym bound to the same secret as the Course credential. The student's SC permitted the participation in such a proof, only if the attendance credit counter in the card was above the preset attendance threshold. Finally, the User Client module (ABC User + GUI) installed on the students' computers offered some additional SC related capabilities. With them, the users could browse the credentials stored on their SCs, change their SC PIN number or unlock it using the PUK value. Moreover, the students could backup and restore the contents of their SCs. This functionality was useful in cases of SC loss or damage so that the user would not lose his attendance credits.

5   Beyond the ABC4Trust Pilot: The Greek School Network and the Envisaged Pilot Extensions

The *Greek School Network*, or GSN for short, is the educational intranet of the Greek Ministry of Education and Religious Affairs that interconnects all schools as well as numerous educational administrative agencies and organizations. It is the largest public network in Greece, with the largest number of users, and has been recognized internationally as a remarkable educational network that promotes the introduction and exploitation of Information and Communication Technologies (ICT) in the Greek educational system.

Because of its crucial educational role and the need to protect students when they access outside sites, the GSN applies strong use site and user certification methods. Depending on their access rights and roles, the GSN entities and users belong to one of the the the following groups: (i) School units, which are provided with multiple accounts to access the network and the GSN services. (ii) Administrative offices, which are also given one or more accounts. (iii) Teachers who are offered personalized services. The identification process for teachers is provided through an automated environment. (iv) Students, who are given access mainly through the school laboratories, but are also provided with personalized services. The identification of the students is performed directly from their schools, with the collaboration of school administration software and GSNs LDAP service. (v) Administrative personnel, who have access through their schools or offices, and are also provided with personalized services.

The number of connected units is, currently, 16.620 schools and 925 administration units. Broadband penetration exceeds 93% for secondary schools, 73% for primary schools and 30% for kindergártens. The number of teachers that have a personal account with GSN is, approximately, 77.000 while the number of students is about 51.000. There is, also, a particularly high demand for telematic services, especially email, emailing lists, websites, blogs, educational video streaming, as well as of social networking and e-class services. In particular, the number of active email boxes exceeds 135.000, while more than 9.000 educational websites are hosted in GSNs servers. Also, 3.515 digital courses have been developed by 890 schools (current school year). More than 10.000 educational blogs and 100 educational communities are provided by GSN, and are visited by more than 150.000 unique visitors per month. Finally, the GSN portal is the most highly visited educational portal in Greece, with more than 220.000 unique visitors in a typical month. All the above data have been recorded as of 23 May 2011.

In all the scenarios that follow the underlying principles that will be implemented are: (i) pupils retain their anonymity (unless it is not permitted by specific service policies, e.g. issuance of an attendance credit) while proving other characteristics of themselves (only the elements required by services, nothing else), (ii) pupils and parents are notified (depending on previous agreement between parents and authorities) when and how pupil information is used by authorities with explanation of the reason for this, and (iii) there is provision for using the pupil information discretely, especially health information which should be accessible by authorities in order to extract useful demographic as well as health aggregate information, which implies the implementation of secure storage and querying mechanisms.

5.1 Scenario 1

1. The pupils are equipped with smart cards with ABC credentials that certify that they are pupils as well as other personal information such as matriculation number, age, grade etc.
2. Pupils are registered at the school they are attending in the beginning of the school year by the school registrar. This process is paper based up to now and even in cases of electronic support, the information remains local and out of reach by education authorities.
3. Special credentials are issued to pupils that certify that they have passed the required health exams or at which health aspects they fail. These health certificates are now paper based and their contents are not transformed in electronic format. Thus, the authorities fail to obtain a global view of the health status of the Greek pupil community while, at the same time, severe privacy problems arise.
4. The pupils can order their books at the beginning of the school year using their credentials. Moreover they can download electronic books, which are available by publishers online to certified users, their credentials.
5. Wherever attendance is required, their smart cards can collect it. In this way, the school principal can keep track, for each pupil, the number of times he/she is absent from school and take appropriate measures when needed.
6. Pupils can order and pay their lunch using their smart cards. The smart card contains information about health problems caused by specific foods and, thus, pupils are restrained from consuming specific types of food which danger of unhealthy for them.
7. They can have access to school premises (indoor gym, library, craft classes) after school hours. Their use of the premises can be certified by their personal information will not be revealed if not necessary.
8. The pupils can, also, evaluate (evaluations are totally absent in Greek schools) informally and in an anonymous way the following:

- School lessons.
- Teacher notes.
- Course books.

9. Pupils can certify themselves and watch supporting online courses and classes.
10. Pupils, teachers, and parents will be given the opportunity to discuss and communicate through a special public area offered by the GSN. Today they use, possibly dangerous, online tools, social networking sites, and discussion blogs that may severely compromise their privacy. Privacy preserving technologies can assure, also, that only eligible (according to age, profession, sex etc.) participate in the various chat areas.

In the envisaged scenarios parents are, also, equipped with SCs that verify that they are, indeed, parents of pupils as well as some other personal information of interest to the educational system. Eligible parents can be informed (either automatically or by the school principal) about absences from classes of their children, school activities their children participate in, possibly inappropriate behavior of their children as well as pupils' grades and progress.

5.2 Scenario 2

This scenario includes the basic characteristics of the previous one. In addition, it can include some safety and privacy properties like using ABC technology for authenticating pupils and proving some of their attributes in order to have access to specific web sites and applications:

We can develop an application tuned for use on pupils' laptops and on school lab computers. This application can verify the users through Privacy-ABCs based authentication according to their roles but without requiring identifying information, such as surname. The basic roles are the following:

1. Pupils: No access to web pages with illegal content but access to school services such as like school chat rooms, School forums, the educational material which is uploaded on the Greek School Network etc.
2. Teachers: They can access various GSN services such as discussion fora for teachers only or for parents and pupils, public educational discussion forums, the educational material which is uploaded on the Greek School Network by all other teachers (e.g. supplementary material or solutions to homework assignments) etc.
3. Parents: They can access a variety of GSN services, such as discussion forums where teachers can, also, participate and exchange views with them, parents only discussion forums, the educational material which is uploaded on the Greek School Network etc.

6 What can, Potentially, Inhibit (or Advance) the Widespread Use of Technological Innovations Such as Privacy-ABCs?

Over the last decade, we have witnessed unprecedented advances in software as well as hardware design and implementation. Especially in the field of security, the advances in theoretical cryptography as well as the construction of highly secure, tamper-resistant hardware devices such as TPMs and smart cards are impressive. Consequently, any security threat, such as the ones our team dealt with during the design and the implementation of our pilot system, could be tackled at a satisfactory level with the appropriate amount of care and effort. Moreover, this should be sufficient to enable the widespread adoption of the Privacy-ABCs innovation by people and organizations alike.

At this point, we should clearly state our view that the other pillar, beyond technology and theory, for adoption of security innovations is users' *trust* towards the innovation. While strong ICT security is a necessary condition for successful security systems, as described in the previous sections, it is by no means (unfortunately) sufficient. In what follows we present the components of a step-wise, trust-driven approach towards the adoption of Privacy-ABCs by people, based on our experiences from the pilot.

The approach involves all stakeholders at the same time and is targeted at convincing them of the usefulness and security of the target system. The principal axes of the approach are the following: (i) Proven technological excellence of the system components. The system should use strong technologies and theoretical primitives. This aspect may be approached using the latest technological advances in ICT security and cryptography. (ii) Use of open source software technologies and publicly available information for maximum transparency and scrutiny. (iii) In field user assessment. After using the system, the users should be asked to evaluate it and provide feedback on its various aspects, such as user-friendliness, efficiency and perceived security. This feedback should be taken into account for improving the system. (iv) Organization of information days before and after system deployment and use. Holding information days before using a system improves users' understanding of its capabilities and operation while information days after the uses have actually used the system help involved people (developers and users alike) understand each other's views and propose improvements on the usability and functionality of the system. These information days should include technical people, normal users, law experts etc.

We will, now, turn to the important role that *social interactions* among users can play in diffusing innovations, such as Privacy-ABCs. As we argued, the lack of trust from potential users can be a major inhibiting factor in making a technologically perfect technology a success. Then one faces the problem of how to convince people to adopt and use this technology. A promising approach is to let them try the technology and see for themselves how good it is, thus removing the trust obstacle. Our belief is that one of the, potentially, most effective ways of introducing the Privacy-ABCs to potential users is to introduce them, initially, to a small group of closely related individuals and then try to introduce them to large numbers of groups of, progressively, larger number of members.

A mathematical result that appears to support this belief is that proved by Young in [15] within the context of innovation diffusion. It is reasonable to regard Privacy-ABCs and their implementation as an innovation, supported by strong mathematical foundations and a carefully implemented, bug-free (to the extend this is possible) reference implementation, to be diffused over a target user population. Within this context, the mathematical results of Young may be applicable. In what follows, we give a brief overview of these results and discuss their connection with our problem achieving widespread adoption of Privacy-ABCs.

Young described in [15] a parameter of social networks (*graphs*, in general) that characterizes the "closeness" of individuals belonging to a social group. According to this parameter, we characterize a set of individuals as *close-knitted* if the following condition holds for every subset of individuals S in the social group:

$$\min_{S' \subseteq S} \frac{d(S', S)}{\sum_{i \in S'} d_i} \geq r.$$

where $d(S', S)$ denotes the number of links between individuals in the sets S' and S and d_i the number of social links that individual i has in total.

This parameter captures, at the same time, two major "closeness" factors for subgroups of the social graph: (i) internal connections (reflected in the numerator of the fraction), and (ii) external connections (reflected in the denominator of the fraction). Then for a social graph to be r-close-knitted, we require the ratio of these two factors to be at least r, i.e. loosely speaking to have strong internal connections and weak external connections.

What Young proved for families of social graphs which have the r-knittedness property is that the time requited for *all* community members to adopt the innovation, given that a subset of them, whose members we call *initiators*, does accept it initially, is bounded and independent from the size of the community. That is, if all the subsets of the community members have strong pairwise links and, at the same time, are weakly connected to outsiders (who may even be negative towards adopting the innovation), then a group of initiators will manage, in the end, to convince all population members to adopt the innovation. We should note, here, that the definition of close-knittedness is a little more complex for graph families, to which the result of Young applies, than the definition for a single graph but it is along the lines of the definition given above.

This mathematical result suggests a way to, successfully, introduce the Privacy-ABCs innovation to large target populations (e.g. citizens of a city or a country). The central idea behind the proposed approach is to introduce the innovation in a *gradual*, *step-wise* manner that involves increasingly larger individual user groups, as potential *initiators*, that are closely knitted, for some parameter r. For example, the Privacy-ABCs system in hand should be deployed, initially, with users forming small groups of closely related individuals, We would like these users to play the role of the innovation initiators. Consequently, in an ideal situation, they should all adopt the innovation in the end after using it. It follows that in order to convince them to adopt the innovation, we should carefully design the use cases and the supporting ICT system so as to avoid any pitfalls that may cause negative feelings and attitude towards the innovation. To this end, it is preferable to deploy the innovation in the least, possible, risky set-up. For instance, we may use simple use cases, avoiding critical or complex scenarios that may either intimidate users or raise (unnecessary) suspicions over the innovation (e.g. financial applications).

The strategy outlined above has a number of positive features, besides convincing potential users of the innovation quality and usefulness. First, it offers the possibility for in-depth testing of the technology and its implementation since the system is used by a small number of people, each time, and with a simple scenario. As the system testing progresses and modifications are done in the system to correct bugs or enhance functionalities, the next innovation diffusion phase may take place using a group with a number of individuals and, potentially, a more complex scenario. Then, having controllable individual groups (due to their small numbers and coherence) offers the possibility to organize and conduct a thorough evaluation of the pilot set-up and the implementation of the pilot set-up giving the opportunity to improve them before the next pilot trial. As a positive side effect, possible negative findings or mishaps during the pilot, stay within a small number of people and gives the opportunity for subsequent improvements without much bad publicity spreading to outsiders.

The approach outlined above is similar to the approach we adopted for our pilot within the ABC4Trust project as well as the one we followed in the pilot of another project of CTI, the PNYKA eVoting project (see [14]). More specifically, in the ABC4Trust case (as in the PNYKA project) we targeted a relatively small group of university students (about 50) in order to ascertain "closeness" among them (closeknittedness) due the fact that they both move about within the same location and discuss with each other daily, strengthening their pairwise social links. Due to the "closeness" among them and from the mathematical result about diffusion of innovation among individuals forming such social graphs, our hope was that in the end, after the pilot, the majority of students would be convinced of the value of Privacy-ABCs and their potential applications, unless of course something went terribly wrong during the pilot operation, which was not the case. This group of students would serve as *initiators* to diffuse, further, the Privacy-ABCs to other students. Indeed, the overall impression of the participants was, in general, positive (see [1]) the received feedback was taken under consideration for further improvements and enhancements.

Given this successful operation, our future plan is to follow the gradual innovation diffusion approach discussed above to introduce Privacy-ABCs related services into the GSN. As we explained, this undertaking should be performed with care running, first, small scale pilots within one school, then to more schools within a small geographical region, continuing in this way until we reach larger numbers of GSN users. Before the next step, the participants' feedback will be taken into account in order to prepare for the next, larger scale, pilot. We believe that through this process Privacy-ABCs will be, eventually, adopted by the majority of the educational community members in Greece, an accomplishment that could not be achieved (as indicated by failures of other, initially promising innovations) if one attempted to diffuse, all of a sudden, the Privacy-ABCs technology in, say, eIdentity cards to the whole user population of the GSN. To put this view in perspective, we will end our discussion with one example of a notable failure of a very promising innovation: eVoting. Our belief is that eVoting has failed to gain much popularity in the various countries that it has been introduced because attempts to introduce it were rather abrupt (even enforced by law) and were targeted to extremely large, virtually unrelated groups of individuals, even whole country populations. In other words, eVoting was introduced to groups of individuals that were not close-knitted and it was, thus, difficult or impossible to adopt and further diffuse the eVoting innovation given, in addition, the misconduct and system failures due to careless design and implementations. The negative discussions of these failures by large numbers of users then created an avalanche effect which actually resulted in the spread of the negative attitude over the whole population which used the eVoting technology.

7 Discussion

We would like to conclude with some lessons learnt from our pilot operation within the ABC4Trust project: a) Modern cryptography and ICT security offer all the necessary tools for building trustworthy Privacy-ABCs systems. b) Security sensitive services and systems should be built using formal design methodologies. c) Privacy preserving services and systems should be designed and built with the end-user in mind. All design steps should be thoroughly documented and explained for later scrutiny by experts as well as non-experts. d) In order to gain wider acceptance, privacy enhancing systems (as any other security sensitive system) should be introduced, gradually, to scenarios of gradually increasing criticality, involving gradually increasing numbers of people over a long time span. e) Finally, a positive attitude towards privacy and Privacy-ABCs can be, potentially, shaped early in the educational system by raising awareness in privacy issues through courses that acquaint pupils with the basics of the Internet, its services as well as its dangers and the protection of their privacy.

Acknowledgement. The research leading to these results has received funding from the European Community's Seventh Framework Programme (FP7/2007-2013) under Grant Agreement no. 257782 for the project Attribute Based Credentials for Trust (ABC4Trust).

References

1. Benenson, Z., Krontiris, I., Liagkou, V., Rannenberg, K., Schopf, A., Schröder, D., Stamatiou, Y.: Understanding and Using Anonymous Credentials. In: 9th Symposium on Usable Privacy and Security (SOUPS 2013) (2013)
2. Bjones, R., Krontiris, I., Paillier, P., Rannenberg, K.: Integrating Anonymous Credentials with eIDs for Privacy-respecting Online Authentication. In: Preneel, B., Ikonomou, D. (eds.) APF 2012. LNCS, vol. 8319, pp. 111–124. Springer, Heidelberg (2014)
3. Brands, S.: Rethinking Public Key Infrastructures and Digital Certificates: Building in Privacy, 1st edn. (August 2000)
4. Brands, S., Demuynck, L., De Decker, B.: A Practical System for Globally Revoking the Unlinkable Pseudonyms of Unknown Users. In: Pieprzyk, J., Ghodosi, H., Dawson, E. (eds.) ACISP 2007. LNCS, vol. 4586, pp. 400–415. Springer, Heidelberg (2007)
5. Camenisch, J.L., Lysyanskaya, A.: An efficient system for non-transferable anonymous credentials with optional anonymity revocation. In: Pfitzmann, B. (ed.) EUROCRYPT 2001. LNCS, vol. 2045, pp. 93–118. Springer, Heidelberg (2001)
6. Camenisch, J., Van Herreweghen, E.: Design and Implementation of the Idemix Anonymous Credential System. Research Report RZ 3419, IBM Research Division. In: Also appeared in ACM Computer and Communication Security (June 2002)
7. Camenisch, J.L., Lysyanskaya, A.: Signature Schemes and Anonymous Credentials from Bilinear Maps. In: Franklin, M. (ed.) CRYPTO 2004. LNCS, vol. 3152, pp. 56–72. Springer, Heidelberg (2004)

8. Camenisch, J.: Protecting (Anonymous) Credentials with the Trusted Computing Group's TPM V1.2. In: Proc. SEC 2006, pp. 135–147 (2006)
9. Camenisch, J., Groß, T.: Efficient attributes for anonymous credentials. To appear in ACM Transactions on Information and System Security (TISSEC) (2011)
10. Cavoukian, A.: Privacy by Design and the Emerging Personal Data Ecosystem (October 2012), http://privacybydesign.ca/content/uploads/2012/10/pbd-pde.pdf
11. Hildebrandt, M.: The Dawn of a Critical Transparency Right for the Profiling Era. In: Bus, J., et al. (eds.) Digital Enlightenment Yearbook 2012, pp. 41–56. IOS Press (2012)
12. Kerschbaum, F.: Privacy-Preserving Computation (Position Paper). Annual Privacy Forum (APF) (2012)
13. Liagkou, V., Metakides, G., Pyrgelis, A., Raptopoulos, C., Spirakis, P., Stamatiou, Y.C.: Privacy preserving course evaluations in Greek higher education institutes: an e-Participation case study with the empowerment of Attribute Based Credentials. In: Preneel, B., Ikonomou, D. (eds.) APF 2012. LNCS, vol. 8319, pp. 140–156. Springer, Heidelberg (2014)
14. Manolopoulos, C., Sofotassios, D., Spirakis, P., Stamatiou, Y.C.: A Framework for Protecting Voters' Privacy In Electronic Voting Procedures. Journal on Cases on Information Technology 15(2) (2013)
15. Young, P.: The Diffusion of Innovations in Social Network. In: Blume, L.E., Durlauf, S.N. (eds.) The Economy as a Complex Evolving System, vol. III. Oxford University Press (2003)

How can Cloud Users be Supported in Deciding on, Tracking and Controlling How their Data are Used?

Simone Fischer-Hübner, Julio Angulo, and Tobias Pulls

Department of Computer Science
Karlstad University, Sweden

Abstract. Transparency is a basic privacy principle and factor of social trust. However, the processing of personal data along a cloud chain is often rather intransparent to the data subjects concerned. Transparency Enhancing Tools (TETs) can help users in deciding on, tracking and controlling their data in the cloud. However, TETs for enhancing privacy also have to be designed to be both privacy-preserving and usable. In this paper, we provide requirements for usable TETs for the cloud. The requirements presented in this paper were derived in two ways; at a stakeholder workshop and through a legal analysis. Here we discuss design principles for usable privacy policies and give examples of TETs which enable end users to track their personal data. We are developing them using both privacy and usability as design criteria.

Keywords: Privacy, transparency, transparency-enhancing tools, usability.

1 Introduction

Transparency of personal data processing is an important principle for the privacy of individuals as well as for a democratic society. As for instance the German constitutional court declared in its Census Decision[1], a society, in which citizens could not know any longer who does, when, and in which situations know what about them, would be contradictory to the right of informational self-determination. For these reasons, transparency of personal data processing is enforced by most western privacy laws, including the EU Data Protection Directive 95/46/EC [9], by granting data subjects extensive information and access rights. Transparency is also an important factor of social trust, since trust in an application can be enhanced if procedures are clear, transparent and reversible, so that users feel in control of their personal data [2], [19]. However, particularly when data are processed in the cloud, multiple processors and subcontractors along a cloud chain can be involved that may belong to different legal entities and may be located in different jurisdictions. End users often lack transparency with regard to who is processing their data, under which conditions, and how they can exercise their data subject rights.

---

[1] German Constitutional Court, Census decision, 1983 (BVerfGE 65,1).

M. Hansen et al. (Eds.): Privacy and Identity 2014, IFIP AICT 421, pp. 77–92, 2014.

The concept of transparency comprises both 'ex ante transparency', which enables the anticipation of consequences before data are actually disclosed (e.g., with the help of privacy policy statements), as well as 'ex post transparency', which offers information about any consequences if data already have been revealed (what data are processed by whom and whether the data processing is in conformance with negotiated or stated policies) [14]. The A4Cloud European Union (EU) Seventh Framework Programme (FP7) project[2] is creating ex ante and ex post transparency enhancing tools to support cloud users[3] in *deciding* on and *tracking* and *controlling* how their data are used by cloud service providers [23].

Transparency Enhancing Tools (TETs) that allow the tracking of the processing of personal data can, however, also endanger privacy, if personal data about a data subject or information about how data have been processed are made available to unauthorised parties (e.g., the information that a psychiatrist has accessed a patient record may reveal sensitive information that the patient may want to keep confidential and that according to Art.8 EU Data Protection Directive 95/46/EC require special protection). Hence, TETs for enhancing privacy should be designed in a privacy-respecting manner.

Moreover, as pointed out in Patrick & Kenny [22], legal privacy principles, such as the transparency principle, have Human Computer Interaction (HCI) implications as "they describe mental processes and behaviour that the data subjects must experience in order for a service to adhere to these principles". In particular, the transparency principle requires that data subjects *comprehend* the transparency and control options, are *aware* of when they can be used, and *are able* to use them. Therefore, another important design criterion for transparency enhancing tools is usability.

In this paper, we will discuss our work, mainly conducted within the scope of both the A4Cloud project and a Google Research Award project, on transparency enhancing tools that are both usable and privacy-preserving. The remainder of this paper is structured as follows. In section 2, we discuss and describe requirements that have HCI implications, which we have elicited through a stakeholder workshop and legal analysis. Section 3 discusses how parts of these requirements for ex ante transparency can be mapped to HCI requirements, principles and design proposals. In section 4, we present ex post TETs that we are developing at Karlstad University and discuss how they are designed to be both privacy-preserving and usable. Section 5 briefly presents related work. Section 6 concludes the paper by discussing some of the remaining challenges for usable and privacy-preserving TETs.

2   Problems and Requirements

Within the scope of the A4Cloud project, we follow a human centred design approach for analysing end user problems and eliciting and testing HCI requirements for TETs. These comprise different methodologies, including stakeholder workshops, user

---

[2] http://www.a4cloud.eu/

[3] In this paper, cloud users refer to both individual user as well as organisations that are outsourcing their data to the cloud. The focus of this paper is however on individual cloud users.

experiments, usability tests, legal analyses and literature studies. This section of the paper reports on the main results emerging from a stakeholder workshop and a legal analysis. Further results from usability tests are described in section 4.2 below.

2.1   End User Challenges - Results from a Stakeholder Workshop

Stakeholder workshops provide an opportunity for active face-to-face interactions between different influential actors who can express their opinions and needs for systems being developed. This workshop method is strongly encouraged during the initial design process, as a way of ensuring that the needs of those who might be impacted by the system are taken into account [20]. In February 2013, a stakeholder workshop was held at Karlstad University to elicit HCI-related requirements for A4Cloud tools including TETs for end users. Participants at the workshop included IT experts of service providers from the private and public sectors that are adopting or are planning to adopt cloud technologies as well consumer organisation representatives who are well aware of the problems that individuals face regarding cloud computing and who thus represent the stakeholder group of individual cloud users. In addition, a lawyer from the Swedish Data Protection Agency (Datainspektionen) was attending the workshop: through her work, she is familiar with the kinds of privacy concerns that data subjects have with regard to the handling of their personal data in the cloud. The results of the stakeholder workshop are reported in detail in Angulo et al. [4]. Most notably, the workshop revealed problems for individual end users with respect to the unclear responsibilities of cloud service providers. In particular, it is often not clear to end users who the data controller is and what liabilities data processors and service brokers have. It is also difficult for them to find out how to obtain redress if something goes wrong and what (national) laws apply. This is especially an issue if Swedish service brokers use services that reside in other countries or if a service provider appears to be located in Sweden (as it has a website in the Swedish language or with a Swedish domain/address/telephone number), but is in fact located in another country.

Furthermore, the shortcomings of trust seals and privacy policies were brought up in the workshop. Often individual end users do not make truly informed choices. It can be easy to deceive people because they often do neither read nor understand legal terms and agreements. There are no established trust seals for cloud services, and even if there were, how would the end users know what labels to trust? It was mentioned that individuals are often not interested in understanding all the details of trust seals, but would rather like to know in general whether their data are "secure".

Another problem that workshop attendees pointed out is that there is usually insufficient support for service cancellation or data export. While registration for a service is usually made easy, it is often made difficult for end users to de-register or terminate a service contract, delete data, or transfer data to other service providers. It is not always clear to end users whether they "own" their own data, as they do not check the terms and conditions carefully.

In conclusion, the stakeholder workshop revealed several end user challenges with regard to privacy policies and the exercising of data subject rights that should be addressed by ex ante and ex post TETs. We will therefore also address these issues in the following sections.

2.2   Legal Requirements for Transparency and User Control

This section discusses essential legal privacy principles for transparency and account-ability for the cloud, for which HCI requirements and principles can be derived. Our legal analysis will mainly refer to the principles of the EU Data Protection Directive 95/46/EC, but we will also cite other legal requirements deriving for instance from the opinions of the Article 29 Data Protection Working Party. In view of the ongoing review of the European legal framework on data protection, our analysis will also take into account legal principles that are being proposed in the draft EU General Data Protection Regulation (GDPR) [10] and the compromise text of the proposed GDPR that was passed by the Committee on Civil Liberties, Justice and Home Affairs (LIBE) of the European Parliament on October 21, 2013 [11].

This section will place an emphasis on legal provisions for transparency and ac-countability for the cloud that have implications for HCI and that thus need to be ad-dressed by the design of graphical user interfaces. These legal provisions mainly comprise transparency rights as well as detective and corrective control rights that data subjects have in regard of data controllers[4]. The proposed EU regulation also highlights the importance of usable transparency and user control by requiring that data controllers have *"transparent and easily accessible policies with the regard to processing of personal data and for the exercise of data subjects' rights"* (Art. 11 draft GDPR) – which according to the compromise text of the GDPR also need to be *concise* and *clear* [11].

Information Rights (Ex Ante Transparency)

Ex ante transparency is a condition for data subjects to be in control and to render a consent[5], which has to be informed, valid. Article 10 of the Data Protection Directive defines what information relating to the processing of their personal data needs to be given to data subjects when information about them are collected and processed. This includes at least the identity of the data controller, and the data processing purposes. Moreover, further information needs to be given for example on the recipients or categories of recipients of the data, on whether replies to questions are obligatory or voluntary and on information about the individual's rights in so far as such further information is necessary to guarantee fair data processing. Such information has to be provided to the data subjects not only when the information is collected from the data subjects, but also when the data have not been obtained from them (Art. 11 Data Pro-tection Directive).

---

[4] According to EU Directive 95/46/EC, a data controller is defined as the entity that alone or jointly with others determines the purposes and means of personal data processing.

[5] The data subject's consent is defined by the Data Protection Directive as "any freely given specific and informed indication of his wishes by which the data subject signifies his agree-ment to personal data relating to him being processed".

The processing of personal data has to be based on one of the grounds that are mentioned in Art. 7 of the Data Protection Directive. The consent of the data subject (Art 7 (a) Data Protection Directive) can be taken as a legitimisation of personal data processing in the cloud. Information that needs to be given to data subjects for a valid (informed) consent should cover at least the elements of information required by Art. 10 Data Protection Directive.

The draft GDPR in Art.14 extends the information that should be provided to data subjects by information about data retention periods, the right to lodge a complaint to the supervisory authority, and – what is especially of relevance in the cloud context – information about the data protection level of a third country or international organisation to which the data controller intends to transfer data.

The compromise text of the GPDR includes a new Article 13a requiring that data controllers use *standardised information policies* for providing the data subject with the following particulars *before* providing information pursuant to Article 14: whether personal data are collected or retained beyond the minimum necessary for each specific purpose of the processing, whether personal data are processed for purposes other than the purposes for which they were collected, whether personal data are disseminated to commercial third parties or are sold or rented out, and whether personal data are retained in encrypted form [11].

Recently, the Art. 29 Working Party discussed in its Opinion 5/2012 on Cloud Computing [7] a lack of transparency in regard to the cloud services' processing operations. Privacy threats may arise from the controller not knowing or not informing the data subjects about the:

- Chain processing that involves multiple processors and subcontractors;
- Data being processed in different geographic locations within the European Economic Area (EEA);
- Data being transferred to third countries outside the EEA;
- Disclosure requests by law enforcement.

The last of these four threats is also important for the reason that, even if data are processed at a services side located in the EEA, data transfers to the United States of America (US) may take place on request by US American law enforcement services.

Furthermore, increased transparency over the chain of data processors and subcontractors is important as, in practice, the roles of data controllers or processors cannot always be clearly assigned to entities. The Art. 29 Working Party, in its "opinion 1/2010 on the concepts of 'controller' and 'processor'", argues that these roles should therefore be determined by "factual elements and circumstances" [6]. The proposed EU data protection regulation also recognises that data processors may, under certain circumstances, have increased control over the data processing and should be made directly accountable to the data subjects (cf. Art. 24, 26 IV).

As discussed above, our stakeholder workshop revealed another transparency problem, namely that data subjects are often not well informed about the applicable consumer laws and rights, especially if cloud brokers or mediators[6] are involved in cross-border eCommerce transactions.

Hence, in a cloud setting, it may be argued that more policy information beyond the minimum that is required by Art. 10 of the Data Protection Directive should be provided to the data subjects, including:

- Contacts and obligations of all data processors along the cloud chain (as far as data processors can be determined ex ante);
- Geographic locations of all data centres along the cloud chain and, in the event that they are located outside the EEA, information about their data protection levels;
- How disclosure requests by law enforcement agencies are handled; and
- Consumer rights and applicable laws.

It will remain a challenge, however, how to inform users of these aspects both unobtrusively and, at the same time, in a way that they can really understand and are conscious of these aspects.

Right of Access (Ex Post Transparency) and Other Data Subject Rights

The EU Data Protection Directive provides data subjects with the right of access to their data. This comprises the right to information about the data being processed, data processing purposes, data recipients or categories of recipients, as well as information about the logic involved on any automatic processing (Art. 12 (a)). This data subject right, which provides ex post transparency, is also a prerequisite for exercising the data subject rights to correct, delete or block data that are not processed in compliance with the Directive (Art. 12 (b)).

The proposed EU Data Protection Regulation, with its Art. 15, extends the information to be provided by the controller to include also information about the data retention period, the right to lodge a complaint with the supervisory authority, and "*the significance and envisaged consequences*" of the data processing at least in the cases of profiling. The data subjects shall also have the right to obtain this information electronically if they have made their requests in an electronic format. Besides, the compromise text even states that "*where possible, the data controller may provide remote access to a secure system which would provide the data subject with direct access to their personal data*" [11]. In addition, the proposed GDPR extends the data subjects' rights by the right to be forgotten (Art. 17 - which is however replaced by a so-called right to erasure in the compromise amendment to GDPR (see [11])) and the right to data portability (Art. 18) and introduces the obligation of data breach notification of the controller to the supervisory authority (Art. 31) and data subject (Art. 32).

Furthermore specific ex post transparency rights are, for instance, provided by the Swedish Data Patient Act [28] to data subjects by requiring that health care providers have to inform patients upon request about who has accessed their medical information.

---

6 A cloud broker or mediator is a third-party that acts as an intermediary between the customer of a cloud service and the seller of this service. It may for instance help to negotiate contracts with cloud providers on behalf of the customers.

3   HCI for Policy Display for Ex Ante TETs

Ex ante TETs include policy tools and languages, such as P3P [29] and the PrimeLife Policy Language PPL [25], which can help to make the core information of privacy policies and information on how far a service side's policy complies with a user's privacy preferences more transparent to an end user at the time that he or she is requested to consent to any form of data disclosure.

As pointed out in [22], legal privacy principles for transparency, consent and data subjects' rights *"have HCI implications as they describe mental processes and behaviour that the data subjects must experience in order for a service to adhere to these principles"*. In particular, the principle of transparency requires that data subjects are aware of and comprehend all privacy policy information. Complex privacy notices are, however, usually neither read nor easily understood. This can be due to the limited cognitive capacity that people usually have, such as limited attention spans memory, as well as a restricted ability to process a large amount of complex information at any one time [22]. Hence, suitable HCI concepts have to be chosen to make the policies displayed by ex ante TETs easily noticeable and understandable.

3.1   Multi-layered Policy Notices

Comprehension of policy information can also be facilitated by a multi-layered structure of policy notices, as it was recommended by the Art. 29 Data Protection Working Party in its opinion on "More Harmonised Information Provisions" [5]. This recommendation takes the approach of structuring complex policies into different layers, where the top layer only provides a short privacy notice with the policy information that is at least required by Art. 10 EU Data Protection Directive (i.e., at least the identity of the controller and data processing purposes). Further detailed policy information can be obtained from the condensed and full privacy notices in other (lower or later) layers. Each layer should offer to the data subjects the information needed to understand the position and make decisions. Examples of user interface (UI) designs for short privacy notices of multi-layered policies are design proposals based on a privacy nutrition label metaphor [17] or PPL (PrimeLife Policy Language) UIs that were elaborated for more complex PPL policy presentations [3].

However, if data are processed in the cloud, it may be argued that more policy information beyond that which is required by Art. 10 should, depending on the circumstances, be displayed to the data subjects to provide transparency. Such information listed in 2.2, may also have to be displayed on the top layer in order to enable users to comprehend the implications of the specific policy.

3.2   Policy Icons

Furthermore, user interfaces, which use real-world metaphors, e.g. in the form of suitable icons, are easier to learn and understand (following Jakob Nielsen's usability heuristics of a "match between system and the real world" [21]). Privacy policy icons have been researched and developed for visualising policy elements in privacy policies with the objective of making the content of legal policy statements easier to access and comprehend. Policy icons should preferably be standardised in the future and be usable across different cultures.

Within the scope of the PrimeLife EU project, a set of policy icons addressing the legal transparency requirements of the EU Data Protection Directive was developed. These icons can be used to illustrate core privacy policy statements in short privacy notices, namely statements about what types of data are collected/processed, for what purposes, and at what processing steps [15]. An intercultural comparison test of the policy icons conducted at Karlstad University with Swedish and Chinese students as test participants gave insights into which icons seem to be well understood by students of both cultures and which icons were understood differently by persons with different cultural backgrounds [12]. Those icons that were easily understood by both Swedish and Chinese students were, for instance, the ones shown in Fig. 1, displaying types of data (personal data, medical data, payment data), the purpose "shipping" and the processing steps (storage, retention).

Fig. 1. Example of well understood PrimeLife policy icons

Other Creative Common-like privacy icons have been initiated by Aza Raskin in 2010 [27] and further developed by a Mozilla-led working group (which, however, stopped its work more than a year before this chapter was written). Interestingly, it includes special icons informing end users about how service providers are handling requests made by law enforcement (see Fig. 2 for examples of the alpha release of icons). As already pointed out, and as it also became apparent after the revelation of the existence of the PRISM program in the summer of 2013, whether and under which conditions data are given to law enforcement is an important aspect that is often not transparent to cloud users.

Fig. 2. Icon proposals (alpha version) by Aza Raskin on the handling of disclosure requests by law enforcement [27]

To meet the demand for higher transparency for data processing in the cloud, further policy icons could be helpful to inform end users about the geographic locations of all data centres along the cloud chain, and in particular whether they are located inside the EEA. In the event that they are located outside the EEA, icons should also include information about their data protection levels.

The compromise amendment of the EU GDPR presents in an annex graphical policy icons to be used by standardised policies in yes/no icon-based tables along with textual descriptions for informing data subjects about policy particulars pursuant to the new Art.13a. While the approach of having standardised policy icons can facilitate an easier recognition and comparison of policy aspects, the icons of the compromise amendment, which were initially suggested and developed by the vice president of the European Parliament, Alexander Alvaro [1], do not seem to be very intuitive in their meaning, and they should definitely undergo further improvements and HCI testing.

4   Ex Post TETs

In this research, we have looked at the architecture and user interfaces of ex ante TETs. An example of such a tool has been named the Data Track. Its description and design is presented in the following sections, along with evaluations of an implemented prototype.

4.1   Data Track

The Data Track is a user side ex post transparency tool, which includes both a history function and online access functions. For each transaction, the history function stores in a secure manner, in which a user discloses personal data to a service, a record for the user on which personal data were disclosed to whom (i.e. the identity of the controller), for which purposes and under which agreed-on privacy policy. The Data Track's user interface version developed under the PrimeLife EU FP7 project provided search functions, which allow users to obtain easily an overview about who has received what data about them, as well as online access functions which allow end users to exercise their rights to access their data at the remote services' sides online and to correct or delete their data (as far as this is permitted by the services' sides). In this way, users can compare what data have been disclosed by them to a services' side and what data are still stored by the services' side, or what data have been implicitly been added (e.g., trust ratings of customers added by an eCommerce company) to the data records stored at the services' side. This allows users to check whether data have been changed, processed, added or deleted (and whether this was in accordance with the agreed-on privacy policy).

Online access is granted to a user if he or she can prove knowledge of a unique transaction ID (currently implemented as a 16-byte random number), which is shared between the user (stored in his or her Data Track) and the services' side for each transaction of personal data disclosure. In principle this also allows anonymous or pseudonymous users to access their data in the services' side.

Furthermore, a user function allowing users to excise the rights of data portability and the right to be forgotten/right to erasure (as proposed by the GDPD and to address precisely the issues pointed out in the context of the stakeholder workshop held by the research team) are developed.

4.2   Graphical User Interface for the Data Track

Complete descriptions of the Data Track proof-of-concept and user interfaces developed under the PrimeLife project can be found in Wästlund & Fischer-Hübner [30]. Usability tests of early design iterations of the PrimeLife's Data Track revealed that many test users had problems to understand whether data records were stored in the Data Track client on the users' side (under the users' control) or on the remote service provider's side.

Therefore, in the A4Cloud project, we have tested alternative HCI concepts consisting of graphical UI illustrations of where data are stored and to which entities data have been distributed. Graphical illustrations of data storage and data flows have a potential to display data traces more naturally, like in real world networks, as discussed in the PRIME deliverable D06.1.f, Section 5.8.1 [17]. Besides, previous research studies suggest that network-like visualisations provide a simple way to understand the meaning behind some types of data ([13], [8] and other recent studies claim that users appreciate graphical representations of their personal data flows in forms of links and nodes [16], [18]).

Therefore, a new UI concept for visualising the users' information in the Data Track tool has been proposed and prototyped at Karlstad University, as shown in Fig. 3. This way of illustrating the tracking of the users' data has been called the "trace view", presenting an overview of which data (with data attributes) have been sent to service providers, as well as which service providers might have the users' data.

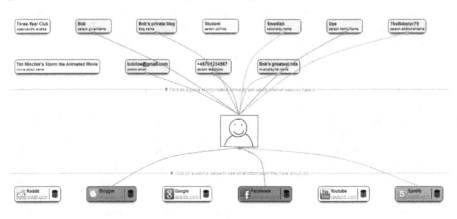

Fig. 3. The trace view user interface of the Data Track

The idea is that users should be able to see all the personal data items stored in the Data Track (displayed in the top of the UI) that they have submitted to services on the Internet (these Internet services are shown in the bottom panel of the interface). If users click on one or many of the Internet services, they will be shown arrows pointing to the information that those services have about them. In other words, they can see a *trace* of the data that the various services have about them. Similarly, if they select one or many data items (at the top of the figure), they will be shown arrows pointing to the Internet services that possess those data items.

Users can also access the data about them stored on the services' side by clicking on the corresponding icons, and are able to correct it or remove it, given that the respective service allows this.

4.3   Usability Evaluation

Usability evaluations of the Data Track's trace view have been carried out in order to test the extent to which users comprehend the ex post transparency features provided by the Data Track. An interactive mock-up of this tool was implemented providing a front-end for users to manipulate its different elements.

A total of 14 participants, aged between 19 and 40 years old, were recruited from different parts of the city of Karlstad in Sweden. They were asked for around 20 minutes of their time to evaluate the graphical interface of a computer program. From the total of 14 participants, 12 indicated that they were "experienced" or "very experienced" with computers; seven were employed at a company, six were students at the university, and one did not specify his occupation. As an introduction to the test, participants were told that they were about to evaluate a program that would let them see a history of the information that they had given to different online companies. They were also told that this program would let them verify that the information that they had released was the same as the information that was stored at the service, and that they could request a service to correct or delete their data if that service allowed it.

To start the test, participants were asked to pretend that they had already disclosed some information to other online companies and that, on this occasion, they were going to purchase a book. In order to complete the transaction, participants were asked to enter their personal information and submit it to this unknown online bookshop. However, they were given a fictitious credit card number to be used to complete the purchase and none of the personal information submitted was actually stored.

A cognitive walkthrough approach was adapted, in which participants were given a series of tasks to complete using the Data Track's user interface. A test moderator notated the answers and comments as the participants carried out the tasks. The order in which the tasks were presented was randomised in order to minimise possible biases. After completing the tasks, participants were asked to complete a post-questionnaire with the intention of capturing their subjective opinions on the interface.

Results revealed that all the participants clearly understood that elements in the bottom panel (cf. Fig. 3) represented different online services to which they had sent information, and the majority of participants (11 out of the total) clearly understood that the elements in the top panel of the interface represented their own information that was sent to online services. Also, it was intuitive for all participants to find out what data items they had sent to a particular service provider (by clicking on one of the services on the bottom panel). All the participants but one found it easy to discover which services had a particular data attribute.

On the one hand, these positive initial observations indicate that participants found the tracing feature of the interface easy to understand, intuitive and informative. On the other hand, participants had a harder time understanding that they could also access the data stored about them on the service's side (which was also a challenge in earlier versions of the Data Track). The reasons for this might be due to the lack of users having mental models of transparency and control features on the services' side, or to the poor affordance and visibility properties of the UI elements that were supposed to allow users to access the services' side data. About half of the participants (eight out of the total), understood that the attributes displayed on the top panel were data that were under their control.

From the results of the post-questionnaires conducted, it is interesting to note that, when asked to rate "how much would you *trust* the Data Track program with the information you give to Internet companies" on a scale from 1 (would not trust at all) to 10 (would trust completely), 30.8% of participants gave a rating of 4, while 61.6% gave a rating of 6 to 8 (just one participant, i.e., 7.7%, gave a rating of 5, and one participant did not answer the question). Moreover, when asked how often they believed that they would use a transparency interface like the Data Track, 11 of the 14 participants indicated that they would use such a program a few times per month or more often (one participant suggested that she/he would use it almost never or never). Similarly, 12 participants responded that they would have the Data Track program turned on so as to track their Internet data releases 75% of the time or more, indicating the desire for this set of users at least to have such transparency tools.

Most test users found the graphical Data Track intuitive and useful. The local Data Track view was well understood by a majority of users. However, further improvements are needed to make users aware and to enable them to understand the control options allowing them to exercise their rights at a service provider side online.

While the current Data Track only allows the tracking of data disclosures to a primary services side, the future Data Track (when combined with transparency logging – see below) will also address more cloud-related scenarios, where users disclose many more data items to many different service providers, who may in turn forward the data to chains of cloud service providers. This consideration forces some redesign of the Data Track user interface, where users should be able to navigate through various elements without the interface being cluttered. **Fig. 4** shows an example illustration of how a more realistic scenario for the Data Track could look, depicting the flow of users' data through the chain of cloud providers.

4.4   Combining the Data Track with Privacy-Preserving Transparency Logging

While the Data Track provides an overview of data disclosures, and the ability to remotely access their data, one key missing aspect is a detailed record of *how* personal data have been processed. A privacy policy provides a description of intended data processor *before* a user discloses data. As data are being processed, *after* data disclosure, the data processor should log a detailed record of how it has processed personal data that are made available to data subjects: This is the goal of transparency logging.

Conceptually, with a detailed record of data processing available concerning personal data, a data subject could *verify* that the *actual* processing on personal data was in line with the processing for which the data subject gave consent to prior to

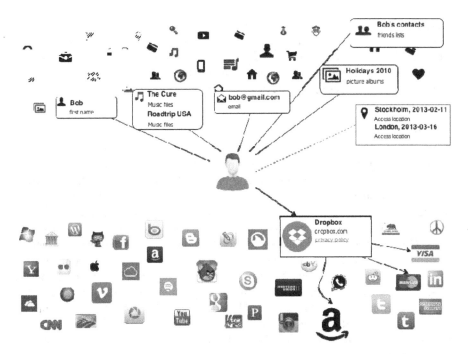

Fig. 4. Mock-up for a graphical Data Track for data a cloud

disclosing data, as stated in the privacy policy presented by the data processor. The detailed record of how personal data have been processed can be seen as the *provenance* of the personal data.

A transparency log contains a detailed record of how personal data have been processed, so the records are also personal data. For example, the records may reveal which doctor has read a patient's medical records in a hospital setting, or which type of car insurance a driver is qualified for based on previous accident history. This means that there is a need for preserving privacy when performing transparency logging. Some key considerations are:

1. Nobody should be able to make undetectable changes to recorded data.
2. Only the intended recipient user of recorded data (i.e., the data subject to whom the log entry refers) should be able to read the data.
3. It should be impossible to correlate data and users.

The first consideration ensures that, once a data processor has recorded data in the transparency log, no changes can be made, be it by the data processor who wishes to hide some processing or a malicious third-party. The second consideration captures the need for secrecy; only the data subject should be able to read this newly created personal data created to make processing of other personal data transparent. Last, but not least, the third consideration minimises the creation of new personal data in the form of metadata. For example, if it was possible to correlate the amount of encrypted data stored for a particular user especially over time, then such information might leak everything from how often the data subject uses the processor's service to particular details about the user's personal data (how data change over time might serve as a signature of a particular event). In [26], the authors describe a cryptographic system for performing transparency logging for distributed systems[7] (e.g., a cloud-based system that provides these properties).

5   Related Work

To the best of our knowledge there is not much previous work on TETs for the cloud that have been designed to be both usable and privacy-preserving. Related work on usable policies, such as [16], [15], are not focused on the cloud context. Related data tracking and control tools for end users are, in contrast to the Data Track, usually restricted to specific applications and cannot be used directly to track data along cloud chains. One example of such related work is the Google Dashboard, which grants its users access to a summary of the data stored in a Google account, including account data and the users' search query history. In contrast to the Data Track, the Dashboard provides access only to authenticated (non-anonymous) users. Related to the Data Track are personal data vaults, such as [19], developed for participatory sensing applications. This includes a logging functionality which allows the display of transactions and transformations of users' data and enables users to track who precisely has accessed their data.

6   Concluding Remarks

Further work is needed to develop and enhance transparency-enhancing tools for the cloud that are privacy preserving and usable. Parts of this team's future work will focus on extending the Data Track to making data processing along the cloud chain more transparent. It will increase the usability of the Data Track's control functions, thereby allowing users to exercise their data subject rights including the right to data portability.

Additional relevant research questions that we would like to address include the following: How can policy interfaces better inform users about the consequences of data disclosures in an unbiased and unobtrusive fashion? How can privacy-preserving ex ante TETs be technically designed to allow users to track who has accessed their data, what logic has been involved in processing their data and what are the consequences of this, while not leaking trade secrets in regard to the data controller's business processes (cf. problem discussed in recital 51 GDPR)?

---

[7] As described above, this system targets at protecting the privacy of individuals whose data are processed. Protecting the privacy of employees processing personal data, whose activities are logged and who can thus be monitored at their working place, is another problem that is outside the scope of this solution. Also, the problem that there may be data referring to more than one data subject is not addressed yet.

Acknowledgements. Parts of this work has been conducted for the EU FP7 project A4Cloud, which received funding from the Seventh Framework Programme for Research of the European Community under grant agreement no. 317550. We especially want to thank our A4Cloud project colleagues, John Sören Pettersson, Erik Wästlund, Eleni Kosta, Maartje Niezen and Karin Bernsmed for cooperation and feedback on the related A4Cloud D:C-7.1 deliverable. Besides, we are very grateful to Marit Hansen and Diane Whitehouse who provided very helpful review comments for this paper to us. The development of the graphical user interfaces for the Data Track was funded by the Google Research Award Project on "Usable Privacy and Transparency II". We want to thank our contact partners at Google for their kind support and fruitful discussions.

References

1. Alvaro, A.: Life Cycle Data Protection Management – Ein Beitrag zur Anpassung der europäischen Datenschutzgesetzgebung an die Erfordernisse des 21. Jahrhunderts (January 30, 2013), `http://www.alexander-alvaro.de/inhalte/lifecycle-data-protection-management-ein-beitrag-zur-anpassung-der-europaischen-datenschutzgesetzgebung-an-die-erfordernisse-des-21-jahrhunderts/`
2. Andersson, C., Camenisch, J., Crane, S., Fischer-Hübner, S., Leenes, R., Pearson, S., Pettersson, J.S., Sommer, D.: Trust in PRIME. In: Proceedings of the Fifth IEEE International Symposium on Signal Processing and Information Technology. IEEE Xplore (2005)
3. Angulo, J., Fischer-Hübner, S., Wästlund, E., Pulls, T.: Towards usable privacy policy display and management. Information Management & Computer Security 20(1), 4–17 (2012)
4. Angulo, J., Fischer-Hübner, S., Pettersson, J.S.: General HCI principles and guidelines for accountability and transparency in the cloud. A4Cloud Deliverable D:C-7.1. A4Cloud Project (September 2013)
5. Art. 29 Data Protection Working Party (2004). Opinion 10/2004 on More Harmonised Information Provisions. European Commission (November 25, 2004)
6. Art. 29 Data Protection Working Party. Opinion 1/2010 on the concepts of "controller" and "processor". European Commission (February 16, 2010)
7. Art. 29 Data Protection Working Party. Opinion 5/2012 on Cloud Computing. European Commission (July 1, 2012)
8. Becker, R.A., Eick, S.G., Wilks, A.R.: Visualizing network data. IEEE Transactions on Visualization and Computer Graphics 1(1), 16–28 (1995)
9. European Commission. Directive 95/46/EC of the European Parliament and of the Council of 24 October 1995 on the protection of individuals with regard to the processing of personal data and on the free movement of such data. Office Journal L. 281 (November 23, 1995)
10. European Commission. Proposal for a Regulation of the European Parliament and of the Council on the protection of individuals with regard to the processing of personal data and on the free movement of such data (General Data Protection Regulation). COM (2012) 11 Final. Brussels (January 25, 2012)
11. European Commission. Proposal for a regulation of the European Parliament and of the Council on the protection of individual with regard to the processing of personal data and on the free movement of such data (General Data Protection Regulation) (COM(2012)0011 – C7 0025/2012 – 2012/0011(COD)). Compromise amendments on Articles 1-29 (Passed October 21, 2013), `http://www.europarl.europa.eu/meetdocs/2009_2014/documents/libe/dv/comp_am_art_01-29/comp_am_art_01-29en.pdf`

12. Fischer-Hübner, S., Zwingelberg, H.: UI Prototypes: Policy administration and presentation - Version 2. PrimeLife Project Deliverable D.4.3.2 (2010), http://primelife.ercim.eu/
13. Freeman, L.C.: Visualizing social networks. Journal of Social Structure 1(1), 4 (2000)
14. Hildebrandt, M.: Behavioural biometric profiling and transparency enhancing tools. FIDIS Deliverable, D7.12. FIDIS EU project (2009), http://www.fidis.net/
15. Holtz, L., Nocun, K., Hansen, M.: Displaying privacy information with icons. In: PrimeLife/IFIP Summer School 2010 Proceedings, Helsingborg, August 2-6 2010. Springer (2011)
16. Kani-Zabihi, E., Helmhout, M., Coles-Kemp, L.: Increasing Service Users' Privacy Awareness by Introducing On-line Interactive Privacy Features. In: IAAC Symposium 2011 (2012) (Online)
17. Kelley, P.G., Bresee, J., Cranor, L.F., Reeder, R.W.: A "Nutrition Label" for Privacy. In: Proceedings of the 5th Symposium on Usable Privacy and Security (SOUPS 2009). ACM, Mountain View (2009)
18. Kolter, J., Netter, M., Pernul, G.: Visualizing past personal data disclosures. In: ARES 2010 International Conference on Availability, Reliability, and Security. IEEE (2010)
19. Lacohée, H., Crane, S., Phippen, A.: Trustguide: Final Report (2006)
20. Maguire, M., Bevan, N.: User requirements analysis. In: Mun, M., Hao, S., Mishra, N., Shilton, K., Burke, J., Estrin, D., Hansen, M., Govindan, R. (eds.) Personal Data Vaults: a Locus of Control for Personal Data Streams, CoNEXT 2010, vol. 17. ACM Digital Library (2002)
21. Nielsen, J.: Usability inspection methods. In: Conference Companion on Human Factors in Computing Systems. ACM (1995)
22. Patrick, A.S., Kenny, S.: From privacy legislation to interface design: Implementing information privacy in human-computer interactions. In: Dingledine, R. (ed.) PET 2003. LNCS, vol. 2760, pp. 107–124. Springer, Heidelberg (2003)
23. Pearson, S., Tountopoulos, V., Catteddu, D., Sudholt, M., Molva, R., Reich, C., Fischer-Hübner, S., Millard, C., Lotz, V., Jaatun, M.G.: Accountability for cloud and other future Internet services. In: IEEE 4th International Conference on Cloud Computing Technology and Science (CloudCom). IEEE (2012)
24. Pettersson, J.S.: HCI Guidelines. PRIME Deliverable D06.1.f. Final Version. PRIME project (2008), https://www.prime-project.eu/
25. PrimeLife, Privacy and Identity Management in Europe for Life - Policy Languages, http://primelife.ercim.eu/results/primer/133-policy-languages
26. Pulls, T., Peeters, R., Wouters, K.: Distributed Privacy-Preserving Transparency Logging. In: Workshop on Privacy in the Electronic Society. ACM (2013)
27. Raskin, A.: Privacy Icons: Alpha Release (2010)
28. Svensk Författningssamling Riksdagen. Patientdatalag 355 (2008)
29. W3C, P3P – The Platform for Privacy Preferences 1.1 (P3P1.1) Specification, W3C Working Group Note (November 13, 2006), http://www.w3.org/P3P/
30. Wästlund, E., Fischer-Hübner, S.: End User Transparency Tools: UI Prototypes. PrimeLife Deliverable D.4.2.2; PrimeLife project (2010), http://primelife.ercim.eu/

Privacy Versus Collective Security
Drivers and Barriers Behind a Trade-off

Bas van Schoonhoven, Arnold Roosendaal and Noor Huijboom*

TNO, The Netherlands
{bas.vanschoonhoven,arnold.roosendaal,noor.huijboom}@tno.nl

Abstract. Many decisions concerning technological development and related policies in the field of protecting the privacy of individuals and security at the societal level include a perceived trade-off between these two interests. Sometimes, this trade-off is made explicitly, but often it is an implicit choice, driven by external factors. This paper assesses a set of factors acting as drivers or barriers towards the development of technologies for privacy and/or societal security. While some of the individual drivers and barriers do not show a clear bias towards security or privacy technology development, the overview gives a clear indication that some powerful factors are biased towards developing and using security technologies, and some other factors are biased towards hindering the development and use of privacy technologies. This bias may threaten the privacy of individuals on the long run and may obscure potential solutions that enhance both security and privacy.

Keywords: Privacy, security, trade-off, drivers, barriers.

1 Introduction

Many decisions concerning technological development and related policies in the field of protecting the privacy of individuals and security at the societal level include a perceived trade-off between these two interests. Security technologies that are developed and deployed to secure society against crime, terrorism or other threats often violate the privacy of individuals. Similarly some privacy technologies hinder security surveillance practices. Sometimes, this trade-off is made explicitly, but often it is an implicit choice, driven by external factors. An important question concerns what these factors are. The phenomenon of the perceived privacy-security trade-off has been recognised in literature before [1]. This research adds to the knowledge concerning this phenomenon by identifying drivers and barriers for the development of privacy and security technologies in order to explain why the trade-off turns out in a certain way.

How exactly the drivers and barriers identified in this paper work out in practice, depends on the specific technology used, the situation in which it is

---

* The authors would like to thank the reviewers and participants of the IFIP Summerschool for their valuable comments

M. Hansen et al. (Eds.): Privacy and Identity 2014, IFIP AICT 421, pp. 93–101, 2014.

applied, and the perceptions of the actors involved. This is not part of this paper, but is developed further in a number of case studies[1] in the PRISMS[2] project. In this paper, first a brief description of security and privacy will be presented. Then, drivers and barriers for development of security and privacy technologies will be discussed. Finally, some conclusions with regard to the impact of these drivers and barriers on the perceived trade-off between security and privacy technology development will be drawn.

2   Security and Privacy

Privacy and security technologies aim at enhancing privacy and security. To understand what these technologies do, it is necessary to have an idea of what security and privacy are. The *European Committee on Standardisation*s working group 161 provides a mainstream definition of security:

> "security is the condition (perceived or confirmed) of an individual, a community, and organisation, a societal institution, a state, and their assets (such as goods, infrastructure), to be protected against danger or threats such as criminal activity, terrorism or other deliberate or hostile acts, disasters (natural and man-made)" [2]

Security as a concept is multidimensional, and generally defined in a very broad sense. It relates to many different scales: international security, national security, corporate security, societal security, and individual security [3].

The concept of privacy has a long history in European and American cultures and it has been defined in many ways. Back in 1890, Warren and Brandeis defined it as "the right to be let alone" [4]. In 1967, the influential privacy researcher Alan Westin described it as "an instrument for achieving individual goals of self-realisation" and "the claim of individuals, groups or institutions to determine for themselves when, how and to what extent information about them is communicated to others" [5].

More recently, researchers have recognised that privacy is a concept that is impossible to fully define in a single definition, and that there are multiple dimensions to privacy, for example as argued by Daniel Solove in his book "Understanding Privacy" [6]. Solove differentiates between different dimensions of privacy according to the type of privacy invasions, e.g. surveillance, aggregation, or intrusion. However, the outlining of privacy problems or intrusions does little

---

[1] These case studies concern biometrics, deep packet inspection (DPI) and internet monitoring, Automated Number Plate Recognition (ANPR), smart grids, and body scanners at airports.

[2] PRISMS stands for "The PRIvacy and Security MirrorS" - Towards a European framework for integrated decision making. The project is part of the EU Seventh Framework Programme and analyses the traditional trade-off model between privacy and security and devises a more evidence-based perspective for reconciling privacy and security, trust and concern.

to provide an overarching framework that would ensure that *individuals* rights are proactively protected.

Rights to privacy, such as those enshrined in the European Charter of Fundamental Rights, require a forward-looking privacy framework that positively outlines the parameters of privacy in order to prevent intrusions, infringements and problems. For our analysis, we use the recent conceptualisation of privacy as seven types of privacy, as identified by Finn, Wright, and Friedewald. These types of privacy are: Privacy of the body, Privacy of behaviour, Privacy of communication, Privacy of data and image, Privacy of thoughts and feelings, Privacy of location and space, and Privacy of association [7].

The concepts of privacy and security partially overlap at the individuals' scale. This is especially visible in the field of information security which is also concerned with data protection. There is no such overlap, however, when comparing security at the societal scale with privacy at the individuals' scale.[3]

3 Collective Security Versus Individual Privacy

Decisions concerning technological development and related policies in the field of protecting privacy and security are made within a certain policy context. The actors involved in the policy arena highly determine the definition of the notions *privacy* and *security* and develop certain *story lines* of the relation between the two notions. To understand the meaning given to the notions and their interrelationship, an extensive discourse analysis has been carried out within the PRISMS project. The discourse analysis shows that actors often perceive the balance between privacy and security as a trade-off; the one issue being at the expense of the other and vice versa. One of the many examples can be found in the Communication of the European Commission on the Stockholm Programme (a five-year plan with guidelines for justice and home affairs) in which it states that "it must also foresee and regulate the circumstances in which public authorities might need to restrict the application of these rules [regarding privacy] in the exercise of their lawful duties [security]" [8]. In other words, it is contended that in some instances privacy has to be restricted in order to enhance security. This perceived trade-off may as well be fed by the rather polarised policy field in which there is a clear distinction between actors who advocate increased privacy and actors who promote more security. Only few actors point to (e.g. technological) possibilities to strengthen both privacy and security at the same time. In addition, privacy and security policies are being developed by distinct policy bodies with their own specific focus (e.g. separate bodies within DG Justice and DG Home Affairs). This rather dispersed policy field and polarised discourse may explain certain technological developments in which the trade-off is visible.

---

[3] We acknowledge that there is a collective value of privacy as well. The research and use cases on which this paper is based, however, concern situations where collective security (e.g. fighting terrorism) counters individual privacy. For instance, the use of body scanners at air-ports concerns public/collective security, but each individual is affected in his privacy.

4   The Trade-off: Drivers and Barriers

In technological developments, a trade-off between security at the societal scale and privacy of individuals is visible. Security technologies are developed and deployed that violate privacy, and similarly some privacy technologies hinder security surveillance practices. For example, advanced surveillance technologies applied in digital and physical environments make it increasingly possible to track and profile individual behavioural patterns, reducing the privacy of these individuals. On the other hand, some privacy enhancing technologies such as communication encryption and onion routing networks hinder online security surveillance practices. To gain a better understanding of how decisions based on this perceived trade-off play out we performed a preliminary analysis of the drivers and barriers that respectively drive security and privacy technological developments, or act as barriers to these developments. The drivers and barriers outlined here are based on a literature study of policy documents, technology roadmaps, foresight studies and impact assessments performed in the PRISMS project. Most drivers and barriers that were identified apply to both security and privacy technology developments, although to a varying extent. We identified the following drivers and barriers.

4.1   Driver 1: Technology and Industry Push

The *military industrial complex* has become a reality by the farewell speech of Dwight Eisenhower in 1961, ending his presidential career. Eisenhower first stipulates the emergence of the military industrial complex, new in the American experience, and in his view the result of the changing approach to arms and armaments after the three large wars in which the United Stated have been involved (the first and second world war, the Korean war). Eisenhower states:

> "Now this conjunction of an immense military establishment and a large arms industry is new in the American experience. The total influence – economic, political, even spiritual – is felt in every city, every Statehouse, every office of the Federal government [...] Only an alert and knowledgeable citizenry can compel the proper meshing of the huge industrial and military machinery of defence with our peaceful methods and goals, so that security and liberty may prosper together."

Eisenhower both addresses the emergence of a complex consisting of industries at arms length of military decision makers and the role and responsibilities of *alert and knowledgeable citizenry* in order that *security and liberty may prosper together*. Several authors indicate that this military-industrial complex meanwhile has experienced a transition into the direction of a security-industrial complex, since the revenues for military undertakings are under pressure. The security-industrial complex is a significant phenomenon in Europe, and is developing at a rapid pace. The pace of these developments is to a large extent based on increasing demand [9]. However, a vested industry also has a significant interest in maintaining and increasing demand for its products and services. Industry, and to some extent research institutions, that are involved in researching and developing technologies for security and privacy provide a *technology push*, or solutions in search of a problem. Since the potential market for societal or national security is much larger than that of individual privacy, there is a strong financial incentive for companies in the security-industrial complex to invest in research and development of surveillance and other security technologies, even if this results in a negative outcome for the privacy of individuals. Companies dedicated to developing privacy protection solutions currently operate mostly in niche markets, and provide a *technology push* to a much lesser extent. In relation to the above, the level of organisation is much higher in the security industry field than in the privacy field. The establishment at the European level, supported by the EU government, of a Group of Personalities and the European Security Research Advisory Board (ESRAB), with a huge influence in the lobbying process, provided these bodies with a steady position. Moreover, these bodies have a strong relationship with industrial companies and are very well supported. On the privacy side, however, it often concerns *voluntary associations* [10] without a clear overarching structure or a social movement with an identifiable base [10].

4.2   Driver 2: Events with High Societal Impact

An analysis performed in the PRISMS project based on the use of keywords related to terrorism and organised crime in CORDIS project objective descriptions shows remarkable increase of projects in these fields from 2004 onwards. A possible explanation for this is that this is a delayed response to a number of high-profile attacks on the EU and its allies, resulting in an increased attention in fighting terrorism and organised crime. These attacks include the September 11 airplane hijack and subsequent attack in 2001 in New York and Washington, the July 7 2005 suicide bombings of the public transport system in London, and the March 11 2004 Madrid train bombings. All these events have had a high impact on the perception of societal security (or the lack thereof) of citizens in the EU, and as a consequence an increased call for security and protection against such terrorist attacks, even at the cost of losing privacy. The interplay between security and privacy as a consequence of high-profile societal events is seen as a possible driver of primarily development of security technologies. Historically, privacy-related incidents (e.g. leaks of large amounts of personal data) have had significantly less impact than the discussed security incidents, and as a consequence the drive for the development of privacy protection technologies because of incidents is much lower [11]. The recent NSA revelations and increased government surveillance can be a driver for privacy technologies. However, any individual privacy enhancing technology that is too difficult for a State to decipher will face difficulties, as was seen with the US government fight against PGP in the 1990's. This can act as a barrier to new privacy technologies. One can also argue that legislation can act as a barrier to privacy technologies. Privacy is secondary to national security in all types of legislation (including Data protection and Human Rights). Generally States do not allow for the total privacy of an individual and this is manifested in legislative policy. Some States have specific legislation to combat certain privacy technologies in the interest of national security. For example the UK Regulation of Investigatory Powers Act 2000, allows authorities to compel a suspect in a criminal or terrorism related investigation to reveal his/her encryption key to enable the access to encrypted data.

4.3   Driver 3: National and EU-level Policy and Regulation

Although national and EU-level regulation tend to be reactive and sometimes fragmented, legislation does act as a driver for organisations to implement certain privacy and security protections, to be compliant with the law [12] [11]. The strength of this driver depends amongst other things on the presence and actions of a supervising authority (e.g. data protection supervisor), and how well organisations understand what they have to do to be compliant, which is an issue especially with regards to privacy. A special case of this driver is the Charter of Fundamental Rights of individuals as argued in the 2010 EU Internal Security Strategy:

> "People in Europe expect to live in security and to enjoy their freedoms: security is in itself a basic right. The values and principles established in the Treaties of the Union and set out in the Charter of Fundamental Rights have inspired the EU's Internal Security Strategy: justice, freedom and security policies which are mutually reinforcing whilst respecting fundamental rights, international protection, the rule of law and privacy [...], transparency and accountability in security policies, so that they can be easily understood by citizens, and take account of their concerns and opinions [13]."

4.4   Driver 4: Citizen Demand for Security and Privacy

Another driver is related to some of the drivers we already mentioned: citizens demand a certain level of security and privacy, and as a consequence a market for products may arise, or governments may setup regulations. Citizen demand plays a role in the application of some surveillance technologies, such as CCTV cameras. A perception of public settings being insecure, e.g. being threatened by crime or violence in city centres, may increase the demand for technologies that are perceived to enhance security, such as surveillance systems. This does not necessarily mean that these solutions are effective in enhancing security [9]. With regard to privacy the same driver applies: citizens demand a certain level of privacy, for example while using internet services, and as a consequence new technologies get developed that fill in this demand. An example is the Do Not Track technology used in web browsers.

4.5   Barrier 1: Privacy and Security not Perceived as Unique Selling Points

Although citizen needs for security and privacy may increase demand for certain technologies that aim to enhance security or privacy, for many services and products security and privacy is not the primary focus, but rather a side issue. For example, for most of the transport sector, transporting goods and passengers is the primary activity, and security and privacy, while important, both do not act as positive selling features that companies advertise [14]. The same is true with regard to privacy: few companies see privacy as a unique selling point that allows them to sell products better or to compete better. Customers do currently not seem to find privacy a distinguishing feature of services, and are not overly willing to pay for enhanced privacy protection [11]. Increasing awareness of the importance of privacy and security with customers may possibly change this barrier into a driver, however. In the EU Security Industrial Policy, aspects such as privacy are mentioned as having a

> "[...]very tangible effect for a company that wants to invest in security technologies. The security industry has to be sure that its products will be compatible with the general opinion of the public. The commercialisation of their new technologies would otherwise be impossible. The financial and human efforts that go into the development and production of a security product can therefore be easily wasted [12]"

4.6   Barrier 2: Lack of Standardisation

Another important barrier to development and use of both security-enhancing and privacy-enhancing technologies is a lack of standardisation [11]. There are several related issues that act as barriers in this: the lack of a clear or commonly held definition of what *security* and *privacy* entails in practice; uncertainty about legal obligations and a fragmented regulatory landscape in the EU with regards to privacy and security; and incompatibility of different kinds of technological solutions with existing systems or other solutions. Some examples of where lack of standardisation hinders technology development and use are a lack of common technical and interoperability standards for automated border control systems, as well as standards for biometric identifiers, or a lack of standards for communication interoperability [12]. For privacy this issue is more pronounced than for security: as privacy is a relatively new issue many companies do not have extensive experience with best practices and reliable knowledge of what precisely to do to enhance privacy is hard to come by.

4.7   Barrier 3: Reactive, not Proactive Approach

Organisations tend to behave reactively and not proactively with regard to privacy protection and security. Similarly, governments tend to formulate regulations and mandatory requirements in response to issues that occur, and not in a proactive manner. Technologies may not be applied because little attention to security or privacy issues was given during the design stage of products and services. The alternatives to such reactive approaches are usually described as *security by design* and *privacy by design*, for example by Ann Cavoukian, the Information Commissioner of Ontario, Canada [15]. A reactive approach may still create a demand for technologies in order to *patch up* security or privacy vulnerabilities in systems and services, but overall we expect that a proactive approach would increase demand for privacy enhancing and security enhancing technologies [12].

5   Conclusion

In the previous sections we discussed a number of key drivers and barriers in the development and application of technologies for privacy and security. Some drivers and barriers have a more pronounced effect on the development of security technologies, for others the effect is stronger on privacy technologies. We argue that there is a clear bias towards developing technologies for societal security, even at the cost of individual privacy, in both the factors driving and hindering technology development. This argument is based on the preliminary assessment performed, which is summarised in the tables below:

Table 1. Bias in factors driving technology development and use

Driver	Biased towards driving ...
Technology and industry push	Security
Events with high societal impact	Security
Government policy and regulation	-
Consumer demand	-

Table 2. Bias in factors hindering technology development and use

Barrier	Biased towards hindering ...
Lack of standardisation	-
Not a unique selling point	Privacy
Reactive approach	Privacy

While some of the individual drivers and barriers do show a clear bias towards security or privacy technology development, the overview gives a clear indication that some powerful factors are biased towards developing and using security technologies, and some other factors are biased towards hindering the development and use of privacy technologies. The drivers and barriers identified here are subject to ongoing developments. For example, with rising privacy awareness in customers, privacy as a unique selling point may become a significant factor driving the development and use of these technologies. The Snowden revelations on the USA PRISM[4] scandal may boost awareness. At this point in time, however, this analysis indicates that there is no level playing field for the development and use of security and privacy technologies: current technological developments tend towards security at the cost of privacy. This bias does not only pose a risk for the privacy of individuals on the long run, but the bias against the development and use of privacy protecting technologies compared to technologies for security at the societal scale and the perceived trade-off between the two may obscure potential solutions that may enhance both security and privacy.

References

1. Solove, D.: Nothing to Hide: The False Tradeoff between Privacy and Security. Yale University Press (2011)
2. Sempere, C.M.: The European Security Industry: A Research Agenda. Technical report (2010)
3. Friedewald, M., Wright, D., Wadhwa, K., Gutwirth, S., Lieshout, M., Bodea, G., Raab, C., Szekely, I., Ploeg, I., Skinner, G., Kimpeler, S., Schuhmacher, J., Goos, K., Finn, R., Lagazio, M., Verfaillie, K., Gonzalez Fuster, G., Veenstra, A., Uszkiewicz, E., Pridmore, J., Valkenburg, G.: Central Concepts and Implementation Plan. PRISMS Deliverable 1.1. Technical report (2012)
4. Warren, S.D., Brandeis, L.D.: Right to Privacy. Harvard Law Review 4(1), 72 (1890)
5. Westin, A.F.: Privacy and Freedom, vol. 97. Atheneum (1967)
6. Solove, D.J.: Understanding Privacy. Harvard University Press, Harvard (2010)
7. Finn, R., Wright, D., Friedewald, M.: Seven Types of Privacy. In: Gutwirth, S. (ed.) European Data Protection: Coming of Age. Number. Springer Science & Business Media, Dordrecht (January 2013)
8. European Commission: Action Plan Implementing the Stockholm Programme. COM/2010/0171 (2010)
9. Wright, D., Székely, I., Friedewald, M., Rodrigues, R., Kreissl, R., Johan, C., Raab, C., Wright, D., Beatrix, V., Goos, K., Hallinan, D., Charles, L., Webster, W., Galdon, G.: Surveillance, Fighting Crime and Violence. IRISS Deliverable 1.1. Technical report (2012)
10. Bennett, C.J.: The Privacy Advocates; resisting the spread of surveillance. MIT Press, Cambridge Massachusetts (2008)
11. van Lieshout, M., Kool, L., van Schoonhoven, B., Bodea, G., Schlechter, J.: Stimulerende en remmende factoren van Privacy by Design in Nederland. Technical report, TNO, Delft (2012)
12. European Commission: Security Industrial Policy: Action Plan for an innovative and competitive Security Industry (2012)
13. European Commission: The EU Internal Security Strategy in Action: Five steps towards a more secure Europe (2010)
14. European Commission: Commission Staff Working Document on Transport Security (2012)
15. Cavoukian, A.: Privacy by Design The 7 Foundational Principles. Security, 7–8 (2011)

---

[4] The USA PRISM program should not be confused with the EU FP7 PRISMS research project.

Privacy in the Life-Cycle of IT Services –
An Investigation of Process Reference Models

Saskia Viktoria Rother and Ina Schiering

{sas.rother,i.schiering}@ostfalia.de

Abstract. During the whole life-cycle of IT services privacy as expressed by user requirements and data protection legislation should be respected. There are several existing assessments for the assurance of privacy requirements in IT services. Other approaches like privacy protection goals allow already the integration in the design of a service. However, unlike information security, privacy is not incorporated in the best practice process reference models that are used to manage the life-cycle of IT services. In this paper widely-used process reference models CMMI and ITIL are analysed. It is investigated for these reference models to what extent privacy is already incorporated and what existing approaches could be recommended otherwise.

Keywords: life-cycle of IT services, privacy, process reference models, CMMI, ITIL.

1 Introduction

Complex IT services often in the form of public cloud services are a vital part of our lives and an increasing amount of personal data is processed in these services. The internet is a main source of information, social networks allow interaction and communication, smart phones with a variety of apps accompany the daily life of people. The next step are devices like e.g. smart watches and monitoring devices e.g. for monitoring sport and other activities. But despite the fact that there is a data protection legislation in Europe since the 90s also today it is not anything but granted that privacy is respected. Concerning smart phone apps see the Opinion 02/2013 on apps on smart devices of the Article 29 Working Party [1]. Additionally, violations of privacy do not only happen during the realisation of a service but often during the operation or evolution of services.

In the European Union the legal framework for the processing of personal data consists of the European Data Protection Directive 95/46/EC [2], the e-Privacy Directive [3] with amendments Directive 2006/24/EC concerning data retention and Directive 2009/136/EC. Since January 2012 there exists a draft of a general data protection regulation [4] which is currently discussed. An interesting aspect of this draft is for example the incorporation of Privacy by Design.

But how to ensure that the regulatory framework is respected during the development, operation and termination of the IT service?

M. Hansen et al. (Eds.): Privacy and Identity 2014, IFIP AICT 421, pp. 102–113, 2014.

In this paper we investigate the approach of integrating privacy requirements in the life-cycle of IT services by incorporating them in process reference models, which describe best practices for the different phases of the service life-cycle.

The connection between data protection regulations and frameworks for information security is investigated in Meints [5]. Here we widen the scope to reference models for the whole life-cycle of IT services. Today process reference models are widely used in organisations: In a recent review of 23 studies about the use of ITIL for IT service management of the APMG, it was mentioned [6, p. 6] that between 28% and 77% of the organisations incorporated in the studies adopted ITIL. As a reference model for development processes CMMI is frequently used according to a survey concerning governance in IT [7, p. 26]. Therefore an overview is given for CMMI, ITIL, and TOGAF, COBIT which are also widely used. CMMI and ITIL are investigated in detail.

In Section 2 we present the process reference models we consider and investigate to which extent privacy requirements are considered and which existing concepts would be appropriate in the context. Afterwards in Section 3 we analyse where links to privacy are already incorporated in the reference models and classify the existing links. After this analysis we investigate in Section 4 which methods to design and control data privacy are available and discuss in Section 5 where these approaches are applicable in the reference models and in the service life-cycle in general.

2   Process-Reference Models in the Service Life-Cycle

The life-cycle of an IT service starts with requirements analysis, incorporates the design and implementation of software, the architecture of the system and the service operation. A typical model to represent these releases is the V-Model. It is a model for system development considering all phases of the development process as requirements, design, implementation, test and maintenance. The form of the "V" suggests that the development of tests is already started after the requirements are specified. During the operation phase continuously new releases of the service are realised and released until the service is terminated.

Therefore in all of these phases the privacy requirements have to be ensured. For each part of the life-cycle there exists process reference models that are widely used and considered as a best practice. Process reference models describe a set of processes and outcomes of processes that are relevant for the designated area.

For the design and implementation of an IT service we consider CMMI [8]. Concerning the development of architectures TOGAF [9] is investigated and as a best practice reference model for IT service management ITIL [10] is considered. As a model for the governance of the service life-cycle we incorporate COBIT [11] in this analysis. The focus of this paper is on CMMI and ITIL.

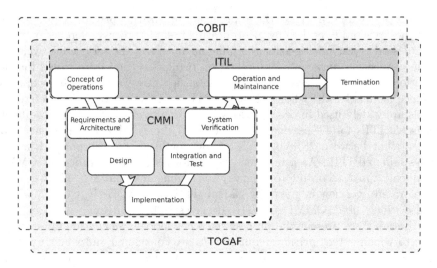

Fig. 1. Reference models and V-model

2.1 CMMI for Development

The Capability Maturity Model Integration (CMMI) for development [8] is developed by the SEI (Software Engineering Institute at Carnegie Mellon University). The aim of this process framework is auditing and process improvement for development processes. The focus there is on organisational processes.

In CMMI practices needed in the development phase are grouped into process areas, (e.g. requirements development (RD), supplier agreement management (SAM), project planning (PP), technical solution (TS), validation (VAL) and verification (VER)). For each process area goals, practices and outcomes of these practices are described to allow for an appraisal (audit) of the development process of the organisation. Based on this process framework the maturity or capability of the development processes of an organisation is investigated. Capability Levels state to what extent the goals and practices in a certain process area are realised. To reach a Maturity Level, a defined set of process areas has to be established within the organisation to a designated level. These levels are initial, managed, defined, quantitatively managed, optimised and are described via generic and specific goals and practices. Therefore CMMI for Development can be used via Capability Levels for the individual improvement of process areas in an organisation whereas Maturity Levels allow for a benchmarking of the whole development process.

2.2 ITIL

The Information Technology Infrastructure Library (ITIL) [10] which is now available in the version ITIL 2011 is a best practise framework for IT service management (ITSM). The focus is on service orientation in information technology which allows for an alignment of IT services with business processes. ITIL is a description of processes, roles and tasks that are needed to provide IT services. There the whole life-cycle of an IT Service is supported with the phases service strategy, service design, service operation and continual service improvement. ITIL can be used as a process framework for an ISO/IEC 20000 certification, the International Service Management Standard for IT service management. Since the focus of ITIL is on the management of IT Services but does not address software development or IT architectures, it could be used in addition to methodologies for these areas.

2.3   TOGAF

The Open Group Architecture Framework (TOGAF) [9] is developed by the Open Group. The framework is focussed on the development of an enterprise architecture. This architecture consists of the domains business, data, application, technology which describe the structure of an enterprise. Besides designing, planning and implementing, such an architecture, the framework provides also assistance for migration planning and governance.

2.4   COBIT

COBIT 5 (Control Objectives for Information and Related Technology) [11] is developed by the ISACA. It is a best-practise framework focussed on governance and management of enterprise IT. COBIT is based on so-called key principles, e.g. meeting stakeholder needs, enabling a holistic approach, separating governance from management. Beside the key principles COBIT is focussed on the notion of enablers. Examples of enabler dimensions are principles, policies and frameworks, processes, organisational structures.

COBIT has an overlap with TOGAF and ITIL, but is not intended to replace these frameworks. The aim of COBIT is to describe requirements concerning these processes unlike ITIL and TOGAF where best practices for processes are described.

2.5   Categorisation of Reference Models

To investigate the consideration of privacy in reference models and recommend existing concepts concerning privacy to fill in gaps, a categorisation of reference models is proposed. First the models can be distinguished concerning the level of detail in which processes are described. There are the possibilities that processes are defined in the form of best or good practices or on the other hand that only requirements for processes are stated.

Reference models like ITIL and TOGAF contain descriptions of abstract best practice processes that can be used as blueprints to define processes for IT service management (ITIL) resp. the development of an enterprise architecture

(TOGAF). The focus of reference models like CMMI and COBIT is to describe merely requirements for processes and other elements needed concerning the models. But there is no guidance for the implementation of the processes. The aim of these reference models is to allow for audits in organisations. This is in particular an element of CMMI where maturity levels are an important aspect of the models.

The other dimension which is investigated here for a categorisation of reference models is the intended audience of the reference model. Reference models can address the technical level or the management level of an organisation. None of the reference models investigated here address the basic technical level of software development or IT operation in detail, i.e. how a backup of a system is realised in IT operation or which rules for static analysis and metrics are used in the development phase of a software project. The reference models addressing the technical level contain processes for the management of development or IT operation. This focus on the management of technical processes can be perceived in ITIL and CMMI. The other models, TOGAF which is focussed on enterprise architectures and COBIT where the aim is the alignment of IT with business goals, have a management perspective.

The focus of this paper is on CMMI and ITIL. Hence reference models with a focus on the technical level are addressed. But these two models already cover all phases mentioned in the V-model (see Figure 1) and the two general approaches of reference models are addressed, i.e. best practice processes and describing requirements for processes. It would be interesting to widen the investigation on frameworks addressing the management level. There TOGAF and COBIT are important frameworks to consider according to [7].

3   Existing Links to Privacy

In the context of these reference models and considerations concerning categorisation, the existing references to privacy are investigated. Here we distinguish the following possibilities how privacy requirements can be integrated.

The strongest form of mentioning privacy is to address directly privacy requirements in the mandatory part of the reference model. Additionally, there are often recommendations concerning privacy in the reference models where requirements to privacy are mentioned or documents are described with a focus on privacy. But these are only recommendations which are not mandatory. Often legal requirements are mentioned in general. This encompasses privacy requirements based on legal regulations. Beside these explicit links to privacy we consider implicit links, e.g. when privacy requirements are defined in the requirements definition phase, as an implication they are tested during the validation and testing phase.

3.1   CMMI

In CMMI for development [8] privacy is not mentioned directly in a mandatory way, but there are references to legal requirements in general and for these legal

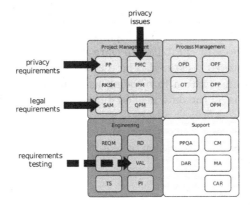

Fig. 2. CMMI and links to privacy

requirements and their implementation examples with a relation to privacy are mentioned. For a better understanding of the references to privacy the respective process areas are described first.

In the following the investigation of the process area project planning (PP) is detailed to illustrate the structure of process areas (see [8]). The aim of this process area is to establish and support project activities. It has 3 specific goals (SG), one of which is "SG2 Develop a Project Plan". There in the specific practice "SP 2.3 Plan Data Management" the management of all data during the project is mentioned which encompasses e.g. requirements, meeting minutes, or specifications. There are example work products for the specific practice mentioned. An example is a document about privacy requirements [8, page 292]. It is not a mandatory document, but an example of a work product. In subpractice 1 of SG 2.3 "Establish requirements and procedures to ensure privacy and the security of data" [8, page 293], privacy is stated.

The next reference can be identified in the process area "Supplier Agreement Management (SAM)". The purpose of this process area is the management of the purchase of products, The legal requirements are mentioned in the examples of the subpractice 6 from the specific practice "SP 2.1 Execute the Supplier Agreement". This subpractice states the management of reviews with the supplier. Review of the supplier's compliance with legal and regulatory requirements is listed as an example [8, page 371].

The process area "Project Monitoring and Control (PMC)" is responsible for measuring progress in the project. An important aspect concerning measuring project progress is the investigation of issues in the project. Privacy issues are named as an example for an issue: The specific goal "SG 2 Manage Corrective Action to Closure" has the sub practice "SP 2.1 Analyse Issues". There in subpractice 1, as an example for issues, privacy issues are mentioned [8, page 278].

Beside that, there are requirements in CMMI, which are often typical privacy requirements, but used in a different context. In the following we state an example: In the basic support process area "Measurement and Analysis (MA)" in the specific practice "SP 1.3 Specify Data Collection and Storage Procedures" there in subpractice 6, it is stated "Who is responsible for data storage, retrieval, and security?". Furthermore in "SP2.3 Store Data and Results" the aspect "Retention period for data stored" is stated. There in subpractice 4 privacy is mentioned "Prevent stored information from being used inappropriately." [8, page 188]. But here the focus is on the data needed during the project. Therefore this is not incorporated in the overview.

An implicit link to privacy is incorporated in the process area "Validation (VAL)". There the aim is the verification of requirements. Hence implicitly also the privacy requirements are tested.

3.2   ITIL

For the reference model ITIL there are mainly privacy requirements mentioned in the Service Design phase as an explicit statement. In the phase Service Design the data and information management is mentioned as technology-related activity. Concerning this activity it is described that legal requirements concerning privacy, security, confidentiality and integrity of data have to be considered. This data and information management can be incorporated in an Information Security Management System (ISMS) that is also mentioned in ITIL.

Implicitly in the phase Service Transition all requirements, hence also the privacy requirements are validated and tested. In the phase Service Operation the service is monitored which should also encompass the privacy requirements and in the Continual Service Improvement a framework for service measurement and improvement concerning the requirements is implemented.

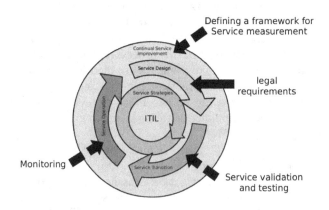

Fig. 3. ITIL and links to privacy

4   Defining and Auditing Privacy Requirements

There are several approaches for incorporating privacy requirements. In the following, we give an overview of approaches for defining and auditing privacy requirements and describe in which part of the service life-cycle they can be applied.

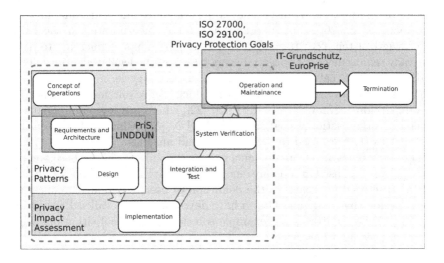

Fig. 4. Categorisation of reference models

The first type of approaches are assessments which are appropriate in the service operation phase of the service life-cycle. These audits are complex tasks, but can be applied to any service also without incorporation into process reference models.

Concerning auditing of European legislation like the data protection directive, assessments like EuroPriSe [12] can be used. Concerning a more general approach which is not focussed on European legislation in ISO 27000 [13] an Information Security Management System is defined. From a more technical point of view this can be investigated with the approach IT-Grundschutz [14], where aspects of privacy are integrated in a detailed security framework.

Beside that in ISO 29100 [15] a privacy framework is defined. In connection with this standard in ISO 29101 a privacy reference architecture is stated. With connection to the process assessment model of ISO 15504 [16] in the draft of ISO 29190 a privacy capability assessment model is proposed where also the maturity of the protection of personal data in an organisation will be addressed.

Instead of auditing a service during the service operation phase there exists also the approach of privacy impact assessments (PIA) [17] which are intended to be integrated in the risk management of the project. See [18] for an overview about PIAs resp. [19] for a detailed report about PIAs and different risk management methodologies. Hence PIAs are conducted already during the start of the project and updated in the next phases and when there are changes in the project. Therefore a PIA is a possibility from the point of view of governance and management to incorporate privacy requirements in the service life-cycle.

Beside these examples of audits and assessments there exists approaches that are also applicable from a more technical point of view. One of these approaches are privacy-specific protection goals. These are based on the security protection goals Confidentiality, Integrity, Availability and are accompanied by goals focussing on privacy, i.e. Transparency, Intervenebility and Unchainability (see Zwingelberg et al. [20]). This approach is already incorporated in the LDSG of Schleswig-Holstein [21]. It can be used in requirements engineering to define the privacy requirements of potential users based on the legal obligations. These stated requirements can be used during the whole life-cycle.

There are also several approaches with a focus on requirements engineering. Here we mention Privacy Safeguard (PriS) [22], where privacy requirements are modelled as organisational goals and LINDDUN [23], which is based on data flow diagrams that are used to perform a thread analysis.

Other approaches also focussing on a technical point of view are based on patterns which are e.g. used in software engineering. The PrimeLife Policy Language [24] is a structured approach to the definition of user requirements concerning privacy. Beside that Doty and Gupta have developed the so called Privacy Patterns [25]. Privacy Patterns are example solutions for typical situations where personal data is used in services.

5   Gaps in the Existing Links to Privacy

How can the existing links to privacy be addressed with existing approaches concerning privacy?

In CMMI in the process area PP [1] privacy requirements should be stated. There in general privacy protection goals are an appropriate tool. Beside that when the service addresses end users, also approaches like the PrimeLife Policy Language can be used. The same argument applies to SAM where project data is addressed. Concerning PMC where during the project also privacy issues should be monitored and corrective actions applied and SAM which addresses the compliance of suppliers with legal requirements during the project especially risk management based approaches like PIAs are useful. Only for the implicit statement of privacy concerning the validation and testing VAL, there is no existing methodology that can be applied.

Concerning ITIL in the Service Design phase legal compliance of services is addressed. There also approaches as privacy protection goals for describing privacy requirements and PIA approaches to check these requirements during the project can be used.

At the end of the development phase assessments like EuroPriSe can be used to check the compliance of the service with legal requirements concerning privacy. But there is a gap concerning testing of privacy requirements during the

---

[1] see Section 2.1 concerning abbreviations

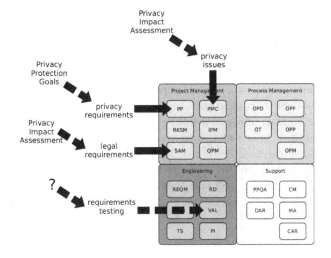

Fig. 5. Gaps concerning CMMI

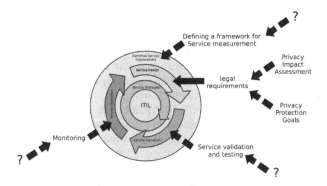

Fig. 6. Gaps concerning ITIL

realisation phase of the project. There is no methodology to check privacy requirements as other requirements via tests that can be performed regularly during the project.

To ensure that the privacy requirements are also preserved during the operation of a service, assessments can be updated resp. repeated periodically as it is addressed in ITIL in general by the Continual Service Improvement. But there exists no methodology to monitor privacy requirements between assessments e.g. after a change of the service. Since these assessments are quite complex this approach is not feasible. Also the implicit links to privacy concerning testing, monitoring and the definition of a framework for service measurement in the form of key performance indicators (KPIs) are not addressed by existing methodologies.

6 Conclusion

During the service life-cycle of IT services there are already various references to privacy in the process reference models investigated here. In most of the cases, especially concerning requirements analysis and auditing there are existing approaches to integrate privacy in reference models.

But at the moment there exists no approach for testing of privacy requirements during the development phase of a service, for monitoring of these requirements during the operation phase of the service and for key performance indicators (KPI). These gaps will be investigated in future work.

Such methodologies could also be used to integrate privacy requirements in light-weight models as agile software development which are often used for the realisation of frequently changing services as cloud services and smart-phone apps.

References

1. Article 29 Data Protection Working Party, WP 202 Opinion 02/2013 on apps on smart devices, European Commission (2013),
   http://ec.europa.eu/justice/data-protection/article-29/documentation/opinion-recommendation/files/2013/wp202_en.pdf
2. Directive 95/46/EC of the European Parliament and of the Council of 24 October 1995 on the protection of individuals with regard to the processing of personal data and on the free movement of such data, http://eur-lex.europa.eu/LexUriServ/LexUriServ.do?uri=CELEX:31995L0046:EN:HTML
3. Directive 2002/58/EC of the European Parliament and of the Council of 12 July 2002 concerning the processing of personal data and the protection of privacy in the electronic communications sector, http://eur-lex.europa.eu/LexUriServ/LexUriServ.do?uri=CELEX:32002L0058:EN:HTML
4. Proposal for a Regulation of the European Parliament and of the Council on the protection of individuals with regard to the processing of personal data and on the free movement of such data (General Data Protection Regulation), http://eur-lex.europa.eu/LexUriServ/LexUriServ.do?uri=COM:2012:0009:FIN:EN:HTML
5. Meints, M.: The relationship between data protection legislation and information security related standards. In: Matyáš, V., Fischer-Hübner, S., Cvrček, D., Švenda, P. (eds.) The Future of Identity. IFIP AICT, vol. 298, pp. 254–267. Springer, Heidelberg (2009)
6. England, R.: Review of recent ITIL studies, APMG (2011),
   http://www.best-management-practice.com/gempdf/Review_ITIL_Studies_White_Paper_Nov11.pdf
7. IT Governance Institute. Global Status Report on the Governance of Enterprise IT (GEIT) (2011), http://www.isaca.org/Knowledge-Center/Research/ResearchDeliverables/Pages/ITGI-Global-Survey-Results.aspx
8. CMMI Product Team. CMMI for Development (2010),
   http://www.sei.cmu.edu/reports/10tr033.pdf
9. The Open Group. TOGAF Version 9.1 (2011),
   http://pubs.opengroup.org/architecture/togaf9-doc/arch/

10. Cabinet Office. ITIL V3 (2011), `http://www.itil-officialsite.com`
11. IT Governance Institute. COBIT 5 (2012), `http://www.itil-officialsite.com`
12. EuroPriSe (European Privacy Seal) (2008),
    `http://www.european-privacy-seal.eu`
13. ISO/IEC. ISO/IEC 27000 - information technology security techniques information security management systems overview and vocabulary (2009)
14. Federal Office for Information Security (BSI). BSI-Standards 100-1 100-2 100-3 100-4 (2008), `http://www.bsi.bund.de/EN/Publications/BSIStandards/BSIStandards_node.html`
15. ISO/IEC. ISO/IEC 29100 - information technology – security techniques – privacy framework (2011)
16. ISO/IEC. ISO/IEC 15504 - information technology process assessment parts 1-5 (2003-2012)
17. Information Commissioners Office. Privacy Impact Assessment Handbook (2009), `http://www.ico.gov.uk/upload/documents/pia_handbook_html_v2/index.html`
18. Wright, D., De Hert, P.: Introduction to privacy impact assessment. Springer (2012)
19. Wright, D., Wadhwa, K., Lagazio, M., Raab, C., Charikane, E.: Privacy impact assessment and risk management, Report for the Information Commissioner's Office (May 2013), `http://www.ico.org.uk/about_us/consultations/~/media/documents/library/Corporate/Research_and_reports/pia-and-risk-management-full-report-for-the-ico.pdf`
20. Zwingelberg, H., Hansen, M.: Privacy protection goals and their implications for eid systems. In: Camenisch, J., Crispo, B., Fischer-Hübner, S., Leenes, R., Russello, G. (eds.) Privacy and Identity Management for Life. IFIP AICT, vol. 375, pp. 245–260. Springer, Heidelberg (2012)
21. Landesdatenschutzgesetz Schleswig-Holstein (2012),
    `http://www.gesetze-rechtsprechung.sh.juris.de/jportal/?quelle=jlink&query=DSG+SH+%C2%A7+21&psml=bsshoprod.psml&max=true`
22. Kalloniatis, C., Kavakli, E., Gritzalis, S.: Addressing privacy requirements in system design: the pris method. Requirements Engineering 13(3), 241–255 (2008)
23. Deng, M., Wuyts, K., Scandariato, R., Preneel, B., Joosen, W.: A privacy threat analysis framework: supporting the elicitation and fulfillment of privacy requirements. Requirements Engineering 16(1), 3–32 (2011)
24. Vimercati, G.N., Paraboschi, S., Pedrini, E., Preiss, F.-S., Raggett, D., Samarati, P., Trabelsi, S., Verdicchio, M.: Primelife policy language (2009)
25. Doty, N., Gupta, M.: Privacy Patterns (2012), `http://privacypatterns.org/`

Forgetting Bits and Pieces

An Exploration of the "Right to Be Forgotten" as Implementation of "Forgetting" in Online Memory Processes

Paulan Korenhof

Privacy & Identity lab
Tilburg Institute for Law, Technology, and Society (TILT)
Tilburg University, Tilburg, the Netherlands
p.e.i.korenhof@tilburguniversity.edu

Abstract. Technology has changed and still is changing our internal and external memory processes. The World Wide Web (Web) can function as an external transactive memory and can store and provide access to personal information for a very long time. The "right to be forgotten or erasure" (R2BFE), article 17 of the proposed General Data Protection Regulation, aims at helping individuals to control the availability of online accessible personal information. This paper takes the term "forgetting" in the article's title seriously and reviews the manner in which the R2BFE implements "forgetting" into the transactive memory on the Web. Exploring the concept of forgetting in this context shows that there is a far broader scale of options to implement digital forgetting than is offered today by the R2BFE. The analysis shows where the R2BFE is insufficient and risks affecting other interests at stake more than is necessary by the application of too narrow a notion of forgetting. This paper suggests that the R2BFE could be transformed into a more successful implementation of "forgetting" in the online transactive memory if it were to draw more heavily on the mechanisms of human forgetting.

Keywords: Data protection, forgetting, Internet, memory, right to be forgotten.

1   Introduction

"The Web Means the End Of Forgetting" [15]: The title of this 2010 article by Rosen expresses the growing concern with personal data available on the World Wide Web (Web)[1] and the potential consequences of permanent availability of these data for individuals; people would be unable to "escape" from their online past. With the increasing number of people that make use of the Web to share and consult information [7, p. 382] such concerns seem justified. In only a relatively short time, the quality and quantity of digital data storage and online accessible information have grown

---

[1] The Web is an application of the Internet. The content of this paper may also be applicable to other applications of the Internet, but to ensure clarity in this paper I have restricted my focus to the Web.

M. Hansen et al. (Eds.): Privacy and Identity 2014, IFIP AICT 421, pp. 114–127, 2014.
© IFIP International Federation for Information Processing 2014

explosively [13]. The dramatic increase and ease with which digital data can be stored have led from a situation that could be described as "forgetting-by-selection" due to limited storage space, to a "remembering-by-default" in our information systems. The technology of the Web is thus influencing what we remember and how we remember.

According to Dodge and Kitchin, stronger growing digital memory technologies mean that "memory should always be complemented by forgetting" [9, p. 441]. In the proposal for the European Union General Data Protection Regulation (GDPR) a "Right to Be Forgotten or Erasure" (R2BFE), article 17 (art. 17 GDPR) was developed in order to provide for such a counterbalance to digital memory. Ideally, the R2BFE aims to help individuals escape their past by targeting information that already exists in the public domain and that "with the passing of time becomes decontextualized, distorted, outdated, no longer truthful (but not necessarily false)" [3, p. 127].

Based on its title, the R2BFE seems to promise people a reinforcement of the forgetting of memories that concern them. However, "forgetting" is a concept that generally takes shape in the human[2] memory process of a singular agent[3] while the R2BFE is directed at information that is shared among agents. The information available on the Web is not only of interest to the agent that is the object of the information, but also to the people that share and consult that information. This makes the concept of human forgetting in such a context challenging to implement.

Taking into account the importance that is assigned to forgetting within the R2BFE, it is important to evaluate how successful the R2BFE could actually be in its implementation of forgetting. By analyzing the R2BFE in the light of human memory processes and the role that the Web plays in human memory, we can get a better idea of the possibilities of how to implement such a concept as human forgetting in relation to data on the Web and subsequently – and more importantly – where the R2BFE may lose out or may be at risk of affecting more than is necessary other interests that are at stake.

So let us assume that art. 17 GDPR was written with the intention to actually provide a "right to be forgotten", then my fundamental question is: **to what extent can we consider the R2BFE to be a successful proposal for implementing forgetting on the Web?** To answer this question I will first describe the concept of "memory", the use of external memory sources and the manner in which agents use the Web as a shared memory. This is followed by a section on "forgetting". Next I will analyze how the R2BFE implements forgetting in the online shared memory and conclude to what extent the implementation of "forgetting" by the R2BFE does justice to the concept of human forgetting and on which fronts it misses out.

---

[2] The focus on human memory and forgetting does not mean that humans are the only species that forget or have a memory process. However, because "biological memory" seemed too broad a topic for this paper and the R2BFE is aimed at human agents, the concepts of memory and forgetting are framed here in human terms.

[3] The agent can be any gender type, including gender X (the third legal gender, for example, in Australia). Because truly gender neutral pronouns like "xe" are still regarded as uncommon, I will refer to an agent as "he/him/his", although this use of the masculine gender is meant to include all options.

2   Memory, External Memory and Transactive Memory

If we want a Web that forgets, we need to get an idea of the semantic content of "forgetting", and for that, we need to know what memory entails. The manner in which we use "our" memory systems has changed and is still changing over time due to technological developments i.e. on the level of information management. Additionally, our memory depends not only on what a single agent can do, but also on what agents can do through social interaction.

To highlight the functioning of our memory in relation to the Web, this section consists of three parts: the concept of "memory", the manner in which we externalise our memory by the use of tools and the manner in which we use the Web in a socially interactive way as a form of external memory, the transactive memory.

Firstly, the concept of "memory". "Memory" is a complex concept that has given rise to much thought in various academic fields [17]. The term "memory" is commonly used for both biological (human) entities and computers (Cf. [6]). This does not mean that these types of memory systems are the same: on the contrary, they differ a lot. For example, the electronic memory system seems far more apt for storing information than the human system; if they would be the same, there would possibly not even be a desire for the R2BFE. However despite (big) differences in its application, the term "memory" is considered applicable for diverse systems because they have something in common that is inherent to memory systems:

> "Any memory system – whether physical, electronic, or human – requires three things, the capacity to *encode*, or enter information into the system, the capacity to *store* it, and – subsequently – the capacity to *retrieve* it." [2, p. 5]

These three elements interact: the manner of *encoding* determines what and how something is *stored*, which will in turn determines what can be *retrieved* [2, p. 5]. The concrete functioning of these three elements can differ according to the type of memory system and entity, but all necessarily comprise the same three elements.

With regard to the human memory process, the brain has special strategies to enhance its memory process with the help of environmental factors. This brings us to the second topic: the use of external tools in the human memory process. Clark points out that "[o]urs are (by nature) unusually plastic and opportunistic brains whose biological proper functioning has always involved the recruitment and exploitation of non-biological props and scaffolds" [8, p. 86]. The use of external tools to increase our cognitive abilities has long been related with the human species: writing is one way that many of us use to think and reflect upon our own thoughts or to remember [8, p. 5]. By using tools to store, alter, combine and transform information we can deal with complex problems and large amounts of information in ways that would be impossible for or require a lot of time and energy from our biological "naked" brains [8, p. 78]. The human brain is good at learning how to use environmental factors and instruments optimally so as to minimize weaknesses like its generally limited memory capacity [8, p. 74-75]. External memory sources can complement this limited capacity by diminishing the amount of information that the biological memory needs to process and store [8, p. 67].

One of these potential external memory sources is the Web. The Web as external memory source differs fundamentally from many other information resources, due its "ontological features" [12, p. 186]. Information on the Web is not bound to a specific physical information source. Digital information is aspatial [19, p. 412]. Because of this, it is easily transported [5, p. 1112]. It is also generally a nonrivalrous good: meaning that the consumption of a good by one person, does not diminish the possibility of its use by others [19, p. 411]. The ontological features of the Web determine the effort that we need to undertake to get access to the information that it contains [12, p. 186]. Together these features determine the degree of "ontological friction" [12, p. 186] of the Web as "infosphere": "the forces that oppose the information flow within (...) the infosphere, and hence (...) the amount of work required for a[n] (...) agent to obtain information" [12, p. 186]. The Web's ontological frictions are low compared to offline, and especially analogue, information sources. Only a device to access the Web is needed and then one can access it almost from anywhere at any time while, if we want for instance to access information in an analogue library, we needs to physically access the building.

Besides its easy accessibility, the digital information on the Web is also easy to store. The storage capacity of digital devices has grown exponentially over the past decade and the quality loss of the stored information is relatively minor [13, p. 67]. Moreover, digital information can be multiplied, and copied easily and flawlessly, without loss of quality and is therefore infinitely expansible [19, p. 411] which can lead to a certain persistence [5, p. 1112]. Additionally the Web provides for easy retrieval of information. By means of search engines and other functions we can scan the Web for certain topics in a great level of detail, and generally we are able to find the desired information even when using vague keywords and search terms [8, p. 153].

The Web is not just a useful tool for us with regard to our memory processes as a singular human being. This fact brings us to a third topic: the Web as a socially interactive memory tool. The Web has a peculiar informational character compared to "classic" resources like libraries and archives. It has a decentralized and anarchic nature [8, p. 149-150]; it is an information source that is created by the minds of many. Everyone with an appropriate device can add information to the Web and often websites are publicly accessible. This gives the Web a special status; it can function as a "transactive memory system" [16].

Wegner[4] introduced the term "transactive memory" to describe the processing and structuring of information within a group of people [20, p. 185]. Transactive memory is "a set of individual memory systems in combination with the communication that takes place among individuals" [20, p. 186]. The notion of transactive memory is based on an analogy between informational group processes and the individual memory process [20, p. 185]. In this sense, the processes of encoding, storage and retrieval have "both internal and external manifestations" [20, p. 188]. People can encode and store information both in themselves and in external sources (including other agents)

---

[4] Daniel M. Wegner, the founding father of the notion of transactive memory, sadly died in July 2013 while I was writing this paper.

and they can retrieve the information they need from these sources and – if made available – from other agents and their external sources [20, p. 188]. Access to a transactive memory allows agents to enhance their own (external) memory stores and to retrieve information that they themselves have never encoded and stored [20, p. 188]. The Web is used as such a transactive memory. Sparrow, Liu and Wegner, in recent research stated that the Internet – this includes the Web – "has become a primary form of external or transactive memory, where information is stored collectively outside ourselves" [16, p. 776]. The features of the Web enable people to easily reach and consult online memory stores, especially search engines and the like effectively facilitate the retrieval of online information [16, p. 776]. The advantage of search engines is that the user does not need to know the location of the information, but that knowledge of the general label is often sufficient. Sparrow at al. conclude that "[w]e are becoming symbiotic with our computer tools, growing into interconnected systems that remember less by knowing information than by knowing where the information can be found" [16, p. 778].

Reciprocal use by agents of each other's memory leads to a transactive memory system "that is larger and more complex than either of the individual's own memory systems" [20, p. 189]. Information from different sources can be linked together and lead to new insights [20, p. 197]. Transactive memory systems thus influence what a group of people remembers and what they individually believe to be true [20, p. 191]. Consequently the Web as transactive memory can influence how we remember and what we remember.

The Web is thus to be seen as a transactive memory system that has a lower degree of ontological friction than traditional libraries or archives. This difference is significant and may lie at the base of a desire to have a R2BFE. The Web's large storage capabilities, its easy access and the fact that everyone can add information to the Web make it into a massive external transactive memory source that memorizes by default. The chief question therefore is: how can the Web "forget"?

3   Forgetting

The R2BFE claims to be – as part of the title of this paper states – a right "to be forgotten". But what is "forgetting"?

Generally forgetting is described in relation to *human* agents. Human agents can be considered "to forget" in both a literal and metaphorical manner.[5] For the purpose of this paper I will only focus on the literal form of forgetting where forgetting is the

---

[5] Making a strict distinction between these two elements of forgetting is not always possible, because they can relate to each other in a reciprocal manner. Metaphorical forgetting relates to instances that are generally described as "forgive and forget": certain information is not literally forgotten by the agent, but the agent will not actively use the information for current decisions. An agent makes a conscious choice to neglect specific memories in certain cases. However, if by this behaviour the information is used less and less and eventually loses its meaningfulness for the agent, there is a fair chance that the information will also literally be forgotten.

occurrence of a glitch[6] in the memory process, a "fail[ure] to remember" [6]. Forgetting can occur as a result of failures in any of the three elements of the memory process. It can be the loss of acquired information (storage), the inability to retrieve stored information (retrieval) and the deterioration of correspondence between the acquired and the retrieved information (encoding) [10, p. 100]. Many nuances are possible, like only losing part of the stored information, being able to retrieve information only partially, a temporary inability to receive certain information or a combination of different failures [10, p. 101]. For the purpose of this paper, I will focus only on the three memory process elements (storage, retrieval and encoding) – although I duly note that reality is far more complex and nuanced than such a basic model.

As stated, forgetting is a glitch somewhere in the three process elements of memory. However not every piece of information is remembered and forgotten equally. The likelihood of a glitch in the encoding, storage and/or retrieval of a specific piece of information in the memory depends on three main factors: the passing of time, the meaning of the information and the regularity with which the information is used [10, p. 100/101]. On the one hand, meaningful and repeatedly used information generally has a longer endurance in the memory; on the other hand, the memory of a certain piece of information generally gets weaker over time [10, p. 100-101][7]. These factors can strengthen or weaken each other. For example, meaningful information may be used more often and thereby remembered better. Additionally, information often loses its value for us over time [1, p. 390], which leads to the increasing chance that it is forgotten eventually. The factors "meaning", "use" and "time" together influence if and till what extent an agent will remember or forget a specific piece of information.

What forgetting entails in relation to human agents is relatively clear. But as described in the previous section of this paper, human agents can extend and share their external memory with others. With regard to the use of external personal memory and external transactive memory, the notion of forgetting becomes increasingly difficult.

Let us start with forgetting in relation to the use of an external memory source by a single human agent. When using an external memory source, the storing of information requires an action of the agent to actively select and encode the information that he wants to store. This extended-by-externalization memory process can show signs of glitches in the extended memory process when the agent interacts with his external memory source: for example, if the agent is unable to retrieve information from an external memory source (i.e. he loses a paper notebook) or if the information in it becomes intelligible (i.e. a cup of coffee is spilt over some of the notebook's pages). Such glitches can be viewed as metaphorical forgetting in the extended memory process. If an agent wants to "forget" information in his external memory store, he will need to actively effectuate the "forgetting" in some way. He could do this by, for instance, destroying the externally stored information or by making sure that it is irretrievable. With the use of most external memory stores (like notebooks), the storing faculty changes from a human memory store that automatically forgets by default into

---

[6] "Forgetting" may also be seen as a feature of the memory process that generates storage space.

[7] Again, this is a basic model of a more complex and nuanced reality.

an external memory store that automatically remembers by default. The "digital turn" of information even strengthened the remembering by default in external memory stores. The previously needed forgetting-by-selection processes due to limited storage space are becoming increasingly unnecessary due to technological developments that enable the increased storage space of digital information [18, p. 349].

Understanding "forgetting" in relation to an external transactive memory is even more challenging, because it does not concern a single agent but multiple agents that may all have different interests at stake. When the transactive memory is stored externally, and especially when in digital format, the transactive memory system will automatically remember by default. The social base of the transactive memory makes it increasingly difficult to see how "forgetting" could work in such a system. The system depends on both the input and output of all agents and is often not under the control of a single agent. All agents that consult the external transactive memory (and not only the ones that add information to it) and/or that are the object of these "memories" have an interest in what is encoded into the memory and what is not, or what is "forgotten". This means that the factors of "meaning", "time" and "use" in the transactive memory differ in their relative importance with regard to the "forgetting" of a specific piece of information depending on the agent in question.

The challenge for the R2BFE is thus to implement the concept of singular human forgetting into the external transactive memory that forms a memory source for multiple agents.

4   R2BFE and Online Transactive Memory

The term "forgetting" in the R2BFE implies human memory, but clearly the R2BFE is not aimed at human memory as such or else it would imply that there is a right to meddle in other people's brains. Rather, the R2BFE is part of the GDPR-proposal and therefore has to be read in the context of personal data protection and information technology systems. The R2BFE, art. 17 GDPR, gives people the "right to obtain from the controller the erasure of personal data relating to them and the abstention from further dissemination of such data" (art. 17 (1) GDPR). The R2BFE thus provides individuals with a right to interfere with digital information that is controlled by others, called data controllers (art. 4 (5) GDPR), and is located on an external memory source. Simply put, the data controller's external memory sources need to "forget".

As pointed out in section two of this paper, external memory sources play an important role in human memory processes because our brains use them as external tools to enhance our memory. Most external memory sources (like stored emails) will have a personal instead of a public nature. Such personal external memory stores cannot be targeted by the R2BFE; art. 2 (2)(d) GDPR states that the processing of personal data "by a natural person without any gainful interest in the course of its own exclusively personal or household activity" falls outside the scope of the GDPR. This is the "household exemption" [4, p. 5]. The target of the R2BFE is thus the external memory shared among people (transactive memory) that lies outside the household. A part of the transactive memory systems is thus safeguarded by the household exemption if it can be considered part of the "household" activity. The scope of what is intended by "household" is therefore very important. The current idea of what is to be considered "household" use includes for a major part the data made accessible by individuals to friends on social networking sites (SNS). The Article 29 Working Party states that many SNS users "operate within a purely personal sphere, contacting people as part of the management of their personal, family or household affairs" [4, p. 3]. However, some exceptions are mentioned: the processing of data on SNS is not considered to be household use when activities extend beyond purely personal or household activity (for instance when the user acts on behalf of a company), when the access to the profile information extends beyond self-selected contacts or when the information is subject to liability under general provisions of national law (such as defamation) [4, p. 5/6]. Due to the household exemption, a large part of the data on social networking sites fall outside the scope of the R2BFE.

With regard to personal websites, the European Court of Justice (ECJ) decided in the Lindqvist ruling that activities on a personal website are not covered by the household exemption when the information on a website could be viewed by an indefinite number of people [11, § 47]. Here we enter the realm of the online transactive memory.

Additionally, the R2BFE tries to account for some of the ontological features of online data – the fact that they can be easily copied, multiplied and transported – in art. 17 (2) GDPR. Art. 17 (2) GDPR deals with third parties who have copied and reproduced data that is challenged by the R2BFE: it compels data controllers to inform third parties that are processing data that were originally published under the responsibility of the data controller, that the subject of the data wants the data to be erased. When the data controller has authorised publication by third parties, the data controller is considered responsible for those publications (art. 17 (2) GDPR).

The household exemption and the Lindquist ruling show that the group of people that can get access to the data play a important role for the criteria whether a certain information source – an external memory source – falls within the scope of the GDPR. The main types of memory that can be targeted by the R2BFE are thus publicly accessible and/or business oriented external transactive memory systems; transactive memory systems that have a big reach and hence can have a substantial group of people that have a legitimate interest in the content of that transactive memory.

The challenge for the R2BFE is to implement "forgetting", a concept that relates to the singular human memory, into a shared transactive memory system that transcends the memory of a single human being. The interests at stake with regard to a specific piece of information expand from one agent to a group of agents with diverse interests. The human memory metaphor can provide guidance on how to implement "forgetting" in online transactive memory systems. It can give guidance on which aspects should play a role in the balancing of interests of the different agents that are stakeholders with regard to the content of an online transactive memory system. In order to evaluate to what extent the R2BFE relates to the concept of human forgetting and implements this notion, I shall review the manner in which the relevant paragraphs of the R2BFE deal with this particular challenge.

The R2BFE targets personal data that relate to a certain individual. Art. 17 (1) GDPR states the grounds on which people have a R2BFE in sub-paragraphs (a) through (d): sub-paragraph (a) grants agents a R2BFE when it concerns data that "are no longer necessary in relation to the purposes for which they were collected or otherwise processed", (b) determines that agents can invoke their R2BFE when the processing of data is based on consent and the agent withdraws this consent or when the period for which the consent is given is expired, (c) entitles agents to a R2BFE if the agent objects to the processing of personal data in accordance with art. 19 GDPR. The data has to be erased, unless the data controller can show compelling legitimate grounds that override the agent's interests (art. 19(1) GDPR), and (d) requires the erasure of data when the processing of the data is not conform the GDPR.

These subparagraphs show the balance of interests between an agent that wants information "forgotten" and the data controller that wants to retain the information. In determining this balance of interests the elements of "meaning" and "time" play a role; the data need to have meaning in order for the data controller to keep it in his external memory source. Art. 17 (1)(a) GDPR contains a temporal and meaning reference that suggests that, with the passing of time, information may lose its relevance for a data controller, in which case the individual's R2BFE prevails. This sub-paragraph restricts a processor's data collection to data that serves the specified purpose for data processing.

The exceptions to what may be forgotten by the enforcement of the R2BFE are also important. These are listed in art. 17 (3) GDPR. Data can be retained (a) when the data is necessary for exercising the right of freedom of expression, (b) for reasons of public interest in the area of public health, (c) historical, statistical and scientific research purposes, and (d) for compliance with legal obligation to retain data and in specific cases described in art. 17(4) GDPR. As these exceptions show, if information has public value the data can be retained. What is important to underline here, is that these exceptions acknowledge the meaning of the data for third parties that consult or make use of the external transactive memory and thus acknowledge their interest with regard to a certain set of topics (the data need to be important for the freedom of expression, public health, historical and/or scientific value).

Additionally the formulation of art. 17 (4)(a) GDPR is interesting: "for exercising the right of freedom of expression". The use of the verb and its conjugation "exercising" suggests that data can be retained if they are part of an ongoing activity of freedom of expression. The question then is: when does this action end? The temporal scope of a freedom of speech activity is an interesting issue, and it is worthwhile debating if the R2BFE is implemented and retains this formulation. Such a discussion however exceeds the scope of this paper.

The R2BFE has some elements that correspond with important factors in the human forgetting process. The most prominent one is the meaning of the information: it is included in terms of whether the data are necessary (meaningful) for the data controller, if the data should be retained due to its public importance (art. 17 (3) GDPR; freedom of expression, public interest in the area of public health, historical, statistical and scientific research purposes) and the meaning of the information for the individual that wants the data to be forgotten. The time-factor of forgetting is less prominent, it is only a factor in art. 17 (1)(a) GDPR. It is notable that any element that acknowledges the importance of the "use" of data in relation to forgetting, the frequency with which the data are used, is missing altogether.

The "forgetting" that is implemented by the R2BFE is initiated by the individual who wants certain data to be forgotten. The R2BFE is thus an externally initiated and enforced form of "forgetting". As the name of the article already indicates, it is a right to *be forgotten and to erasure*. The first paragraph shows that "erasure" is the dominant feature of the article, because the R2BFE gives individuals the "right to obtain from the controller the erasure of personal data". By erasing information the R2BFE operates on the storage level of the transactive memory process and thereby applies a black-and-white notion of forgetting: data are either erased or not. This is in contrast with the concept of human forgetting which can also play a role at the process levels of encoding and retrieval, and may vary in gradations of forgetting: in human terms, information can be partially or temporally forgotten.

However, there is (minor) potential in the in the second and fourth paragraph of the article of the R2BFE for it to be applied to the two levels of retrieval and/or encoding. Art. 17 (2) GDPR compels data controllers "to inform third parties which are processing such data, that an individual requests them to erase any links to (...) that personal data". An erasure of hyperlinks would be an interference with the transactive memory process on the level of retrieval. The question, however, is whether a controller can request third parties to remove the links while retaining the information on his own website due to one of the exceptions of art. 17 (3) GDPR. In this situation, the information would be more difficult to retrieve, but not impossible to retrieve for people who know what they are looking for and where to look. Also, it is unclear whether an individual could use the R2BFE only to have links removed, and not the content itself: for instance, if the agent wants to retain the content for sentimental reasons, but not draw attention to it because it is outdated.[8]

Art. 17 (4) GDPR mentions several cases where data controllers can refrain from erasing data, but have to restrict its processing. Sub-paragraph (b) and (c) are interesting in the light of "forgetting". A controller is allowed to restrict the processing of data instead of erasing them, when (b) the data controller needs to maintain the data for the purposes of proof, (c) the processing of the data is unlawful, but the individual requests the restriction of the use of the data instead of erasure. In the case of (b) the interference of the R2BFE works on the levels of retrieval and encoding in the transactive memory process: the data may only be retrieved for the purpose of providing proof and no additional information may be encoded, nor may the already encoded information be altered. Roughly the same goes for (c), with the difference that the request for the retention of the data is initiated by the individual. However, paragraph

---

[8] What plays an important role here is whether a search engine can be considered to be a data controller. This is one of the central legal questions in the Google versus Spain case (case number C-131/12) that is currently still under discussion by the ECJ. Advocate General Jääskinen stated in his advice to the court that search engines cannot be considered data controllers. The question is: will the court hold the same interpretation of the law? Opinion of Advocate General Jääskinen, 25 June 2013, Case C-131/12.

four of the article seems to be focused on internal company processes and not aimed at online publicly accessible content.

In sum, the R2BFE is largely concentrated on erasure on the storage level and only minimally allows for other – more fine-grained – applications of "forgetting" that may deal with the same issue at hand. Possibilities to use implementations of "forgetting" on the process levels of encoding and retrieval are the exception rather than the rule.

5   Learning from Forgetting by the Human Memory

As stated earlier, the human memory metaphor can provide valuable guidance on how to implement "forgetting" in online transactive memory systems. Its rich mechanisms of forgetting provide for a better understanding of which aspects can and should play a role in the balancing of the interests of different stakeholders in online transactive memory systems and give guidance for implementations of more gradual and balanced forms of "forgetting". A straightforward erasure of data is a too narrow understanding of "forgetting".

The "forgetting" implemented by the R2BFE needs to take place somewhere in the transactive memory process of encoding, storage and retrieval. The element of retrieval seems to be a very significant part in the use of the Web as transactive memory; people can get access to information they did not even know existed through the use of search engines [16]. Cues in search engines can lead to search results that individuals were not originally looking for and search results can provide for new insights by showing information that can be combined serendipitously. The R2BFE would obtain means to more nuanced implementations of "forgetting" if it were to be able to impede for instance, the retrieval of information by search engines. Links could be erased or moved to a harder-to-access area (e.g., an area that requires a user login or an area that can be found only with the use of very specified retrieval cues in a search engine), or certain results in search engines could be downranked.[9]

On the level of encoding, there may be possibilities to anonymize, pseudonymize or encrypt information or certain – identifying – parts of the data (this in return will influence the extent of retrieval of the information). Additionally, one can think of encoding more contextual and actual information with memory items, so that people who consult the transactive memory view updated instead of possibly outdated information. Such forms of forgetting or updating of the memory could be a less heavy and more goal-effective means of forgetting than erasure of data on the storage level.

Hold-ups in the retrieval process or obscuration in the encoding process would obviously interfere with the interests of individuals who try to consult the transactive memory. However, they will have a greater chance of retrieving the "forgotten" information or at least part of it – with some effort – than would be the case if the information were to have been erased altogether. An implementation of forgetting on the level of encoding and/or retrieval would be therefore a less extensive integration

---

[9] The search engine Google uses ranking algorithms to deal with certain issues, see for example http://googleblog.blogspot.nl/2010/12/being-bad-to-your-customers-is-bad-for.html (last accessed 8 November 2013).

of forgetting in the online transactive memory than the erasure of the content itself. Using less far-reaching measures than the plain erasure of data could be beneficial for the interests of others. It could include access to: the historical and scientific value of information, the freedom of speech, or personal interests of others. Also an individual self can have a need for different "grades" of forgetting rather than plain erasure.

With an eye on the balancing of interests between the individual who wishes certain personal information to be forgotten and the users of the transactive memory, it will be worthwhile to pay attention to factors that influence the memory process – of which "meaning", "time" and "use" are the most important ones.

In its current form, the R2BFE neglects the frequency with which information is used as a factor that affects the forgetting process. Allocating a role to the "use" of information as a factor that either enforces or prevents "forgetting" can be a helpful element in weighing up the balance of various interests. "Forgetting" information on a website that is hardly viewed makes more sense than "forgetting" information that is consulted several hundreds of times a day. Integrating "use" as a factor could benefit the interests of third parties, which as consulting parties are now only taken into account by means of the exceptions to the R2BFE. "Use" as a factor that could oppose "forgetting" provides a possibility for concrete evaluation: measuring how often something is viewed is technically easy on the Web. Additionally giving more attention to the factors "time" and "meaning" – not just for the data controller, but also for the third parties who consult the transactive memory – could help in providing the R2BFE with the right tools to oversee a good balance of interests.

Additional and especially technical research is needed to obtain better understanding of the possibilities of how to implement more sophisticated forms of "forgetting" in the online transactive memory. This will enable us to shape and implement a R2BFE that is more fine-tuned and based on a more nuanced process of forgetting that will be better equipped to balance between an individual's need to be forgotten and the other interests at stake.

6   Conclusion

Technology has changed and is still changing our internal and external memory processes. The Web – as discussed in this paper – is one of those technological developments that affects the way we remember and what we remember in fundamental ways. We have moved from external memory stores with limited storage space that therefore had to "forget"-by-selection to memory stores with ever-growing storage space that "memorize"-by-default.

The R2BFE aims to deal with the possible negative consequences of the shared online memory by providing people with a means to have some of their data in the online transactive memory "forgotten". Implementing "forgetting" into such systems is difficult, because the concept of forgetting originates from a single agent's internal memory process. Instead of functioning as forgetting within a singular agent, the R2BFE has to implement forgetting in an external transactive memory that affects the interests of multiple agents. The current wording of the R2BFE does this with limited success.

The manner in which the R2BFE implements "forgetting" is mainly a "right to erasure" of content and operates thereby mainly on the storage level of the external transactive memory process. The present possibilities for the R2BFE to operate on the level of encoding and retrieval are very limited. The R2BFE thus uses a narrow interpretation of "forgetting". While "erasure" is black-and-white (information is either erased or it is not), "forgetting" provides for a big greyscale. Additionally, of the factors that influence the occurrence of forgetting, only the "meaning" of the information for diverse agents plays a significant role. "Time" as a relevant factor to either enforce or avert forgetting is only marginally acknowledged in the R2BFE and "use" is not acknowledged at all.

The R2BFE could be transformed into a more successful implementation of "forgetting" in the external transactive memory if it were to draw more heavily on the mechanisms of human forgetting. Despite the fact that the human memory is based on a single agent, the human concept of memory shows us that there are more levels in information processes in which we could interfere to achieve "forgetting". Instead of the plain erasure of information we could interfere on the level of encoding or retrieval, which can also lead to successful "forgetting".

Furthermore, the factors "meaning", "time", and "use" provide for a better understanding of which aspects play a role in every agent's relation to (memorized) information and thereby to information in the external transactive memory. These factors give guidance as to which aspects can and should play a role in the balancing of the interests of the different stakeholders in online transactive memory systems: not just the agents that are the object of the memory or the data controller, but also, very important, the third parties that *use* the external transactive memory as memory and may rely on it.

Acknowledgments. This research is conducted within the Privacy and Identity Lab (PI.lab) and funded by SIDN.nl (http://www.sidn.nl). Additionally I would like to acknowledge the help of the IFIP Summer School participants, my anonymous reviewers, and Bert-Jaap Koops, Ronald Leenes and Diane Whitehouse by providing me with very helpful and much appreciated comments and suggestions.

References

1. Ambrose, M.L.: It's About Time: Privacy, Information Lifecycles, and the Right to Be Forgotten. Stanford Technology Law Review 16, 369–422 (2012)
2. Anderson, M., Eysenck, M.W., Baddeley, A.: Memory. Psychology Press, London (2009)
3. de Andrade, N.N.G.: Oblivion, The Right to Be Different from Oneself. Reproposing the Right to Be Forgotten. In: VII International Conference on Internet, Law & Politics. Net Neutrality and Other Challenges for the Future of the Internet, IDP. Revista de Internet, Derecho y Política, vol. 13, pp. 122–137 (2012)
4. Article 29 Working Party, WP 163, Opinion 5/2009 on online social networking
5. van den Berg, B., Leenes, R.: Audience Segregation in Social Network Sites. In: Proceedings for SocialCom2010/PASSAT2010 (Second IEEE International Conference on Social Computing/Second IEEE International Conference on Privacy, Security, Risk and Trust), pp. 1111–1117. IEEE, Minneapolis (2010)

6. Concise Oxford English Dictionary, 11th edn.
7. Castells, M.: The information Age: Economy, Society, and Culture, 2nd edn. The Rise of the Network Society, vol. I. Wiley-Blackwell, Chichester (2010)
8. Clark, A.: Natural-Born Cyborgs: Minds, Technologies, and the Future of Human Intelligence. Oxford University Press, Oxford (2003)
9. Dodge, M., Kitchin, R.: 'Outlines of a World Coming into Existence': Pervasive Computing and the Ethics of Forgetting. In: 34 Environment and Planning B: Planning and Design, pp. 431–445 (2007)
10. DuDai, Y.: Memory from A to Z. Oxford University Press, Oxford (2004)
11. European Court of Justice, case C-101/01, Criminal proceedings against Bodil Lindqvist
12. Floridi, L.: The Ontological Interpretation of Informational Privacy. Ethics and Information Technology 7(4), 185–200 (2005)
13. Mayer-Schönberger, V.: Delete: The Virtue of Forgetting in the Digital Age. Princeton University Press, Princeton (2009) (used print: 2011)
14. Proposal for a General Data Protection Regulation, COM(2012) 11 final (January 25, 2012), Download: http://ec.europa.eu/justice/data-protection/document/review2012/com_2012_11_en.pdf (last accessed November 8, 2013)
15. Rosen, J.: The web means the end of forgetting. The New York Times 21 (2010)
16. Sparrow, B., Liu, J., Wegner, D.M.: Google effects on memory: Cognitive consequences of having information at our fingertips. Science 333(6043), 776–778 (2011)
17. Sutton, J.: Memory. In: Zalta, E.N. (ed.) The Stanford Encyclopedia of Philosophy, 2012th edn. (Winter), http://plato.stanford.edu/archives/win2012/entries/memory/ (last accessed November 8, 2013)
18. Szekely, I.: The Right to Forget, the right to be Forgotten; Personal Reflections on the Fate of Personal Data in the Information Society. In: Gutwirth, S., Leenes, R., De Hert, P., Poullet, Y. (eds.) European Data Protection: In Good Health?, pp. 347–363. Springer Netherlands (2012)
19. Vafopoulos, M.: Being, space, and time on the Web. Metaphilosophy 43(4), 405–425 (2012)
20. Wegner, D.M.: Transactive memory: A contemporary analysis of the group mind. In: Mullen, B., Goethals, G.R. (eds.) Theories of Group Behavior, pp. 185–208. Springer, New York (1986)

An Advanced, Privacy-Friendly Loyalty System

Milica Milutinovic, Italo Dacosta, Andreas Put, and Bart De Decker

KU Leuven, Dept. of Computer Science, iMinds-DistriNet
firstname.lastname@cs.kuleuven.be
http://distrinet.cs.kuleuven.be/

Abstract. Loyalty systems are a very popular service employed by retailers in order to measure and reward customer loyalty. However, currently deployed systems introduce many privacy risks, as the users' data
is completely controlled by retailers. In this work we tackle this issue by
investigating the requirements posed on a privacy-friendly loyalty system
and proposing a new design for a digital loyalty system. With this novel
approach, the users are given more control over their data, but retailers
are still able to measure their loyalty and perform (authorised) data collection. Additionally, the functionality of the design is flexible and allows
for deployment of more advanced services.

Keywords: loyalty system, privacy, user profiles, anonymous credentials.

1 Introduction

The retailing business has changed significantly over the last decades. The competitive environment has led to the development of new services that incentivise
customer loyalty. Examples are the loyalty points system or personalised advertisement and offers. Although these approaches may increase user satisfaction,
they also bring significant privacy concerns. In order to make personalised offers
to the customers, or to reward their loyalty, the service providers simply record
all their purchases. This data is then used to determine preferences or to measure
customers' loyalty.

With this approach, users disclose information that is not required for de-
livering these services. Only a part of the revealed data would suffice to have
fully featured services. When taking part in the aforementioned schemes, the
customers are usually not aware of the magnitude of information that is collected or even how it will be handled. Data mining techniques are increasingly
powerful and collected data can reveal much more than even privacy-wary users
would suspect. Most importantly, these services do not require users' identities,
but some providers nonetheless collect it. This provides a direct link between
the behaviour and the identity of the customer. An additional concern is also
the protection of the databases that store this data. Even with major providers,
they can suffer from deliberate or accidental leakages [5].

Even though these services are becoming increasingly ubiquitous and privacy
concerns are not negligible, little attention is given to developing solutions that

M. Hansen et al. (Eds.): Privacy and Identity 2014, IFIP AICT 421, pp. 128–138, 2014.
© IFIP International Federation for Information Processing 2014

would protect the privacy of the users. Some providers shy away from employing these services, in order to avoid customers' negative reactions [16]. A recent survey indicates that almost 30% of customers believe that too much information is collected through the loyalty services, leading 24% of users to decline taking part in them [9]. This shows that a change in current practices is necessary.

Next to the aforementioned issues, an additional drawback of the existing systems is the practical aspect. With current deployment, the users are required to carry a physical card for every provider that offers a loyalty scheme. This can significantly affect user experience, taking into account the abundance of offered schemes. This is illustrated with a US survey suggesting that an average household is subscribed for 14 loyalty programs, while actively participating in almost half of them [3]. There are solutions, which offer simple transfer of loyalty cards to the smartphone [1,2], but usability problems may arise as barcode detection and accuracy require multiple scanning attempts [4].

Contributions. In this work we tackle the aforementioned issues by designing a privacy-friendly loyalty system able to offer advanced services. We allow even privacy-concerned users to benefit from loyalty schemes by providing the means for them to control disclosure of their data. At the same time, service providers are still able to perform (authorised) data collection. To the best of our knowledge, this work also represents the first proposal in this area that explores using anonymous credentials technology for these services. By employing anonymous credentials on smartphones, the functionality of the design becomes more flexible and offers more advanced services, such as service providers collaboration or brand loyalty. This proposal aims to preserve the incentives for all the involved stakeholders - not only users, but also service providers. Additionally, by developing electronic loyalty cards that the users can carry and use with their smartphones, there is no longer the need for the users to carry a number of physical cards with them at all times.

Moreover, this work is applicable to users with different privacy preferences. Work of Hinz et al. [12] identifies three groups of users, classified according to their privacy concerns. The first group represents the users that are *privacy unconcerned* and are willing to reveal personal data even for small economic incentives offered by the provider. The second group are *pragmatic* users that do want to protect their privacy, but are willing to disclose portions of their personal information for the right rewards. The third group are users that are *privacy concerned* and are not willing to disclose personal information or participate in customer loyalty programs, regardless of the offered incentives. Our proposal is applicable to all three groups of users. Namely, the users can choose their level of anonymity and disclose selected information that would allow obtaining appropriate levels of incentives.

2   Related Work

Privacy is recognised as an important concern in the loyalty schemes [13,12]. However, there is not a significant body of research addressing this issue.

Proposals for improving privacy in the loyalty systems usually focus on unlinkability of the loyalty points issued to the user. In [14] the authors propose to have a batch of user loyalty cards available to users for anonymous download. While this allows the users to remain anonymous towards the system, the service provider cannot measure their loyalty, which imposes significant limitations and at the same time removes incentives of the retailers. A solution proposed by Enzmann and Schneider [10] uses blind signatures to avoid linking loyalty points in the issuing and the redeeming phase. Even though the users can collect loyalty points, there is no robust mechanism that prevents the users from sharing or merging their loyalty points. Additionally, in both approaches, there is no option for the retailer to record any data, even with user consent. Contrary to these proposals, we try to tackle the privacy issues of the loyalty systems, while preserving the incentives for all involved stakeholders. We also aim at providing new functionality, which is advantageous for the service providers, but also the customers.

The data that the loyalty systems collect about their users is also employed to personalise the delivered services. Those include personalised advertisements, offers and coupon issuance. While there is limited work on the topic of privacy in loyalty systems, there are related research proposals that try to tackle privacy-preserving personalisation of accompanying services. Work by Hardt and Nath [11] allows users to choose the amount of personal information that is to be disclosed to an ads server in order to be offered with personalised advertisement. The user sends (part of) her preferences to the ads server, which are used for coarse-grained filtering of ads that are sent to her. The user application then performs the final filtering of the received ads based on more detailed personal information. This way, the user is presented only with relevant advertisement and can still choose her level of privacy. A proposal of Partridge et al. [15] tries to solve personalised coupon delivery with user privacy protection. Namely, it uses locality sensitive hashing, allowing the server to send all coupons encrypted to a user, while she would only be able to decrypt the ones that are targeting her behaviour. Similarly to the described research efforts, our proposal allows to have the personalised services, while users have complete control over the level of data disclosure.

3   Loyalty System Design Requirements

We identify the following requirements that need to be achieved by a privacy-friendly loyalty system design. These requirements are also guiding the design decisions for the proposed system.

- *Unlinkability.* The design of the system should not allow the service provider to link different purchases of one user or to link purchases with user's personal information, without user's explicit authorisation.
- *Anonymity and selective disclosure.* Users of the loyalty system should be able to choose their level of anonymity. They may opt for remaining completely anonymous towards the provider, or may decide to disclose (a part of) their personal information.

- *Points unforgeability and double-spending prevention.* The users should not be able to create new points or reuse valid loyalty points.
- *No unauthorised points sharing.* The users should not be able to share or merge the loyalty points they obtain, unless they are authorised to do so (e.g. in a family loyalty scheme).
- *Flexibility.* The system design should be flexible to support different scenarios and different types of interaction between the user and the service provider.
- *Extensibility.* The design should allow ease of deployment of new services.
- *Deployability.* The proposed system design should not require any additional hardware at the user side which would impede system reception.
- *Compatibility.* The novel loyalty system should be compatible with the existing systems and be able to run in parallel.

4 Approach

The existing loyalty systems are based on sweeping user profiles maintained by service providers, which record all the personal information, loyalty information and shopping behaviour of users. When interacting with the store, the user only needs to authenticate by showing the loyalty card and disclosing the unique loyalty number. This number points to the profile of the user stored in the provider's database. The provider adds to the profile all the information from this latest interaction, such as the purchased items and obtained loyalty points. This, however, allows the service provider to record much more data than is actually needed for the service in question. Additionally, the authentication mechanism itself does not ensure that the user who is using the card is actually the user that was issued with it. In order to solve these issues, the approach of this proposal is to keep all user data on her device and disclose only chosen portions of it. At the same time, when authenticating, the users prove that they are legitimate system users and the loyalty tokens that are issued to her cannot be transferred to other entities without authorisation.

In order to provide such a privacy-preserving loyalty system design, we employ anonymous credentials technology. The loyalty card is issued to the user as an anonymous credential. It records their identifying data[1] and other information that is related to the service, such as the unique loyalty card number. As different usages of loyalty credential should not be linkable, we assume usage of Idemix credential technology [7]. In the interaction with the service provider, the user can choose which part of the data she wishes to disclose[2]. She may decide only to prove the fact that she is a legitimate user of the loyalty service offered by

---

[1] This information can remain hidden from the service provider throughout the card's lifespan. It can also be utilised if the user decides to disclose parts of it, but also prove the validity of the data.

[2] The system design assumes that the payment protocol protects user anonymity, i.e. the user does not disclose her identity or enable the service provider to link her purchases through the payment process, e.g. by using e-cash or involving an external payment service.

that service provider. The service provider thus maintains profiles with different levels of anonymity, but is ensured that the interacting customers are authorised loyalty system users.

As different levels of disclosure are possible, the users are incentivised to reveal more data by appropriate rewards, such as higher discounts or vouchers. The users may choose to only collect the default number of points and thus only prove that they possess a valid loyalty credential. The points are obtained independently and the user does not need to reveal their previous count. This is an additional improvement for the privacy, as it further reduces the possibility of making links between different user–provider interactions.

The second level of disclosure is allowing the provider to link the purchases the user makes. In this case, the user would reveal the unique loyalty number contained in the loyalty credential. This value is an attribute in the user's credential and therefore cannot be forged by other users. As an alternative, the provider can also be presented with a pseudonym based on the credential secret and some public value, allowing him to link the purchases in a pseudonymous profile. This way the user is able to reset her profile by changing her pseudonym.

Finally, privacy unconcerned users can disclose any data recorded in their credential, which the service provider is assured has been approved at the time of credential issuing.

4.1 Threat Model

The attacks to the loyalty system can originate from both internal and external attackers. Internal attackers can be legitimate users of the system, who may try to forge points, double-spend them or merge them without authorisation. Internal attacks can also be mounted by the retailer–or service provider–if he tries to obtain more data than the user authorises him to. On the other hand, an external attacker is an adversary who is not a legitimate participant in the loyalty scheme and who tries to defeat the system by attempting to use the loyalty system as a legitimate user without subscribing for it, and additionally forge loyalty points in order to obtain offered rewards.

4.2 Loyalty Points

Users can have a number of points issued to them. The points are linked to their anonymous credential and are not transferable. At the same time, the service provider does not have to acquire any unique data (e.g. identity or the unique loyalty card number). Additionally, with this approach, unauthorised points sharing or merging is prohibited. The users are not able to merge points linked to two different cards, i.e. anonymous credentials. Also, sharing the card would require sharing the credential itself, which is prohibited with existing credential sharing-disincentivising schemes. However, this approach still allows to offer *family cards* to the customers. That ensures that customers can still benefit from the family scheme, while not compromising their privacy. Each family member is issued with a loyalty card which can be used independently, while the loyalty points are pooled together.

4.3 Advanced Services

With the proposed approach, new possibilities are opened, and new services can be developed within this system. As an example, the users can collect *brand-specific loyalty points* which are not retailer-specific. This allows the brand to incentivise and reward user loyalty directly. Also, different retailers can cooperate and loyalty obtained at one can be used to retrieve benefits with the other. For instance, users can be issued special points for all eco-friendly products they purchase and proving that they have obtained a certain number of points can allow them to gain benefits in an environmentally friendly store, or even with the government, which can offer certain incentives, such as specific tax reductions.

5 Cryptographic Building Blocks

This section provides an overview of the cryptographic building blocks used in the proposed system design.

- **Commitments.** Commitment schemes enable an entity to commit to a set of values while keeping them secret. These schemes are comparable to sealed, opaque envelopes. When a commitment is issued to a verifier, the user cannot change the values she committed to, without it being detectable by the verifier. The commitment hides the values chosen by the user, but still allows for proving certain properties of the committed values.
- **Blind signatures.** Blind signature are signing schemes that allow to hide the contents of a message when it is signed [8]. The concept is comparable to envelopes lined with carbon paper. The party that wishes some document to be signed by an authority, but still hidden from it, can enclose the document in such an envelope. The authority then signs the closed envelop and when the requesting party opens the envelope, it is presented with the signed document.
- **Zero-knowledge proofs of knowledge.** Proofs of knowledge in cryptography, are proofs in which one party, the prover, proves to a verifier that she holds certain knowledge [6]. With zero-knowledge proofs of knowledge, a prover can convince a verifier that a certain statement is true, without revealing any additional information.

6 Privacy-Preserving Protocols

In this section, we provide an overview of the protocols for issuing loyalty cards, obtaining and using loyalty points. We also present how to extend the offered services, without making any changes to the design of the system.

6.1 User Registration

In order to participate in the loyalty scheme, the users initially need to register with a designated credential issuer in order obtain a loyalty credential. For user convenience, the protocol for issuing the anonymous credentials can also be performed through an online service. A standard protocol for issuing multi-show Idemix credentials [7] is used. The issuer can therefore be the provider itself, since the usage of the credential will not be linkable to the registration stage. In case of online issuance, interested users would initially contact and establish a secure connection with a trusted issuing party. They would possibly need to prove some personal information, such as identity, address and email address. For proving personal attributes, the electronic ID can be used, and other information, such as email or telephone number can be verified by the issuing party by simply sending a validation code to be returned. The user also chooses a random number to be included in her credential, but sends only a commitment to it, so that the issuing party cannot learn its value. The issuer applies a random offset to this value and the result represents loyalty card secret, which remains hidden from the issuer. The user is then issued with an anonymous credential which records her personal information, a loyalty credential number chosen by the issuer and the loyalty secret. The credential is stored and managed on the user's smartphone.

6.2 Obtaining Loyalty Points

When making a purchase and obtaining loyalty points, the user can choose her level of anonymity. In this work we describe the protocol in which the user remains completely anonymous towards the store, as the other levels of privacy can easily be derived from it. The only additional action that would be required from the user is to simply show or prove properties of attributes contained in her credential. Those can be the unique loyalty credential number or even her identity.

When a user makes a purchase and is to be awarded with a certain number of points, she initially creates a commitment to her loyalty secret, the number of points and the epoch that applies[3], and blinds this commitment. Using zero-knowledge proof of knowledge protocols, she proves that the blinded commitment is correctly created and that is contains the value from her credential. The store than verifies the proofs and checks that the correct epoch identifier and number of points are used. If these checks pass, the store signs this data and sends the signature to the user. The user then removes the blinding factor from the signature thus obtaining provider's signature on the commitment. The user finally stores the commitment and its opening information, number of earned points and the epoch together with the unblinded signature, which represents the points she has earned.

---

[3] The epoch number represents an indication of the period when the points were obtained. They are used, so that the service providers can limit the validity of the loyalty points.

In order to avoid any kind of linkability, the service provider should not issue unique numbers of points. With every purchase, the points can be divided into predefined amounts that are issued separately. This is an additional requirement that protects from the already limited possibility of service provider linking different purchases.

6.3   Using Loyalty Points

When a user wishes to redeem previously collected points in order to obtain certain benefits, the procedure is as follows. The user would give the store the collected signatures on the commitments, previously unblinded, along with the numbers of points they were mapped to and the epochs they were obtained in. The user also provides proof that the commitment is linked to her credential and that it is correctly created, using expected epoch and number of points. The store is then able to verify the applicability of the epochs in which the points were obtained and if the commitments were used before[4]. The store then verifies the validity of the signatures and the provided proofs. If all the checks are successful, the provider sums up all the points the user was issued with. It also stores the commitments and the corresponding epochs in order to detect and prevent double spending of the used points.

Optionally, these protocols can be simplified. It is possible is to omit the proof of having the loyalty secret in the user's credential. This step assures the store that the points are only spent by the user who obtained them. Therefore, in case points sharing is permitted, this step can be skipped.

6.4   Advanced Services

Obtaining and using the loyalty points represent the basic functionality of the loyalty system. The designed protocols also allow for deployment of more advanced services, without introducing threats to user privacy.

Family Loyalty Card.   The described scheme is applicable to family loyalty service. In order to merge the points they collect, family members only need to link their loyalty credentials at the time of issuing. One member initiates the process by choosing the random value for the creation of the loyalty secret and registers with the issuing party. At that point it is also required to specify how many family members will be participating in the loyalty scheme. After obtaining the credential with the loyalty secret created from the chosen random number with an offset applied by the issuer, the user distributes the chosen random number along with the loyalty number to the other members. They can then approach the issuing party, reveal the loyalty number they wish to have included in their credential, and obtain their loyalty cards, i.e. anonymous

---

[4] It checks the database where used commitments are stored together with their epochs. Once the epoch becomes invalid, the database can be cleared from the corresponding entries.

credentials with the same loyalty secret and loyalty card number included in them. The loyalty secret is the same for all the users, as the issuer stores and reuses the offset used for a specific card number. The issuer is able to verify that only the specified number of users obtains the credentials with the same loyalty number and loyalty secret.

In case of the family scheme, collection of points is performed in the same way as by the individual users. The collected signed commitments are stored in a joint cloud storage together with their opening information, so that a family member can merge and use them collectively. When the commitments are opened, any family member can successfully prove that they have been constructed as a function of an attribute contained in her credential.

Brand Loyalty. The described scheme allows for brands loyalty, where the users would be issued loyalty points for purchases of specific brands' products. The only difference in the protocols is that the the brands identifier would be added to the commitment that is signed, similarly to the epoch identifier. The user is then able to prove that the points she was issued are linked with a specific brand giving her the appropriate benefits.

Privacy-Preserving Personalisation. The system can be easily extended to encompass personalised services. For instance, for personalised coupon delivery, the users can collect specific tokens when making purchases. The tokens would indicate the category of their interest and would be issued linked to the user's credential in a similar way as the loyalty points. When wanting to obtain personalised coupons, the user would prove that she was issued with a set of tokens, similar to showing the gathered points. This way the user can remain anonymous and her shopping behaviour would not be transparent to the provider or linkable to a profile, while the service provider can be ensured that the shown behaviour has not been fabricated or shared.

7   Discussion

This section discusses the protocols from the point of view of the requirements listed in Section 3.

- *Unlinkability.* When interacting with the service provider, the user by default does not disclose any unique or identifying information. For obtaining points, the user discloses only a blinded commitment to her loyalty secret. When the points are redeemed, the user shows the commitment itself, which cannot be linked to the initial blinded commitment.
- *Anonymity and selective disclosure.* By utilising anonymous credentials as loyalty cards, the users can choose their level of anonymity. No personal data from the credential is disclosed to the provider, unless the user explicitly authorises such an action.

- *Points unforgeability and double-spending prevention.* Since the users do not have the secret signing key of the provider, they cannot create valid signatures that would allow them to use points that are not authentic. They can also not reuse their obtained points, as the service provider checks for every received commitment whether it was seen before.
- *No unauthorised points sharing.* All the points that are issued are linked to the credential of the interacting user, and thus cannot be shared or merged amongst different users. It is however possible that users would lend the credential itself to another user, but that is less likely as the loyalty credentials are bounded to their smartphones, which also contain sensitive information. The loyalty credential sharing can also be prevented with existing schemes for disincentivising sharing.
- *Flexibility.* The system is applicable to different scenarios and can be utilised in both online and offline shopping.
- *Extensibility.* As described in the previous text, the design allows deployment of new services, such as brand loyalty or personalised coupon delivery.
- *Deployability.* No special hardware is required for the utilisation of the proposed system. The users can participate in the loyalty scheme with their smartphones.
- *Compatibility.* The loyalty system is compatible with the existing implementations and can run in parallel. The users that do not own a smartphone or are not privacy-concerned can continue using the plastic loyalty cards and have the service provider maintain their data and loyalty points.

8   Concluding Remarks

This paper describes an enhanced loyalty system that provides benefits to providers while respecting user privacy. It also represents the novel approach for employing anonymous credentials technology in the loyalty systems design. Defense against described attacker models is provided by the properties of anonymous credentials. The customers are able to prove that they are subscribers of the loyalty system and choose the data they want to disclose. They are also ensured that the service provider has learned nothing more. Additionally, unauthorised parties cannot create valid credentials and the service provider is assured that he is interacting with legitimate users.

Both service providers and users benefit from the proposed design. Even the most privacy-concerned customers can use the system as they can choose the level of information disclosure. Optionally, they can collect points completely anonymously, even without the possibility of the provider linking different purchases. The service providers are able to perform authorised data collection, contrary to existing proposals. Such a system offers competitive advantage, as users are more enticed to select an option that ensures their privacy. Furthermore, this proposal provides new functionality, such as brand loyalty, i.e. brands themselves can measure and reward user loyalty, or privacy-preserving personalisation of loyalty services.

Acknowledgements. This research was funded by the IWT-SBO Project Mob-Com (A Mobile Companion).

References

1. Cardstar, http://www.cardstar.com/
2. FidMe, http://www.fidme.com/en/home.html
3. Getting a Business Lift from Loyalty program. Facts and Statistics, http://www.loyaltyleaders.org/facts.php
4. http://gadgetwise.blogs.nytimes.com/2010/10/15/cardstars-vision-problem/
5. Sony PlayStation data breach, https://www.privacyrights.org/data-breach-asc?title=Sony
6. Bellare, M., Goldreich, O.: On defining proofs of knowledge. In: Brickell, E.F. (ed.) CRYPTO 1992. LNCS, vol. 740, pp. 390–420. Springer, Heidelberg (1993)
7. Camenisch, J.L., Lysyanskaya, A.: An efficient system for non-transferable anonymous credentials with optional anonymity revocation. In: Pfitzmann, B. (ed.) EUROCRYPT 2001. LNCS, vol. 2045, pp. 93–118. Springer, Heidelberg (2001)
8. Chaum, D.: Blind signatures for untraceable payments. In: CRYPTO, pp. 199–203 (1982)
9. eMarketer. To keep users happy, loyalty programs must walk a fine line, http://www.emarketer.com/Articles/Print.aspx?R=1009958
10. Enzmann, M., Schneider, M.: A privacy-friendly loyalty system for electronic marketplaces. In: 2004 IEEE International Conference on e-Technology, e-Commerce and e-Service, EEE 2004, pp. 385–393 (March 2004)
11. Hardt, M., Nath, S.: Privacy-aware personalization for mobile advertising. In: Proceedings of the 2012 ACM Conference on Computer and Communications Security, CCS 2012, pp. 662–673 (2012)
12. Hinz, O., Gerstmeier, E., Tafreschi, O., Enzmann, M., Schneider, M.: Customer loyalty programs and privacy concerns. In: Proceedings of BLED (2007)
13. II Hann, H., Hui, K.L., Lee, T.S., Png, I.P.L.: Consumer privacy and marketing avoidance. In: Equilibrium Analysis: Essays in Honor of. Cambridge University Press (2005)
14. Marquardt, P., Dagon, D., Traynor, P.: Impeding individual user profiling in shopper loyalty programs. In: Danezis, G. (ed.) FC 2011. LNCS, vol. 7035, pp. 93–101. Springer, Heidelberg (2012)
15. Partridge, K., Pathak, M.A., Uzun, E., Picoda, C.W.: Privacy-preserving smart coupon delivery architecture. In: 5th Workshop on Hot Topics in Privacy Enhancing Technologies (HotPETs 2012), pp. 94–108 (2012)
16. Sackmann, S., Strüker, J.: Electronic Commerce Enquête 2005: 10 Jahre Electronic Commerce - Eine stille Revolution in deutschen Unternehmen. Konradin IT-Verlag (2005)

Securus: From Confidentiality and Access Requirements to Data Outsourcing Solutions

Jens Köhler and Konrad Jünemann

Karlsruhe Institute of Technology (KIT), Steinbuch Centre for Computing (SCC),
Karlsruhe, Germany,
{jens.koehler,konrad.juenemann}@kit.edu

Abstract. To preserve data confidentiality in database outsourcing scenarios, various techniques have been proposed that preserve a certain degree of confidentiality while still allowing to efficiently execute certain queries. Typically, several of those techniques have to be combined to achieve a certain degree of confidentiality. However, finding an appropriate combination is not a trivial task, as expert knowledge is required and interdependencies between the techniques exist. Securus, an approach we previously proposed, addresses this problem. Securus allows users to model their requirements regarding the information in the outsourced dataset that has to be protected. Furthermore, queries that have to be efficiently executable on the outsourced data can be specified. Based on these requirements, Securus uses Integer Linear Programming (ILP) to find a suitable combination of confidentiality enhancing techniques and generates a software adapter. This software adapter transparently applies the techniques to fulfill the specified requirements and can be used to seamlessly outsource and query the data. In this paper, we present an outline of Securus and extend our previous work by highlighting the differences to other approaches in the field. Furthermore, we show how Securus can be extended to allow for more efficient solutions if the attacker's capabilities can be modeled by the user.

1 Introduction

Preserving the privacy of individuals in today's service landscape is an ongoing research topic that gains even more importance with the trend of service outsourcing. Besides the protection of personal information that is necessary to make access control decisions [3], enforcing the confidentiality of personal data that is processed by third parties constitutes a challenge [2,12]. Ensuring confidentiality when outsourcing databases is both necessary to protect sensitive information and to adhere to privacy laws in many cases. One approach to tackle this problem is to establish a trust relationship with the external provider using *Service Level Agreements* (SLAs) [13] or by relying on laws for being able to hold the external provider accountable [16]. However, in many cases either no trust relationship can be established or (regional) laws forbid relying on trust alone. In these cases, technical means have to be used to preserve confidentiality [14].

M. Hansen et al. (Eds.): Privacy and Identity 2014, IFIP AICT 421, pp. 139–149, 2014.

A naive solution that technically preserves data confidentiality is to completely encrypt the whole database prior to outsourcing. However, queries on entirely encrypted data cannot be efficiently executed. It is thus better to selectively apply encryption techniques and partitioning the database on *multiple*, non-colluding external providers, as this way a tradeoff between data confidentiality and efficient query execution can be achieved [4,7,10,11,15]. However, it requires expert knowledge to choose a suitable set of existing techniques for a given scenario that protect confidential information while maximizing query efficiency. Furthermore, the choice highly depends on which parts of the data are considered sensitive and how the data will be queried.

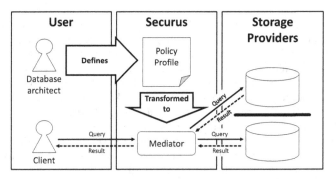

Fig. 1. Overview of the general Securus concept [14]

In this paper, we describe the *Securus* (**S**ecure and **E**fficient **C**loud **U**tilization **R**elying **U**pon **S**chemes) framework [14] that enables users to define which information of the outsourced data requires protection and which queries are executed on the data in a *policy profile* (see Figure 1). Furthermore, a set of available *storage providers* (SPs) to which the data will be outsourced can be specified.

Attacker model: The worst case Securus protects against is that each SP constitutes an honest-but-curious attacker or is compromised by one. We assume that the attackers a) do not collude and b) do not have background knowledge on data inserts/deletions/updates or incoming queries that can be used to infer information on data records. For instance, knowing that SELECT...WHERE name='john' is the most frequently executed query can be used to reveal encrypted names of the result records of the most frequently executed queries.

Based on the policy profile, Securus chooses a matching set of confidentiality enhancing techniques and generates a *mediator* software component that automatically applies them before outsourcing the data. Users can utilize mediators to transparently execute queries on the outsourced data, i.e., without taking the applied confidentiality enhancing techniques into account. Securus provides strong performance guarantees in terms of induced overhead during query executions, regardless of the outsourced dataset's composition.

The paper is structured as follows: We summarize related work and existing approaches Securus builds on in Section 2. In Section 3, we introduce the components of policy profiles and show how we adapted the building blocks of

Table 1. Catalog of security mechanisms for different queries and substitution categories. The ✓ symbol indicates that no security mechanisms need to be applied, ✗ indicates that no security mechanisms are known that have the required properties.

Query	Plaintext	Deterministic Substitute	Probabilistic Substitute
Equality Selection	✓	Det. Encryption & Hash indices [7,4]	✗
Range Selection	✓	Bucket Hash Indices [10]	✗
Aggregation	✓	Homomorphic Encryption [11,15]	Homomorphic Encryption [11,15]

the policy profile (and thus the policy transformation process) to reflect the assumed attacker's knowledge more precisely compared to the already published version of Securus [14]. In Section 4 we show how to transform policy profiles into an outsourcing solution. As addition to our previous work [14] we highlight the differences between Securus and other existing approaches and provide an extended evaluation of our approach in Section 5. Finally, the paper is concluded in Section 6.

2   Related Work

In the *Database-as-a-Service* community, several contributions that share the goal of confidential data outsourcing exist. These can be categorized into approaches that encrypt data in a way that allows for the execution of specific queries [4,7,10,11,15], approaches that only encrypt parts of the data [17] and approaches that protect sensitive information by fragmenting the data on several non colluding providers [5,1].

Various *security mechanisms* have been proposed that encrypt attribute values while still allowing the efficient execution of queries containing *equality selections* (e.g. ...WHERE name='Doe') [4,7], *range selections* (e.g. ...WHERE age<30) [10] and *aggregations* (e.g. SELECT SUM(salary)...) [11,15]. These security mechanisms can be categorized as shown in Table 1. We distinguish between mechanisms that map equal plaintext values on the same encrypted values (*deterministic substitute*) and mechanisms that map equal plaintext values on different encrypted values that cannot be distinguished (*probabilistic substitute*). While an attacker with background knowledge like the frequency distribution of an attribute can infer information from deterministic substitutes [4,8], no information can be inferred from probabilistic substitutes. However, in our model it is also impossible to evaluate equality or range selections on them. While cryptographic methods to search probabilistically encrypted data exist [18,6], the proposed methods require to "touch" every data record instead of using indexing structures or reveal information upon processing queries that can be used to distinguish records in a similar way deterministic ciphertexts do. Homomorphic encryption schemes enable the storage provider to aggregate encrypted values before returning the query result to the client.

Additionally to these security mechanisms, the approach to protect sensitive attribute combinations by fragmenting the critical attributes across multiple SPs has been proposed [1]. For instance, while the attribute name and the attribute salary of a dataset may be viewed in plaintext by the attacker, the combination of them might be considered sensitive. Therefore, plaintext attribute values of name have to be stored by another SP than plaintext attribute values of salary.

CryptDB [17] is an approach that initially encrypts all attributes of the database that is outsourced to an external SP. Once a query needs to be executed, the key for the relevant attributes is passed to the SP. Thus, the SP incrementally unveils attributes and is able to execute queries efficiently. While providing performance guarantees regarding query execution, the protection of sensitive attributes cannot be guaranteed and depends on the query workload.

Securus makes use of both security mechanisms *and* attribute fragmentation to fulfill the user's requirements. Previous approaches [5,9] also propose to let the user specify which information contained in the data is sensitive and the query workload that will be executed on the data. They provide heuristics to find the best-effort attribute fragmentation that protects confidential relationships between attributes and produces as little overhead as possible for the given workload. Securus goes beyond true fragmentation and considers storing particular attributes at multiple SPs to allow for a more efficient query execution. Furthermore, Securus allows the user to specify hard performance requirements that must not be violated (cf. Section 5.1).

3   Policy Profiles

Before Securus can generate a mediator, the user has to specify his particular requirements in a *policy profile*. Besides the attributes that are contained in the dataset that is outsourced, the user defines the following three types of policies:

- **Access Policies** (APs) describe the queries that have to be efficiently executable. For instance, the AP [Name,Salary] expresses, that queries like SELECT * FROM db WHERE Name=''xy'' AND Salary=10000 have to be efficiently executable. Besides equality selections, Securus also supports range selections and aggregation. For the sake of simplicity and space constraints we do not introduce them in this paper.
- A **Confidentiality Constraint** (CC) [1,5,9,19] constitutes a set of attributes that are considered sensitive if they are combined. For instance, the CC [Name,Salary] expresses that no name should be mapable on a salary value and vice versa. However, revealing the names *or* the salaries to an SP is tolerable. A special case are CCs containing a single attribute: [Salary] expresses that the salaries are sensitive and must not be revealed to any SP.
- **Inference Constraints** (ICs) specify a set of attributes. By including an attribute in the ICs it can be expressed that the assumed attacker is not

able to infer any information from deterministically encrypted values of the attribute[1]. In particular, this assumption holds for attributes that are guaranteed to be unique [8]. We are aware of the fact that ICs constitute very crude assumptions that users cannot confidently make in many scenarios. However, they provide an "interface" that enables us to explore a more fine-grained modeling of the attacker's capabilities in our future research. For instance, ICs could be derived from a more fine-grained attacker model specified by users.

4 Policy Transformation

4.1 General Concept

The workflow of an example mediator that was automatically generated by Securus is shown in Figure 2. To outsource a dataset (e.g. *Employees*), the attribute values of each record are encrypted probabilistically and put in the *main table* that can be stored by an arbitrary SP. As the probabilistic ciphertexts are indistinguishable for the SPs, no CC is violated. However, while it is possible to request specific records, no other queries can be executed based on the main table. Therefore, for each AP an *index table* that allows for efficient query execution is stored by at least one SP. Index tables contain attribute values in plaintext or protected by a security mechanism that does not prohibit the efficient execution of queries that comply to the AP (cf. Section 2). Thus, queries can be executed efficiently based on the according index table.

However, index tables might violate CCs. For instance, consider two index tables that store the attributes {address} and {disease} in plaintext, respectively. If those two index tables are stored by the same SP, this would violate the CC [address,disease]. The violation of CCs might be prevented by distributing the index tables on multiple, non colluding SPs and/or selectively applying security mechanisms on the attributes of the index table. For instance, in Figure 2, the CC [name,salary] is not violated as neither SP1 nor SP2 store both name and salary in plaintext or as deterministic ciphertexts that an attacker with – for instance – knowledge about the frequency of attribute values might infer plaintext values from. The CC [name,age] can be satisfied even though both attributes have to appear together in one index table to satisfy the AP [name,age]. This is due to the defined IC {age} that specifies, that it is assumed that the attacker cannot infer information from deterministically encrypted attribute values. Therefore, it suffices to encrypt age in index table 1 deterministically to comply with CC [name,age].

4.2 Solving the Puzzle

Finding an appropriate distribution of the index tables on the SPs that minimizes the required application of security mechanisms and satisfies the defined

---

[1] For instance, if an attacker would know the most frequently occurring attribute value, he could reveal the most frequently occurring deterministic ciphertext.

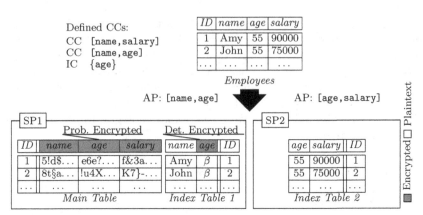

Fig. 2. Exemplary mediator generation

APs, CCs and ICs is not a trivial task and can be shown to be NP-hard. Securus reduces the problem of finding a suitable solution on an *Integer Linear Programming* (ILP) problem. ILP is a well understood mathematical model to specify optimization problems. ILP problems consist of constraints that define feasible solutions and an optimization criterion that characterizes the optimal solution.

While the exact formulation of the ILP problem is out of scope of this paper, we introduce the basic ideas. We utilize the constraints of the ILP to model the policies defined in the policy profile:

- **Access Policies**: To satisfy an AP, every attribute of the AP has to be stored in plaintext or as deterministic substitute by at least one SP to allow for an efficient execution of equality and range selections (cf. Table 1). The SP that stores all attributes of an AP may also store the AP's index table.
- **Confidentiality Constraints**: A CC is satisfied if at each SP at least one contained attribute is not revealable. To guarantee that, for each SP it must hold that at least one of the attributes contained in the CC is not stored at all, stored as probabilistic substitute or stored deterministically encrypted and contained in the specified ICs.

In order to apply security mechanisms only when necessary, we define the optimization criterion of the ILP as follows:

$$min \sum_{j \in SPs} \sum_{i \in Attributes} (d_{i,j} + p_{i,j}) \tag{1}$$

where

$$d_{i,j} = \begin{cases} 1, \text{if SP j stores deterministic substitutes of attribute i} \\ 0, \text{else} \end{cases}$$

$$p_{i,j} = \begin{cases} 1, \text{if SP j stores probabilistic substitutes of attribute i} \\ 0, \text{else} \end{cases}$$

The versatile nature of the ILP optimization criterion allows us to consider fine-grained performance differences of security mechanisms and database systems of the SPs in future work.

Once the ILP problem is solved by existing ILP solvers the solution of the ILP problem can be used to derive an optimal distribution of the index tables across the SPs and to determine which security mechanisms need to be applied on the attributes of the index tables. For instance, from Table 1 it can be deduced that if SP1 may store attribute *age* as deterministic substitute, hash indices can be used in an index table that should enable efficient queries that contain an equality selection on *age* (cf. Figure 2).

5   Evaluation

5.1   Benefit of Redundantly Storing Attributes

One feature that distinguishes Securus from previous approaches is that while encryption *and* fragmentation is used to protect data confidentiality, we do not enforce *true* fragmentation of the attributes on the SPs. In many scenarios, true fragmentation is an unnecessarily strict way of fulfilling confidentiality constraints. For instance, consider the example depicted in Figure 3. While *gender* and *ZIP* must not be stored by the same SP to satisfy the CC [gender,ZIP], it is legitimate to store *age* at both SPs. True fragmentation would dictate that *age* may only be present at a single SP in plaintext.

ID	gender	age
1	m	30
2	m	50
3	m	40
4	f	20
5	f	40
6	f	40

Exemplary index table at SP1
(AP: [gender, age])

ID	ZIP	age
1	76131	30
2	51362	50
3	76131	40
4	51362	20
5	76131	40
6	51362	40

Exemplary index table at SP2
(AP: [ZIP, age])

Fig. 3. Exemplary index tables at two SPs. APs: [gender, age], [ZIP, age], CC: [gender, ZIP]

The example shown in Figure 3 also illustrates the advantages of storing attributes redundantly at multiple SPs. Consider the query SELECT ID FROM index table 1 WHERE gender=f AND age=50. This query would return zero records as no record matches the query. However, if the attributes were truly fragmented and *age* would not be part of index table 1 but of index table 2, the query would have to be reformulated to SELECT ID FROM index table 1 WHERE gender=f. Consequently, records 3-6 would be transmitted to the mediator and would then all be discarded when evaluating the second part of the query: SELECT * FROM results WHERE age=50. Thus, for this example, three records would have been transmitted unnecessarily due to true fragmentation.

Table 2. Time required to generate a mediator from policy profiles of various sizes

Number of policies/elements					Duration (s)	
Attr.	APs	ICs	CCs	SPs	mean	max
10	5	1	10	3	0.004	0.056
20	10	2	40	4	0.015	0.217
20	15	2	10	4	0.016	0.330
40	40	3	50	4	0.555	8.169
40	40	3	60	4	0.658	6.714
80	40	3	40	4	0.036	0.812
80	60	3	80	4	0.887	16.602
80	80	3	100	4	5.474	692.235

Furthermore, the example illustrates why Securus can provide hard performance guarantees for specified APs. Securus enforces that for each specified AP, an index table that holds all attributes of the AP exists. Thus, instead of having to evaluate parts of the query in the mediator, queries can be entirely executed by the SPs. As shown in the example above, true fragmentation can not guarantee that all returned records are part of the query's result. In fact, the number of unnecessarily transmitted records depends on the datasets structure. As the example shows, it is possible that, to answer a query that would not return any results at all, half of the dataset needs to be transmitted to the mediator first. Thus, client-side validation whether a record is really contained in the result or not can lead to a massive and potentially unpredictable performance overhead.

5.2 Policy Transformation Performance

To evaluate the policy transformation performance, we randomly generated policy profiles of different sizes and measured the time needed to transform the policy profiles into mediators. For each policy profile size, we generated 5000 policy profiles. We ran the Gurobi solver[2] on a commodity computer with 4GB RAM and a 2.93GhZ Dual Core CPU to conduct the measurements shown in Table 2. The results show that Securus scales well for reasonably sized scenarios. The maximum transformation time was less than 693 seconds even for datasets with 80 attributes, 80 APs and 100 CCs. This is feasible, as mediator generation only has to be performed once, initially.

5.3 Discussion

Securus allows the definition of APs that guarantee an efficient query execution of the according queries and CC that prevents SPs from viewing attribute combinations or even from inspecting single attribute values. Policy profiles that are inherently unsolvable exist. As a trivial example, consider a policy profile with

---

[2] http://www.gurobi.com

a CC $[a_1,a_2]$ and an AP $[a_1,a_2]$. The CC and the AP contradict each other: both attributes have to be present at an SP in plaintext or as deterministic substitutes to satisfy the AP, however, at least one attribute must not be stored as plaintext or as deterministic substitute to satisfy the CC. In future work, we will investigate how to support the user in resolving policy conflicts. In particular, the solution will tell the user *why* his policy profile is infeasible.

In terms of query constructs, Securus supports equality and range selections as well as aggregation. It can be easily extended to support further query constructs such as LIKE or GROUP operators. Just like the range and equality selections, these would have to be bound to a required representation (e.g., plaintext or deterministic substitute) at the SP.

We assume that the CCs, APs and ICs are known by the user before generating the mediator and are not subject to changes. However, CCs might change in reality, for instance, due to shifting legal requirements concerning privacy. APs might change due to the arising demand to efficiently execute queries that have not been addressed by existing APs. To account for changing policies, a new mediator has to be generated and the dataset has to be re-outsourced.

The proposed concept considers each SP as an honest-but-curious attacker. Unlike other approaches [17,9], we do not assume that the attacker is not capable of monitoring operations on the data or queries. We only assume that the attacker lacks applicable background knowledge on the executed operations and queries such as the frequency distribution of executed queries. In particular, using Securus an SP without background knowledge can not violate CCs by monitoring the effects of an insert operation on the data tables. In future work we plan to extend Securus to also address attackers *with* background knowledge on incoming queries.

6   Conclusion

We presented an outline of Securus, a framework that simplifies data outsourcing by allowing users to specify their requirements in terms of data confidentiality and queries that have to be efficiently executable. Based on this information a software adapter is generated that can be used to outsource the data compliantly to the specified requirements and that can execute the specified queries efficiently. We extended our previous publication of Securus [14] by highlighting the differences to other data outsourcing frameworks in this paper. One major difference constitutes that Securus makes use of both fragmentation and encryption techniques, but also stores attributes redundantly at multiple SPs for a more efficient query execution if this does not undermine the required data confidentiality. Furthermore, it was shown that Securus can provide hard performance *and* confidentiality guarantees. We altered the policy model of the originally published version of Securus by specifying ICs that make assertions on the assumed attacker's knowledge. In future work, we can utilize the strict semantics of ICs to pursuit one of our future research directions: enabling users to model the attacker's capabilities in a fine-grained manner. Furthermore, we aim to explore methods to resolve conflicting requirements and to adapt the approach to consider fine-grained performance differences of both security mechanisms and database backends. Although Securus abstracts from confidentiality enhancing techniques, users are still required to specify which information needs protection. Enabling users to accurately define their company's individual confidentiality needs constitutes an interdisciplinary challenge that needs to be addressed not only in computer science but also in law and social sciences.

References

1. Aggarwal, G., Bawa, M., Ganesan, P., Garcia-Molina, H., Kenthapadi, K., Motwani, R., Srivastava, U., Thomas, D., Xu, Y.: Two can keep a secret: A distributed architecture for secure database services. In: Proc. of CIDR (2005)
2. Armbrust, M., Fox, A., Griffith, R., Joseph, A., Katz, R., Konwinski, A., Lee, G., Patterson, D., Rabkin, A., Stoica, I., Zaharia, M.: Above the clouds: A Berkeley view of cloud computing. Technical report, Berkeley (2009)
3. Camenisch, J., Dubovitskaya, M., Lehmann, A., Neven, G., Paquin, C., Preiss, F.-S.: Concepts and languages for privacy-preserving attribute-based authentication. In: Fischer-Hübner, S., de Leeuw, E., Mitchell, C. (eds.) IDMAN 2013. IFIP AICT, vol. 396, pp. 34–52. Springer, Heidelberg (2013)
4. Ceselli, A., Damiani, E., De Capitani di Vimercati, S., Jajodia, S., Paraboschi, S., Samarati, P.: Modeling and assessing inference exposure in encrypted databases. ACM Transactions on Information and System Security (TISSEC) (2005)
5. Ciriani, V., De Capitani di Vimercati, S., Foresti, S., Jajodia, S., Paraboschi, S., Samarati, P.: Combining fragmentation and encryption to protect privacy in data storage. ACM Transactions on Information and System Security (TISSEC) (2010)
6. Curtmola, R., Garay, J., Kamara, S., Ostrovsky, R.: Searchable symmetric encryption: improved definitions and efficient constructions. In: Proc. of the 13th ACM Conference on Computer and Communications Security (CCS). ACM (2006)
7. Damiani, E., De Capitani di Vimercati, S., Jajodia, S., Paraboschi, S., Samarati, P.: Balancing confidentiality and efficiency in untrusted relational DBMSs. In: Proc. of the ACM Conf. on Computer and Communications Security (CCS) (2003)
8. De Capitani di Vimercati, S., Foresti, S., Jajodia, S., Paraboschi, S., Samarati, P.: On information leakage by indexes over data fragments. In: Proc. of the 1st Int. Workshop on Privacy-Preserving Data Publication and Analysis (PrivDB) (2013)
9. Foresti, S.: Preserving Privacy in Data Outsourcing. Springer (2011)
10. Hacıgümüş, H., Iyer, B., Li, C., Mehrotra, S.: Executing SQL over Encrypted Data in the Database-Service-Provider Model. In: Proc. of SIGMOD (2002)
11. Hacıgümüş, H., Iyer, B., Mehrotra, S.: Efficient execution of aggregation queries over encrypted relational databases. In: Lee, Y., Li, J., Whang, K.-Y., Lee, D. (eds.) DASFAA 2004. LNCS, vol. 2973, pp. 125–136. Springer, Heidelberg (2004)
12. Harauz, J., Kaufman, L.M., Potter, B.: Data Security in the World of Cloud Computing. IEEE Security and Privacy (2009)
13. Jaatun, M.G., Bernsmed, K., Undheim, A.: Security sLAs – an idea whose time has come? In: Quirchmayr, G., Basl, J., You, I., Xu, L., Weippl, E. (eds.) CD-ARES 2012. LNCS, vol. 7465, pp. 123–130. Springer, Heidelberg (2012)
14. Jünemann, K., Köhler, J., Hartenstein, H.: Data outsourcing simplified: Generating data connectors from confidentiality and access policies. In: Proc. of the Workshop on Data-intensive Process Management in Large-Scale Sensor Systems (CCGrid-DPMSS) (2012)

15. Mykletun, E., Tsudik, G.: Aggregation queries in the database-as-a-service model. In: Data and Applications Security XX, pp. 89–103 (2006)
16. Pearson, S.: Toward accountability in the cloud. IEEE Internet Computing 15(4), 64–69 (2011)
17. Popa, R.A., Redfield, C., Zeldovich, N., Balakrishnan, H.: Cryptdb: protecting confidentiality with encrypted query processing. In: Proc. of the 23rd ACM Symp. on Operating Systems Principles (SOSP), pp. 85–100. ACM (2011)
18. Song, D.X., Wagner, D., Perrig, A.: Practical techniques for searches on encrypted data. In: Proc. of the IEEE Symposium on Security and Privacy (S&P) (2000)
19. Xiong, L., Goryczka, S., Sunderam, V.: Adaptive, secure, and scalable distributed data outsourcing: a vision paper. In: Proc. of the Workshop on Dynamic Distributed Data-intensive Applications, Programming Abstractions, and Systems (3DAPAS) (2011)

Problem-Based Consideration of Privacy-Relevant Domain Knowledge

Rene Meis

paluno - The Ruhr Institute for Software Technology – University of Duisburg-Essen
`rene.meis@paluno.uni-due.de`

Abstract. Especially for a privacy analysis, an adequate and accurate consideration of domain knowledge is needed. Domain knowledge is often only implicitly given and mainly stored in the minds of domain experts. It is important to make this implicit knowledge explicit and to use it in the privacy analysis of a software system. To our knowledge, no privacy-aware requirements engineering approach exists yet which explicitly considers the elicitation of privacy-relevant domain knowledge. This paper presents an extension of the problem-based privacy analysis (ProPAn) method. The extension consists of three parts. First, we elicit the relevant domain knowledge based on questionnaires which are derived from the stakeholder analysis literature. Second, we present generic patterns which can be instantiated to represent the elicited knowledge. Last, we extend the definitions of ProPAn's privacy graphs to take into account the domain knowledge.

1 Introduction

The quality of a privacy threat analysis strongly depends on the domain knowledge which is considered during the analysis. In general, the elicitation of domain knowledge for the development of a software system has a limited scope. Only those stakeholders and domains are identified that directly take part or are part of a functionality of the system-to-be. We will call these stakeholders *direct stakeholders*. But privacy threats in software systems can also stem from *indirect stakeholders* whose privacy is vulnerable or who possibly affect the privacy of other stakeholders. Another source of privacy threats is the missing domain knowledge about the behavior and further usages of legacy systems which are part of the system-to-be.

In this paper, we will consider privacy requirements, expressing that personal information of *stakeholders* shall not be accessible by *counterstakeholders*. In contrast to the term *attacker* a counterstakeholder may obtain personal data about the stakeholder involuntarily. We have a *privacy threat* for a privacy requirement in our system if there is an information flow from the stakeholder to a domain that is accessible by the counterstakeholder. Note that privacy has more facets than information flow and access control, such as transparency and intervenability [14].

This paper presents an extension of the Problem-based Privacy Analysis (ProPAn) method [4] considering the elicitation, modeling, and use of domain knowledge. ProPAn provides assistance for the initial steps of any given privacy analysis, which is to figure out those parts of the system where personal information of stakeholders can be disclosed by counterstakeholders. The focus of ProPAn, as we presented it in [4], is the

M. Hansen et al. (Eds.): Privacy and Identity 2014, IFIP AICT 421, pp. 150–162, 2014.

privacy analysis based on the functional requirements that have to be satisfied by the system-to-be. The extension of ProPAn that we present in this paper adds the consideration of domain knowledge to the privacy analysis. For a structured elicitation of the domain knowledge, we use questionnaires. Requirements engineers shall answer these questionnaires in cooperation with domain experts. On the basis of the answers of the questionnaires, we model the domain knowledge using the UML4PF-tool [5] on which ProPAn's tool-support is built. To assist the requirements engineer in the modeling process, we extended the ProPAn-tool[1] with wizards that generate the domain knowledge diagrams based on the answers of the questionnaires. Further, we extended the privacy threat graph generation of ProPAn such that the modeled domain knowledge is used.

The rest of the paper is structured as follows. First, we introduce the problem frames approach, UML4PF and ProPAn, as background of this paper in Section 2. In Section 3, we present the contribution of this paper. Section 4 presents the results of the empirical validation of our questionnaires. Then we discuss related work in Section 5. Finally, Section 6 concludes the paper and describes our future work.

2   Background

The problem frames approach, UML4PF, and ProPAn are described in this section.

Problem Frames Approach. The problem frames approach is a requirements engineering approach proposed by Jackson [8]. The first step of the problem frames approach is to create a *context diagram*. A context diagram represents the environment (e.g. stakeholders, other software) in which the machine (i.e. software) shall be built. The context diagram consists of domains and connections between them. Jackson distinguishes the domain types causal domains that comply with some physical laws, lexical domains that are data representations, and biddable domains that are usually people. Connections between domains describe the phenomena they share. Both domains can observe the shared phenomena, but only one domain has the control over a phenomenon (denoted by a "!"). Then the problem of building the system-to-be is decomposed until subproblems are reached which fit into problem frames. Problem frames are patterns for frequently occurring problems. An instantiated problem frame is represented as a problem diagram which in addition to a context diagram also contains a requirement. A requirement can refer to and constrain phenomena of domains. Both relations are expressed by dependencies from the requirement to the respective domain annotated with the referred to or constrained phenomena. An example for a context diagram and a problem diagram is given in Fig. 1 in Section 3.

We use the UML4PF-framework to create problem frame models. UML4PF consists of a UML profile which comes with stereotypes that allow to represent problem frame diagrams as UML class diagrams. The UML4PF-tool stores all diagrams in one global UML model. Hence, we can perform analyses and consistency checks over multiple diagrams and artifacts of the software development process. A more detailed description can be found in [5].

---

[1] Available at http://www.uni-due.de/swe/propan.shtml

ProPAn. ProPAn extends the UML4PF-framework with a UML profile for privacy requirements and a reasoning technique. A privacy requirement in ProPAn consists of two domains of the system-to-be, namely a *stakeholder* and a *counterstakeholder*. It states that the counterstakeholder shall not be able to obtain personal information of the stakeholder using the system-to-be. The reasoning technique identifies the domains to which personal information of the *stakeholder* can flow. The information flow of the whole system is represented by the global information flow graph which is automatically generated by the ProPAn-tool from the requirements represented as problem diagrams. Formally, the global information flow graph $\mathcal{G}$ is a directed graph with domains as nodes and edges annotated with problem diagrams. An edge (d_1, p, d_2) : Domain $\times$ ProblemDiagram $\times$ Domain denotes that there is a possible information flow from domain d_1 to domain d_2 which stems from the requirement of problem diagram p. Due to the semantics of problem diagrams, there are possibly information flows from each domain in the problem diagram to the domains constrained by the requirement. In this paper, we annotate the edges in the graphical representation of the privacy graphs with the requirements of the problem diagrams. An example for a global information flow graph is the not dashed part of Fig. 3 in Section 3.

From $\mathcal{G}$ the stakeholder information flow graph $\mathcal{S}_s$ is generated, which is a subset of $\mathcal{G}$. $\mathcal{S}_s$ is generated for the stakeholder s of the privacy requirement, and it shows the possible information flows starting from the stakeholder s. Stakeholder information flow graphs are printed with thin lines and filled arrowheads.

Additionally, our technique identifies the domains to which the *counterstakeholder* c has access. This information is captured in the counterstakeholder graph $\mathcal{C}_c$. This graph is generated for the counterstakeholder c of the privacy requirement. $\mathcal{C}_c$ is of the same type as the information flow graphs, but its edges have a different semantics. An edge $(c, p, d) \in \mathcal{C}_c$ denotes that the counterstakeholder c may gain information from the domain d due to problem diagram p. Counterstakeholder graphs are represented with bold lines and empty arrowheads.

For a privacy requirement with stakeholder s and counterstakeholder c, $\mathcal{S}_s$ and $\mathcal{C}_c$ are combined to the privacy threat graph $\mathcal{T}_{s,c}$. This graph shows possible privacy threats of the system-to-be where the privacy of stakeholder s can be harmed by the counterstakeholder c. An example is shown in Fig. 4 in Section 3. Based on the problem diagrams and a given privacy requirement, all graphs are automatically generated by the ProPAn-tool. For more details see [4].

3   Domain Knowledge Extension of ProPAn

The extension of ProPAn for the consideration of domain knowledge consists of the steps *elicitation*, *modeling*, and *use*. Before these steps are presented in more detail, we introduce our running example that we use to illustrate our method.

Running Example. We use a subsystem of an electronic health system (EHS) scenario provided by the industrial partners of the EU project *Network of Excellence (NoE) on Engineering Secure Future Internet Software Services and Systems (NESSoS)*[2] to illustrate our method. This scenario is based on the German health care system which

---

[2] http://www.nessos-project.eu/

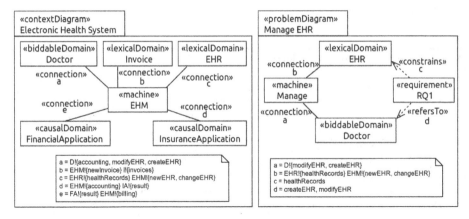

Fig. 1. Context diagram and problem diagrams of the EHS scenario

uses health insurance schemes for payment purposes. The context diagram of the EHS is shown in Fig. 1. The electronic health machine (EHM) is the machine to be built. It has to manage electronic health records (EHR) which are created and modified by doctors (functional requirement RQ1). Additionally, the EHS shall support the doctor to perform the accounting of patients. The accounting shall be based on the information stored in the health records. Using the insurance application it is possible to perform the accounting with the respective insurance of the patient. In the case that the insurance company does not bear the (complete) treating costs, the EHS shall create an invoice for the patient (RQ2). Patients shall be invoiced using a financial application (RQ3). The problem diagram for the functional requirement RQ1 is shown in Fig. 1. The not dashed part of Fig. 3 is the generated global information flow graph for the considered subsystem of the EHS.

The two privacy requirements that come into mind are that the doctor's privacy shall be protected against the financial and insurance applications. A privacy requirement about the patient cannot be expressed yet because the patient is not part of the problem frames model. We assume that the requirements engineer decided to leave out the patient because the patient does not directly interact with the machine.

Elicitation. For the elicitation of the domain knowledge, we use questionnaires. All questions aim at the elicitation of indirect (counter)stakeholders or at the identification of hidden information flows in the considered system. Indirect (counter)stakeholders are (counter)stakeholders who are not considered yet because they are not directly part of the system-to-be. We distinguish two kinds of questions. Questions with the prefix 1 elicit counterstakeholders who can gain personal information from the domain. Questions with the prefix 2 elicit stakeholders of whom the domain provides personal information. We developed questionnaires for causal/lexical and biddable domains that refine these two question types. For the elicitation process, we have to consider all domains of the context diagram and to answer the corresponding questionnaires.

Table 1. Domain knowledge elicitation questionnaire for causal and lexical domains

No.	Question
1	**Elicitation of Counterstakeholders**
1.1	Is there a competitor that also uses the domain?
1.2	Could the domain be attacked by a hacker?
1.3	Does the domain provide information to legislators or law enforcement agencies?
1.4	Is the domain also used in other systems? State possible counterstakeholders that have access to the domain in these systems.
2	**Elicitation of Stakeholders**
2.1	Is the domain also used in other systems? State possible stakeholders of these systems from whom information is accessible through the domain.
2.2	Is initially personal information of stakeholders stored in the domain?
2.3	Does the domain store or process personal information of stakeholders directly, indirectly, or implicitly connected to it?

First, we consider all causal and lexical domains of the context diagram. The questionnaire for causal and lexical domains is shown in Table 1. We refined the first question type using the Volere stakeholder analysis template [2] which suggests the *negative stakeholders* competitor (question 1.1) and hacker (question 1.2). Furthermore, we refined question type 1 by asking for the *baseline stakeholder* legislator (question 1.3) suggested by [13]. Additionally, we added the possible counterstakeholder law enforcement agency to question 1.3. Competitors, hackers, legislators, and law enforcement agencies are all possible indirect counterstakeholders that are usually not considered as direct stakeholders of a software system. Questions 1.4 and 2.1 elicit (counter)stakeholders that can gain or provide personal information due to a re-use of a domain. Previous privacy analyses of the domain in other systems can be re-used to answer these questions. Especially lexical domains can already be filled with personal information, e.g. an existing database with contact information of customers. Question 2.2 elicits the stakeholders of this personal information. Systems may contain hidden information flows, i.e. storage or processing of personal information of stakeholders that are directly, indirectly, or implicitly connected to the domain. Question 2.3 elicits to which stakeholders a hidden information flow exists from the domain.

In the EHS example, we have to consider these questions for the domains EHR, insurance application, and financial application. Because of space limitations, we do not consider the insurance application for the domain knowledge elicitation in this paper. For the EHR, we have no indirect stakeholders that have access to the domain because this domain shall only be accessible using the EHS. But we have the indirect stakeholder *patient* because the EHRs may initially contain personal information about patients (question 2.2). The financial application (FA) is part of other systems and we identify its employees and customers as indirect (counter)stakeholders, due to questions 1.4 and 2.1. Furthermore, the application is considered to be a possible source of hacker attacks (question 1.2). The list of all (counter)stakeholders that we elicited for the FA using the questionnaire can be found in Table 4 in Section 4.

Second, we consider all biddable domains of the context diagram. The questionnaire for biddable domains is shown in Table 2. Question 1.1 aims at the trustworthiness of

Table 2. Domain knowledge elicitation questionnaire for biddable domains

No.	Question
1	**Elicitation of Counterstakeholders**
1.1	Is the domain vulnerable to social engineering attacks?
1.2	Does the biddable domain provide information to another biddable domain?
1.3	Does the biddable domain provide information to legislators or law enforcement agencies?
2	**Elicitation of Stakeholders**
2.1	Does the biddable domain get information of another biddable domain?
2.2	Does the biddable domain act on behalf of customers or wards (e.g. children)?

Table 3. Excerpt of the answer template for the EHS scenario

Dom \ Question	1.2	1.4	2.1	2.2
EHR	-	-	-	Patient
FA	Hacker	Employee, Customer	Employee, Customer	-
Doctor	Family of Patient	/	Family of Patient	Patient

a biddable domain in the system-to-be. With this question, we want to identify indirect stakeholders with whom the biddable domain possibly shares information that comes out of the system-to-be. Hence, question 1.1 elicits the source of so-called *social engineering attacks*. Questions 1.2 and 2.1 elicit implicit communications between biddable domains in the system. Question 1.3 is the same as question 1.3 from the previous questionnaire. Question 2.2 elicits those indirect stakeholders for whom a direct stakeholder acts on behalf of. These indirect stakeholders are of high relevance for the privacy analysis because personal information of those indirect stakeholders is stored and processed in the system-to-be in all likelihood.

In the EHS example, we only have the doctor as biddable domain. Hence, questions 1.2 and 2.1 are not relevant. For simplicity reasons, we do not consider question 1.1 because doctors are bound to professional discretion and hence we have no indirect counterstakeholders to which they provide information. It would be possible to consider corrupted doctors who break their professional discretion, and to elicit the stakeholders to whom they possibly provide information. All those stakeholders that we would consider as relevant are listed in Table 4 in Section 4. When we consider question 2.2, we identify the patients of the doctor, which can be seen as both customers and wards (i.e. persons who are being cared for by other persons). Doctors create health records on behalf of the patients whose personal information is stored in the records. The answers of the questionnaires are summarized in answer templates as shown in Table 3

It is reasonable to extend both questionnaires with questions specific to an application domain to give further assistance for the elicitation process. The questionnaires are easily extensible with questions aiming at the elicitation of privacy-relevant counterstakeholders (question type 1) and stakeholders (question type 2).

Modeling. We use *domain knowledge diagrams* to model the domain knowledge, elicited using the questionnaires. Domain knowledge diagrams are already part of the UML4PF-profile, for the representation of indicative statements. A domain knowledge

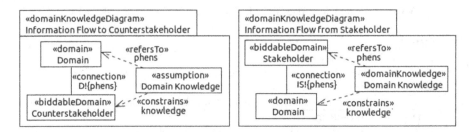

Fig. 2. General pattern for a domain knowledge diagram with an information flow from (left) / to (right) the indirect (counter)stakeholder

diagram consists of an indicative statement, which is represented by the stereotype *DomainKnowledge*, and the domains referred to or constrained by the domain knowledge. The stereotype *DomainKnowledge* is specialized into the stereotypes *Fact* and *Assumption*. Facts are statements that are always true and assumptions only hold under specific circumstances. In general, we have presented two kinds of elicited domain knowledge. First, we elicit the indirect counterstakeholders who can gain information from the system-to-be (question type 1). Second, we elicit the indirect stakeholders of whom personal information is possibly stored and processed in the system-to-be (question type 2). The identified indirect (counter)stakeholders are modeled as biddable domains in all above cases. To represent the first kind of domain knowledge, we create a domain knowledge diagram by instantiating the pattern shown in Fig. 2 on the left-hand side. In the other case, we instantiate the pattern shown in Fig. 2 on the right-hand side. The domain *Domain* will be instantiated with the domain for which we answered the question, the *(Counter)Stakeholder* with the newly identified biddable domain, the title of the domain knowledge diagram and the domain knowledge with an appropriate name. Additionally, we have to decide whether the domain knowledge is a fact (a truth that always holds) or an assumption (a statement that could also be false under some circumstances). A dependency with the stereotype *refersTo* starting from the domain knowledge points to the source of the information flow and a dependency with the stereotype *constrains* starting from the domain knowledge points to the target of the information flow.

In the EHS example, we instantiate the patterns according to the answer template in Table 3. For example, the first variant is instantiated for the domain *Financial Application* with the indirect counterstakeholder *Hacker*. The second variant is instantiated for the domains *EHR* and *Doctor* with the indirect stakeholder *Patient*. Due to space limitations, we do not show the instantiated domain knowledge diagrams.

Use. The domain knowledge can now be used for the generation of the information flow graphs and the counterstakeholder graph. In a domain knowledge diagram d, we have a possible information flow from the referred domain r to the constrained domain c, analogous to the possible information flows stemming from the problem diagrams [4]. Hence, we allow edges annotated with domain knowledge diagrams in the information flow graphs and add the edges (r, d, c) : Domain $\times$ ProblemDiagram $\times$ Domain for all domain knowledge diagrams to the global information flow graph. If a

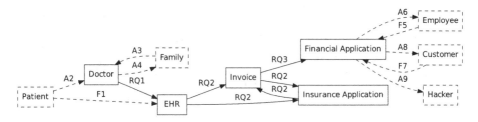

Fig. 3. Global information flow graph for the EHS with indirect stakeholders

Fig. 4. Privacy threat graph for patient and hacker

counterstakeholder c is constrained in a domain knowledge diagram d, then the counterstakeholder has possibly access to the information of the referred domain r. Hence, we add the edge (c, d, r) to c's counterstakeholder graph $\mathcal{C}_c$. With this additional rules for the graph generation, the privacy threat graphs now also provide possible threats that stem from indirect (counter)stakeholders.

In our example, it is now possible to consider the patient as a stakeholder whose privacy we want to protect. Additionally, hackers, as well as employees and customers of the financial application, can now be considered as counterstakeholders. From this small example, we can see that the elicitation of further domain knowledge is essential for a useful privacy analysis. The new global information flow graph is shown in Fig. 3 and the threat graph for the stakeholder patient and the counterstakeholder hacker in Fig. 4. The elements added by the proposed extension of ProPAn are drawn dashed.

Tool-Support. We extended the ProPAn-tool[1] for the consideration of domain knowledge as described in this paper. The extension consists of a wizard that asks the user the questions of the questionnaires for all domains of the context diagram and directly creates the needed domain knowledge diagrams based on the domain knowledge patterns. Furthermore, the graph generation algorithms are extended such that they also consider the elicited (counter)stakeholders captured in domain knowledge diagrams.

4 Empirical Evaluation

We evaluated our questionnaires for the elicitation of indirect (counter)stakeholders during the presentation of this paper at the summer school. After the introduction of ProPAn and the running example, the audience of the presentation was randomly split into two groups. Both groups had 10 minutes time to identify indirect (counter)stakeholders for the doctor and the financial application of the running example. One group had to guess

---

[1] Available at http://www.uni-due.de/swe/propan.shtml

Table 4. Summarized results of the evaluation (privacy-relevant cells are printed in **bold** font)

Indirect Stakeholder	Doctor S	Doctor C	Fin. App. S	Fin. App. C	Sum
Insurance companies	0 4 4	**8 9 17**	0 1 1	**1 6 7**	9 20 29
Patients	**5 8 13**	**1 6 7**	**0 5 5**	0 0 0	6 19 25
Other doctors	**4 5 9**	**5 6 11**	0 0 0	0 2 2	9 13 22
Nurses and staff	**3 3 6**	**5 6 11**	0 0 0	0 0 0	8 9 17
Pharmacy companies	**2 2 4**	**3 6 9**	0 1 1	**1 1 2**	6 10 16
Government and politicians	0 0 0	**5 2 7**	0 0 0	**1 6 7**	6 8 14
Family of patients	**4 2 6**	**0 4 4**	0 0 0	0 0 0	4 6 10
Hacker	0 0 0	0 0 0	0 0 0	**0 7 7**	0 7 7
Law enforcement agencies	0 1 1	**0 2 2**	0 0 0	**1 3 4**	1 6 7
Financial companies	0 2 2	**2 1 3**	0 0 0	0 0 0	2 3 5
Provider of financial app	0 0 0	0 0 0	**1 0 1**	**3 1 4**	4 1 5
Friends and family of doctor	0 0 0	**0 4 4**	0 0 0	0 0 0	0 4 4
Journalist	0 0 0	**1 2 3**	0 0 0	**0 1 1**	1 3 4
Researchers	0 1 1	**1 2 3**	0 0 0	0 0 0	1 3 4
Customers of financial app	0 0 0	0 0 0	**0 2 2**	**1 0 1**	1 2 3
Doctor	0 0 0	0 0 0	**0 2 2**	**0 1 1**	0 3 3
Employees of financial app	0 0 0	0 0 0	**0 3 3**	0 0 0	0 3 3
Social engineering attacker	0 0 0	**0 3 3**	0 0 0	0 0 0	0 3 3
Competitor of financial app	0 0 0	0 0 0	0 0 0	**0 2 2**	0 2 2
Employers	0 0 0	**1 1 2**	0 0 0	**0 0 0**	1 1 2

indirect stakeholders without assistance and the other group used the developed questionnaires for the elicitation. The questionnaires used in the experiment can be found in the Appendix. There were 12 participants in the control group (without assistance) and 15 in the questionnaire group.

We consider twenty indirect (counter)stakeholder from the overall amount of thirty indirect (counter)stakeholders identified by the participants of the experiment as relevant. These are listed in the first column of Table 4. The following columns contain three numbers and show how often the indirect stakeholder was identified as stakeholder (S) or counterstakeholder (C) for the doctor and the financial application, respectively. The first number in these columns indicates how often the indirect stakeholder was considered by the control group, the second how often by the questionnaire group and the third gives the total amount of considerations. We printed a cell of the table in bold font if we consider the indirect stakeholder of the row as a relevant stakeholder (S) or counterstakeholder (C) for the domain in the column in a privacy analysis.

Based on the relationships that we consider as relevant, we computed the average precision, specificity, accuracy, and recall of both groups shown in Table 5. The precision and specificity of both groups is above 90%. The questionnaire group identified a few more unexpected indirect (counter)stakeholder relationships (false positives) than the control group, which leads to a smaller precision and specificity. The questionnaire group has a slightly larger accuracy than the control group. The recall of both groups lies below 20%, which is surely caused by the limited time of 10 minutes the participants had for the elicitation. Nevertheless, the questionnaire group

Table 5. Precision, specificity, accuracy, and recall of both groups

Group	Precision	Specificity	Accuracy	Recall
control group	93,39%	97,91%	41,67%	12,82%
questionnaire group	90,65%	93,33%	44,97%	20,17%

identified 1,5 times more correct indirect (counter)stakeholder relationships. In summary, the questionnaires seem to help to increase the number of correct identified indirect (counter)stakeholders and their relationships to the domains of the context diagram significantly. The trade-off of the questionnaires is that the precision and specificity is slightly decreased. But this is reasonable because our main focus is the elicitation of all relevant indirect (counter)stakeholders for the privacy analysis.

5   Related Work

In this section, we discuss privacy-aware requirements engineering and stakeholder analysis methods that are related to this work.

Privacy-Aware Requirements Engineering. The LINDDUN-framework proposed by Deng et al. [6] is an extension of Microsoft's security analysis framework STRIDE [7]. LINDDUN adds the seven privacy threats linkability, identifiability, non-repudiation, detectability, information disclosure, content unawareness, and policy/consent noncompliance to STRIDE. In contrast to ProPAn, the system to be analyzed is modeled as a data flow diagram (DFD), which has to be set up carefully for the analysis. ProPAn is based on a problem frames model which is assumed to be already existing and which can systematically be created using the problem frames approach [8]. Additionally, LINDDUN has to be carried out manually.

The PriS method introduced by Kalloniatis et al. [9] considers privacy requirements as organizational goals. The impact of the privacy requirements on the other organizational goals and their related business processes is analyzed. The authors use privacy process patterns to suggest a set of privacy enhancing technologies (PETs) to realize the privacy requirements. PriS is a goal-based approach, whereas ProPAn is problem-based. In addition, the PriS method has to be carried out manually.

Liu et al. [10] propose a security and privacy requirements analysis based on the goal and agent-based requirements engineering approach i^* [15]. The authors integrate the security and privacy analysis into the elicitation process of i^*. Already elicited actors from i^* are considered as attackers. Additional skills and malicious intents of the attackers are combined with the capabilities and interests of the actors. Then the vulnerabilities implied by the identified attackers and their malicious intentions are investigated in the i^* model. In contrast to our work, the approach of Liu et al. is goal based and it does not elicit additional privacy-relevant stakeholders for the analysis.

Stakeholder Analysis. Stakeholder analysis originates from information systems research [11]. We describe the research of requirements engineers on this field.

Sharp et al. [13] present a method for the identification of stakeholders for requirements engineering. The authors distinguish four groups of *baseline stakeholders*, namely users, developers, legislators, and decision-makers. For each baseline role, the method identifies *supplier stakeholders* who provide information, *client stakeholders* who process or inspect the products, and *satellite stakeholders* who interact or support the baseline stakeholders and vice versa.

Alexander and Robertson [2] recommend a combination of two methods. The first method is the onion model [1] for the identification of stakeholders. The model arranges different generic stakeholder roles around the product, which is the center of the onion. The distance of a stakeholder to the product expresses how directly the stakeholder interacts with the product. The second method is the usage of the Volere stakeholder analysis template [12]. This template suggests 72 stakeholder roles that are divided into 14 stakeholder classes which again are divided into 4 categories of stakeholder classes. The template shall elicit stakeholders that hold relevant knowledge for the project.

The stakeholder analysis approaches all aim at the identification of stakeholders that are relevant to successfully complete a project. In contrast, we are interested in those stakeholders whose privacy is affected or those counterstakeholders that can harm the privacy of stakeholders in the system-to-be and not at the time of development.

6   Conclusion and Future Work

In this paper, we extended ProPAn with a structured method for the consideration of privacy-relevant domain knowledge. Three steps are necessary for the extension of ProPAn. First, we elicit the relevant domain knowledge based on questionnaires. Second, we introduce two generic patterns that can be instantiated to represent the elicited domain knowledge in the UML model. Third, we extend the definition of the global information flow graph and the counterstakeholder graph such that the domain knowledge is also considered in the privacy threat graphs. To support our method, we extended the ProPAn-tool[1] with the presented questionnaires from which the corresponding domain knowledge diagrams are generated.

The proposed questionnaires can easily be extended to provide better support for the elicitation of privacy-relevant indirect (counter)stakeholders. Our extension improves the expressiveness of the ProPAn-method because ProPAn can now consider both indicative and optative statements for the privacy analysis. Despite the fact that the amount of 27 participants of the empirical evaluation at the summer school is not representative and that the participants were no experts in the health care domain, it yields promising results. The evaluation shows that the questionnaires help to significantly increase the amount of identified privacy-relevant indirect (counter)stakeholders, while the amount of those who are not relevant is slightly increased. The questionnaires itself will generally not lead to a comprehensive and correct list of indirect (counter)stakeholders, but they give guidance for the elicitation process that has to be performed by requirements engineers in cooperation with domain experts.

As future work, we want to investigate how to prioritize privacy threats by the risk they cause. This prioritization can then be used to narrow down the amount of threats that has to be considered for development. Furthermore, we plan to extend ProPAn with specific analyses for privacy requirements such as unlinkability, transparency, and

---

[1] Available at http://www.uni-due.de/swe/propan.shtml

intervenability. Furthermore, ProPAn shall be extended to bridge the gap between the problem and the solution space. Therefore, we want to suggest PETs that can be chosen to implement a specific privacy requirement. The work of Deng et al. [6], Kalloniatis et al. [9], and Antón et al. [3] will serve as a starting point for this work. The application of ProPAn and the extension presented in this paper to an industrial-size case study and further empirical evaluations are also part of our future work.

Acknowledgment. We thank Maritta Heisel, Azadeh Alebrahim, Kristian Beckers, Stephan Faßbender, Denis Hatebur, Marit Hansen and the anonymous reviewers for their constructive and valuable comments on earlier versions of this paper.

References

1. Alexander, I.F.: A taxonomy of stakeholders: Human roles in system development. IJTHI 1(1), 23–59 (2005)
2. Alexander, I.F., Robertson, S.: Understanding project sociology by modeling stakeholders. IEEE Software 21(1), 23–27 (2004)
3. Antón, A.I., Earp, J.B., Reese, A.: Analyzing website privacy requirements using a privacy goal taxonomy. In: RE, pp. 23–31. IEEE Computer Society (2002)
4. Beckers, K., Faßbender, S., Heisel, M., Meis, R.: A problem-based approach for computer aided privacy threat identification. In: Preneel, B., Ikonomou, D. (eds.) APF 2012. LNCS, vol. 8319, pp. 1–16. Springer, Heidelberg (2014)
5. Côté, I., Hatebur, D., Heisel, M., Schmidt, H.: UML4PF – a tool for problem-oriented requirements analysis. In: Proceedings of RE, pp. 349–350. IEEE Computer Society (2011)
6. Deng, M., Wuyts, K., Scandariato, R., Preneel, B., Joosen, W.: A privacy threat analysis framework: supporting the elicitation and fulfillment of privacy requirements. In: RE (2011)
7. Howard, M., Lipner, S.: The Security Development Lifecycle. Microsoft Press, Redmond (2006)
8. Jackson, M.: Problem Frames. Analyzing and structuring software development problems. Addison-Wesley (2001)
9. Kalloniatis, C., Kavakli, E., Gritzalis, S.: Addressing privacy requirements in system design: the PriS method. Requir. Eng. 13, 241–255 (2008)
10. Liu, L., Yu, E., Mylopoulos, J.: Security and privacy requirements analysis within a social setting. In: Proceedings of the 11th IEEE International Requirements Engineering Conference, pp. 151–161 (2003)
11. Pouloudi, A.: Aspects of the stakeholder concept and their implications for information systems development. In: HICSS (1999)
12. Robertson, S., Robertson, J.: Mastering the Requirements Process, 2nd edn. Addison-Wesley Professional (2006)
13. Sharp, H., Finkelstein, A., Galal, G.: Stakeholder identification in the requirements engineering process. In: DEXA Workshop, pp. 387–391 (1999)
14. Westin, A.F.: Privacy and Freedom. Atheneum, New York (1967)
15. Yu, E.: Towards modeling and reasoning support for early-phase requirements engineering. In: Proceedings of the 3rd IEEE International Symposium on Requirements Engineering, RE 1997, pp. 226–235. IEEE Computer Society, Washington, DC (1997)

Appendix: Questionnaires of the Experiment

As mentioned in Section 4, we split the audience of the presentation of this paper during the summer school randomly into two groups. One group got the developed questionnaire shown in Fig. 5 and 6. The other group was the control group and got the questionnaire shown in Fig. 7.

	Elicitation of	UNIVERSITÄT DUISBURG ESSEN
June 20, 2013	**Privacy-Relevant Domain Knowledge**	*Open-Minded*

What is your expertise in requirements engineering?

□ expert   □ high   □ medium   □ low   □ none

Questionnaire for the Doctor

1.1 Is the **doctor** vulnerable to social engineering attacks? State possible indirect counterstakeholders, who could perform a social engineering attack on the **doctor**.

_____

_____

1.2 Does the **doctor** provide information to another biddable domain of the system? State possible connections between the **doctor** and other biddable domains.

_____

_____

2.1 Does the **doctor** get information from another biddable domain of the system? State possible connections between the **doctor** and other biddable domains.

_____

_____

2.2 Does the **doctor** act on behalf of other people (e.g. customers, children)? State indirect stakeholders the **doctor** acts on behalf of.

_____

_____

Fig. 5. First page of the developed questionnaire

Elicitation of
Privacy-Relevant Domain Knowledge

Questionnaire for the Financial Application

1.1 Is there a competitor that also uses the **financial application**? State possible indirect counterstakeholders, who also use the **financial application**.

1.2 Could the **financial application** be attacked by a hacker? State possible hackers that could attack the **financial application**.

1.3 Provides the **financial application** information to legislators? State possible legislators to which the **financial application** provides information.

1.4 Is the **financial application** also used in other systems? State possible counterstakeholders that have access to the **financial application** in these systems.

2.1 Is the **financial application** also used in other systems? State possible stakeholders of these systems from whom information is accessible through the **financial application**.

2.2 Is initially personal information of stakeholders stored in the **financial application**? State stakeholders from whom the **financial application** possibly provides personal information.

Fig. 6. Second page of the developed questionnaire

What is your expertise in requirements engineering?

☐ expert   ☐ high   ☐ medium   ☐ low   ☐ none

Identify indirect (counter)stakeholders and state their relation to the Doctor.

Identify indirect (counter)stakeholders and state their relation to the Financial Application.

Fig. 7. Control group questionnaire

Extending Signatures of Reputation*

Emmanuelle Anceaume[1], Gilles Guette[1], Paul Lajoie-Mazenc[1],
Thomas Sirvent[2], and Valérie Viet Triem Tong[3]

[1] IRISA – Université de Rennes 1 – CNRS, France
`firstname.lastname@irisa.fr`
[2] DGA Maîtrise de l'information,
IRMAR – Université de Rennes 1, France
`thomas.sirvent@m4x.org`
[3] SUPELEC, France
`valerie.viettriemtong@supelec.fr`

Abstract. Reputation mechanisms are a powerful tool to reduce the
potential risk of interacting with almost or completely unknown users in
environments in which there is no incentive to behave trustworthily, e.g.
in open and large-scale systems. However, by collecting feedback about
users, reputation mechanisms can easily be manipulated to deduce users'
profiles; thus, these mechanisms jeopardize users' privacy, which clearly
compromise their wide adoption. Privacy-preserving reputation mechanisms have recently been proposed to solve this issue. All the proposed
designs either rely on a trusted central authority to handle the casting
of votes and the derivation of reputation scores, or are based on a distributed environment and use cryptographic tools (e.g. non-interactive
zero-knowledge proofs of knowledge and homomorphic encryption) to
demonstrate the validity of votes and reputation scores. However, to the
best of our knowledge, all the proposed distributed mechanisms produce
solely monotonic reputation scores: whatever the outcome of an interaction, a service provider's reputation can never decrease. In this article,
we propose a distributed privacy-preserving reputation mechanism handling both positive and negative votes. This is achieved by combining
algorithms and tools from both the distributed and the cryptographic
communities.

Keywords: Distributed reputation mechanism, privacy, non-monotonic
reputation score.

1 Introduction

In large scale and dynamic networks such as the Internet, most interactions occur
between unknown users. When users invest time or money in such interactions,
this may induce a severe risk. For instance, in e-commerce transactions, a buyer
– or client – has no guarantee that the item on sale will be sent or even that

---

* This work has been partially supported by the French ANR project AMORES,
`http://amores-project.org`

M. Hansen et al. (Eds.): Privacy and Identity 2014, IFIP AICT 421, pp. 165–176, 2014.
© IFIP International Federation for Information Processing 2014

its real state is consistent with its description. Hence, there is a crucial need for clients to determine to what extent an interaction with a given user is safe. In the following, we call *service providers* the users that provide a given service, and *clients* the users that wish to obtain a given service.

Reputation mechanisms come out as an effective tool to assess this risk, and indirectly foster trust and motivate cooperation in large scale and open systems. Indeed, similarly to the word-of-mouth reputation, a reputation mechanism allows clients to form an opinion on the behavior of an unknown service provider through a *reputation score*. A reputation score is a mathematical object (e.g. a number or a percentage) computed from the set of votes cast by the past clients of the targeted service provider. Reputation scores can either be computed by a central entity – like in eBay[1] – by the users themselves [1–4] or by the targeted entity [5]. Users evaluate the risk of interacting with the targeted service provider according to his reputation score. Reputation mechanisms are thus an efficient tool to encourage service providers to trustworthily behave. On the other hand, the reputation of misbehaving service providers gradually decreases, which quickly dissuades potential clients from interacting.

In order to maintain reputation scores up to date, clients are regularly requested to send their feedback regarding their past interactions with service providers. Unfortunately, by collecting feedback from clients, reputation mechanisms can easily be manipulated to deduce users' profiles (both clients' and service providers') and thus to jeopardize their privacy. This is achieved by compromising users' *anonymity* and the *unlinkability* of their interactions [6]. Pfitzmann and Hansen's taxonomy [7] states that a user is anonymous if an attacker cannot identify him among a group of users; and that any two interactions are unlinkable if an attacker cannot tell whether they involve the same users. Privacy-preserving reputation mechanisms have recently been proposed to solve this issue. Proposed designs either rely on a trusted central authority to handle the vote casting and reputation score derivation [8], or use cryptographic tools (e.g. non-interactive zero-knowledge proofs of knowledge and homomorphic encryption) to demonstrate the validity of votes [5]. By protecting users' identities and by guaranteeing the unlinkability of their actions, Resnick et al. [9] have shown that it gives supplementary incentives for the clients to feed the reputation mechanism with honest feedback without fearing retaliation. However, to the best of our knowledge, none of the existing privacy-preserving reputation mechanisms can handle both positive and negative votes. Note that a negative vote is a vote reflecting a dissatisfied client, but not necessarily a negative vote in the mathematical sense. Negative votes allow reputation scores to exactly reflect misbehaving service providers. In particular, negative votes allow to protect the system against service providers that initially behave correctly to gain a high reputation, until they suddenly turn malicious and attract clients in fraudulent transactions. Indeed, handling both positive and negative votes is recognized as a real scientific challenge [5].

---

[1] http://www.ebay.com

In this article, we present the main principles of a reputation mechanism preserving the privacy of clients and service providers in a distributed way. This mechanism is inspired from the *signatures of reputation* proposed by Bethencourt et al. [5]. The most important feature of our proposal is the handling of both positive and negative votes. To the best of our knowledge, this is the first mechanism handling such a feature in a privacy-preserving distributed context.

The remainder of this article is organized as follows. We present the state of the art of privacy-preserving reputation mechanisms in Sect. 2, with a focus on the signatures of reputation of Bethencourt et al. [5]. In Sect. 3, we define the privacy and security properties that our mechanism guarantees. We then present the tools used in our proposal in Sect. 4, and how they are used during an interaction between a client and a provider in Sect. 5. Finally, we conclude in Sect. 6.

2   State of the Art

Pavlov, Rosenschein and Topol [10] were the first ones to propose a reputation system guaranteeing the privacy of its users in a distributed way. In contrast to subsequent works, their notion of privacy is limited to the non-disclosure of clients' votes. Androulaki et al. [8] go a step further by proposing a reputation mechanism preserving the anonymity of both service providers and clients through pseudonyms, anonymous credentials and blind signatures. On the other hand, and despite their reliance on a correct (but curious) central authority, their mechanism does not guarantee that the reputation score of a given service provider reflects its past behavior. Indeed, a service provider s_1 can easily collude with another one s_2 by giving to s_2 the *repcoins* (i.e. anonymous positive votes) he has received so that s_2 can ask the central authority to increase his own reputation score with these irregularly received repcoins. Guaranteeing the non transferability of reputation is crucial when dealing with malicious service providers. In addition, and as mentioned above, negative votes are not handled by this mechanism.

Bethencourt, Shi and Song [5] propose a cryptographic primitive called *signature of reputation*, allowing any user to advertise the services he provides with his reputation without divulging any private information. Both clients and service providers preserve their anonymity through one-time pseudonyms. The construction of signatures of reputation does not rely on any trusted central authority. Rather, each service provider computes signatures of reputation based on cryptographic votes built by his past clients. The reputation of a service provider is the count of *distinct* clients who granted him votes. This avoids ballot-stuffing attacks, i.e. attacks where a single client votes multiple times for a service provider to raise or lower his reputation. Bethencourt et al.'s system makes extensive use of Non-Interactive Zero-Knowledge proofs of knowledge (NIZK) [11]. Basically, such proofs allow to prove the knowledge of an equation solution without disclosing it. This allows both clients and service providers to prove statements such as "this pseudonym is well-formed" or "this signature of reputation is valid" without disclosing their identity. The first drawback of their solution is that NIZKs require high computational power, bandwidth, and storage capacity. For instance, a signature of reputation computed on 100 votes takes about 50MB of storage, which is too large to be practical. The second issue is, as for all existing privacy-preserving reputation mechanisms, that reputation scores do not reflect dissatisfied clients. This is a clear impediment to the wide adoption of such privacy-preserving mechanisms. In the following, we propose a mechanism that does take into account the discontentment of clients.

3   Modelling and Main Expectations of Our Proposal

In this section, we first introduce the model and the terminology used throughout this work. Then, we present the properties that fully characterize our privacy-preserving reputation mechanism.

3.1   System Model

We consider a large scale and open system populated by clients and service providers. We assume that both clients and service providers communicate over an anonymous communication network, e.g. Tor [12]. Both clients and service providers interact via pseudonyms they generate themselves. We do not make any assumption regarding the behavior of both parties. In particular, clients may abruptly end their interaction prior to having cast their votes, and service providers may devise strategies to manipulate their own reputation, or steal the reputation of another service provider. More generally, any number of users may collude in the objective of breaking the anonymity of some other user.

3.2   Reputation Mechanism

First, we make a difference between a *transaction* and an *interaction*. A transaction represents the exchange of the service between a service provider and a client, while an interaction consists of the transaction and all the communications between the client and the service provider allowing to take into account the outcome of the transaction. Any meaningful reputation mechanism involves the following three phases. The first phase allows any service provider to prove its current reputation to any requesting client. Then, when the requirements of both parties are satisfied, the transaction takes place. Finally, the client casts a vote reflecting the quality of the transaction. Note that in order to face non-cooperative clients, that is clients disengaging from the interaction prior to having cast a vote, a mechanism attesting that a transaction did occur between both parties need to be implemented. Such proofs of interaction must appear in the reputation score of service providers.

3.3 Properties

We now present the properties that fully characterize our reputation mechanism.

Property 1 (Privacy of service providers). *The privacy of service providers is preserved if, when a client votes for an honest service provider, this service provider is anonymous among the service providers with an equivalent reputation.*

Property 2 (Privacy of clients). *The privacy of clients is preserved if:*

1. *An honest client is anonymous among all clients;*
2. *The interactions of a client with different service providers are unlinkable.*

In addition to both privacy properties, we present the properties that guarantee that no attacker can take advantage of our reputation mechanism.

Property 3 (Correctness of a reputation mechanism). *A reputation mechanism is correct if the following six properties hold.*

Unforgeability of votes *If a service provider has received n votes, then this service provider was involved in at least n transactions;*

Unforgeability of interaction proofs *If a service provider proves that n transactions occurred, then this service provider was involved in at least n transactions with distinct clients;*

Unforgeability of reputation scores *A service provider cannot prove a fake reputation score;*

Non-repudiation of votes *If, at the end of a transaction between a client and a service provider, the client casts a vote, then his vote updates the reputation score that was proved at the beginning of the interaction;*

Non-repudiation of interaction proofs *At the end of a transaction between a client and a service provider, the service provider can prove that the transaction occurred;*

Impact limitation *The impact of a single client on the reputation score of a service provider is limited.*

The unforgeability and non-repudiation properties are standard properties in reputation systems, and most systems ensure them. On the other hand, the non-repudiation of votes prevents colluding service providers from using a "good" service provider to prove his reputation – and attract clients – and then behaving maliciously and giving the negative votes to another service provider. Finally, the impact limitation property prevents ballot-stuffing attacks. Note that Bethencourt et al.'s signatures of reputation [5] guarantees those properties. However, since there are no negative votes, service providers have no interest in repudiating a vote. In the following section, we present the tools we use to guarantee all these properties.

4   Principles of Our Reputation Mechanism

Our proposal aims at enhancing the signatures of reputation proposed by Bethencourt et al. [5] by handling negative votes. Taking into account negative votes implies major modifications with respect to the implementation of the mechanism. Specifically, in Bethencourt et al.'s mechanism, service providers locally store votes cast at the end of their interaction with their clients, and compute their reputation score by aggregating the received votes. In particular, they can keep only a subset of them, which clearly makes negative votes useless. We propose to improve upon this solution by guaranteeing that negative votes are taken into account. This is achieved by making both reputation scores and votes of service providers publicly available in order to prevent anyone from modifying or hiding them. Our proposition accomplishes this without jeopardizing the privacy of clients.

4.1   Preserving the Privacy

In order to preserve the privacy of both clients and providers (Prop. 1 and 2), these entities must prove that they belong to the system without revealing their identity (in the following, we use the term *credential* as a synonymous of identity), and prove the correctness of their computations without revealing the values used in these computations. Similarly to Bethencourt et al. [5], we use Non-Interactive Zero-Knowledge proofs of knowledge (NIZK) to solve these issues.

Furthermore, the reputation scores displayed by providers are approximations of their exact reputations. Indeed, if two different pseudonyms prove that "82.476% of my clients are satisfied", it is highly plausible that those pseudonyms belong to the same provider, which breaks this service provider's anonymity. Thus, providers only prove approximations of their reputation score: showing that "between 80% and 85% of my clients are satisfied" yields roughly the same information as before, but enlarges the anonymity set of the provider.

4.2   Correctness of the Mechanism

Unforgeability of votes, interaction proofs and reputation scores. In order to guarantee the properties of unforgeability (i.e. unforgeability of votes, interaction proofs and reputation scores), we use anonymous proxy signatures [13]. They preserve the privacy of both clients and service providers due to their compatibility with NIZKs. To participate in the system, each user (i.e. clients and service providers) register with a registration authority which generates the user's credentials and certificates. With anonymous proxy signatures and NIZKs, a user can then use his certificate to prove that he sent a message or made computations without disclosing his credential among all registered clients, or service providers. Several messages or computations can be linked to a unique hidden certificate (using the same randomization of the certificate). By doing so, a client can emit a vote for a service provider, without knowing the credential of the service provider, but with the guarantee that his vote will affect the reputation score of the service provider who proved his reputation at the beginning of the interaction.

Non-repudiation of Votes and Interaction Proofs. In the context of anonymous reputation mechanisms, both clients and service providers have antagonist expectations. Clients require that each of their votes (in particular negative ones) be taken into account, while providers expect their privacy to be preserved. However, if the provider remains anonymous when the client casts his vote, he has the opportunity to reject a negative vote simply by not revealing his identity; indeed, the vote cannot be assigned to any provider. On the other hand, if the provider reveals his identity prior to the voting phase, his privacy is broken, and the client may change both his behavior and his vote according to the provider's identity. In the same way, the provider wants to get a proof of interaction testifying that a transaction took place, while the client wishes to stay fully anonymous.

To deal with such opposite concerns, we propose to build a trusted and distributed third party through *share carriers*. At the beginning of each interaction the client and the service provider choose share carriers among the system's users so that no one controls a majority of them, even if some of the share carriers can be malicious. The role of share carriers is to obtain the identity of the service provider, prior to the vote, and disclose this identity after the vote if the service provider behaves incorrectly. The same process is used for the non-repudiation of interaction proofs. The choice of share carriers is done at the beginning of each interaction. This choice is jointly handled by both the client and the service provider that wish to engage into a given transaction. This prevents any collusions between a malicious client (or a malicious service provider) and a set of malicious share carriers. The choice of share carriers is the outcome of a nonce-based interactive protocol between the client and the service provider. To prevent some of the share carriers from disclosing any sensitive information (i.e. the identity of the provider, or the interaction proof), any information is shared using Verifiable Secret Sharing (VSS) [14]. A VSS is a (t, n)-threshold cryptographic scheme dividing a secret into n shares, such that any t shares allow any user to recompute the secret. On the other hand, less than t shares yields no information about it. Share carriers can also verify the consistency of all shares and the correctness of the secret, so that they cannot be bilked by neither the client nor the provider in the sharing process.

Impact Limitation. To guarantee the impact limitation property, we follow the strategy given by Bethencourt et al. [5] that allows to detect whether any two votes on a given service provider were cast by the same client. This detection is made through an indicator that fully characterizes a given couple (client, provider), independently of the client and provider pseudonyms. Such an indicator is called *invariant*. In Bethencourt et al.'s reputation mechanism, an invariant is somehow a positive vote, and a service provider proves his reputation score by proving that he obtained enough distinct invariants. In our construction, the invariant is used as an interaction proof, and appears in votes, to detect multiple votes from the same client for the same provider. Note that even if the invariant is unique for a given couple, it is impossible to compute the client's credential from the invariant and the service provider's credential. Furthermore, two providers cannot distinguish whether they have interacted with the same clients or not.

In our scheme, the invariant is computed during a three steps interaction. First, the provider masks his identity, and sends the result to the client. The client then computes a masked invariant, based on the masked identity of the provider and his own identity, and sends it to the provider. Finally, the provider removes the mask, and obtains the plain invariant.

5   Protocol of Interaction

In the previous section, we have presented the tools used to guarantee both the privacy of providers and clients (Props. 1 and 2), and the mechanism's correctness (Prop. 3). We now detail the interaction protocol between a client c and a service provider p, and describe how these tools are used. An interaction is made of four successive stages.

1. Service provider p proves his reputation to client c.
2. Both c and p choose the distributed third-party for the interaction.
3. Both c and p commit themselves to the interaction by sharing a secret.
4. Once the transaction is over, they both participate to update p's reputation; there are three variants of this stage:
   (a) both c and p are correct and help each other by respectively casting a vote and getting a proof of interaction
   (b) c is malicious and refuses to help p to get a proof of the interaction,
   (c) p is malicious and refuses to help c to rate him.

We assume that, at the beginning of each interaction, p receives a certificate on his credential and his reputation.

5.1   Proof of Reputation

To prove his reputation, p sends his pseudonym nym_p and his reputation rep_p to c and proves that he knows a certificate on his reputation thanks to a NIZK. Namely, p demonstrates that he knows

- cred_p such that nym_p was issued from cred_p, and
- cert_p certifying $\langle \text{cred}_p, \text{rep}_p \rangle$

Once c has checked the proof and if he is comfortable with the reputation score of p, then c engages an interaction with p. Note that all the proofs (i.e. reputations and computations) are done through NIZKs.

5.2   Choosing the Share Carriers

Both c and p need to choose the share carriers they will rely on throughout their interaction as presented in Section 4.2. The number n of chosen share carriers depends on two system parameters – the total number N of user, and the proportion m of malicious users – and on the maximal probability P of having a collusion among the share carriers, that is of having more than $n/2$ malicious share carriers. Table 1 shows n for multiple values of N and m, for $P = 2^{-80}$.

Table 1. Required number of share carriers to prevent collusions as a function of N (total number of share carriers) and m (percentage of malicious share carriers)

m \ N	100	500	1,000	5,000	10,000
5%	9	45	53	61	61
6%	11	51	59	69	69
7%	13	55	67	75	77
8%	15	61	73	83	85
9%	17	67	79	93	93
10%	19	73	87	101	103

To choose the share carriers, both c and p use a hash function H (e.g. SHA-256 [15]), with h-bits outputs, and proceed as follows.

1. c chooses a random nonce r_c and commits himself to r_c by sending $H(00 \parallel r_c)$ to p;
2. p chooses a random nonce r_p and sends it to c;
3. c sends r_c to p;

The share carriers are the $\left\{ \lfloor H(01 \parallel r_p \parallel r_c \parallel i) \times N/2^h \rfloor, i \in \{0, \ldots, n'-1\} \right\}$, where all users are labelled $0, \ldots, N-1$ and n' is set so that the set contains exactly n distinct share carriers.

5.3   Completion of a Transaction

Once both client c and service provider p have agreed on the set of share carriers, c must make sure that p will allow him to cast a vote whatever the issue of the transaction. Similarly p must be guaranteed that c will allow him to get a proof of interaction whatever the issue of the transaction. In both cases this is achieved by having c and p commit to secrets, which they share among the share carriers. From Sect. 4.2, computation of the invariant requires that both c and p be involved in an interaction, we use it as the proof of interaction between c and p. Thus, the secret of c is the masked invariant while the one of p is its credential cred_p. Hence, even if either c or p disconnect after the transaction, the other one will be able to reconstruct either p's identity for c

or the invariant, that is the proof of interaction, for p. Once computed, p sends his masked credential to c, c computes the masked invariant and both share their secret among the share carriers. Suppose that client c wants to split a secret $x \in \mathbb{Z}_k$ into n shares and allows its reconstruction with any t of them. Then, c randomly chooses $a_j \in \mathbb{Z}_k, j \in \{1, \ldots, t-1\}$, defines $a_0 = x$, and $q : z \mapsto \sum_{j=0}^{t-1} a_j z^j$. Client c sends the i-th share $q_i = q(i)$ to the i-th share carrier. Client c also computes commitments C_{a_j}, C_{q_i} to each a_j and q_i with a homomorphic commitment scheme (such as the SXDH commitments [11]). The main property of such commitments is that if C_{z_1}, C_{z_2} are commitments to $z_1, z_2 \in \mathbb{Z}$, then $C_{z_1} \cdot C_{z_2}^\lambda$ is a commitment to $z_1 + \lambda z_2$. For each share, c also computes two NIZKs: the first one is a proof that C_{q_i} is a commitment to q_i. The second one is a proof that all the share are consistent, i.e. a proof that $C_{q_i} \cdot \prod_{j=0}^{t-1}(C_{a_j})^{-(i^j)}$ is a commitment to 0; indeed, thanks to the homomorphic and commitment properties, this proof demonstrates that

$$q_i = \sum_{j=0}^{t-1} a_j \left(i^j \right) = q(i).$$

Once the secrets have been shared and verified, c and p can proceed with the transaction. Figure 1 illustrates the interactions described in Sect. 5.2 and 5.3.

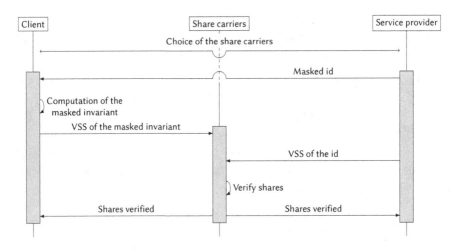

Fig. 1. Preparation phase of the transaction between a client and a service provider

5.4 Casting a Vote

Once both c and p have finished their transaction, the reputation of p can be updated thanks to c's vote (if any), or in the negative thanks to the proof of interaction. There are three different outcomes of the protocol according to both c and p behaviors, that is, depending on whether they are willing to give their secrets.

Suppose that both behave correctly. Then c simply gives his vote and the masked invariant to the share carriers, who transmit the masked invariant to p. Note that sending the masked invariant to the share carriers save them from recomputing it from their shares. Then, p reveals his credential to c and computes the invariant. Afterwards, the vote is cast on p and p's reputation is updated with c's vote.

Now assume that p refuses to reveal his credential. Then the share carriers give p's shares to c once c has cast his vote, allowing c to obtain p's identity. Thus, c is able to compute the invariant and to emit the vote.

Finally suppose that c refuses to give the masked invariant to p. Then whether c has given his vote to the share carriers or not, the share carriers give c's shares to p, which allows p to compute the invariant and obtain the proof of interaction. Figure 2 shows the vote emission when both c and p are correct.

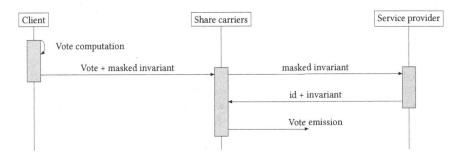

Fig. 2. Vote emission

6   Conclusion

In this article, we have presented a reputation mechanism addressing two main issues of reputation mechanisms: preserving all users' privacy *and* computing reputation scores based on both positive and negative ratings. There were already systems addressing those two issues, but, to our knowledge, none addressed both of them at the same time. We achieve this thanks to cryptographic schemes such as zero-knowledge proofs, verifiable secret sharing, and anonymous proxy signatures. Furthermore, our proposition is independent of the reputation model; that is, our system can integrate any reputation model [1,4], preferably one using both positive and negative ratings, and limiting the impact of a single client on a given provider.

Our proposal works in a distributed fashion: no trusted central authority is required for either the correctness or the users' privacy. However, this requires many certifications done by all the possible share carriers, which might be too expensive for a large-scale system. For future work, we intend to quantify those costs for an implementation. If they are too high, we will study to what extent a central authority could lower these costs while preserving the users' privacy.

References

1. Jøsang, A., Ismail, R.: The beta reputation system. In: Proceedings of the 15th Bled Electronic Commerce Conference, pp. 41–55 (2002)
2. Yu, B., Singh, M.P.: Distributed reputation management for electronic commerce. Computational Intelligence 18, 535–549 (2002)
3. Anceaume, E., Ravoaja, A.: Incentive-based robust reputation mechanism for p2p services. In: Shvartsman, M.M.A.A. (ed.) OPODIS 2006. LNCS, vol. 4305, pp. 305–319. Springer, Heidelberg (2006)
4. Anceaume, E., Guette, G., Lajoie-Mazenc, P., Prigent, N.: Viet Triem Tong, V.: A privacy preserving distributed reputation mechanism. In: Proceedings of the IEEE International Conference on Communications (ICC) (2013)
5. Bethencourt, J., Shi, E., Song, D.: Signatures of reputation. In: Sion, R. (ed.) FC 2010. LNCS, vol. 6052, pp. 400–407. Springer, Heidelberg (2010)
6. Steinbrecher, S.: Enhancing multilateral security in and by reputation systems. In: Matyáš, V., Fischer-Hübner, S., Cvrček, D., Švenda, P. (eds.) The Future of Identity. IFIP AICT, vol. 298, pp. 135–150. Springer, Heidelberg (2009)
7. Pfitzmann, A., Hansen, M.: A terminology for talking about privacy by data minimization, v0.34 (2010)
8. Androulaki, E., Choi, S.G., Bellovin, S.M., Malkin, T.: Reputation systems for anonymous networks. In: Borisov, N., Goldberg, I. (eds.) PETS 2008. LNCS, vol. 5134, pp. 202–218. Springer, Heidelberg (2008)
9. Resnick, P., Zeckhauser, R.: Trust among strangers in internet transactions: Empirical analysis of ebay's reputation system. Advances in Applied Microeconomics 11, 127–157 (2002)
10. Pavlov, E., Rosenschein, J.S., Topol, Z.: Supporting privacy in decentralized additive reputation systems. In: Jensen, C., Poslad, S., Dimitrakos, T. (eds.) iTrust 2004. LNCS, vol. 2995, pp. 108–119. Springer, Heidelberg (2004)
11. Groth, J., Sahai, A.: Efficient non-interactive proof systems for bilinear groups. In: Smart, N.P. (ed.) EUROCRYPT 2008. LNCS, vol. 4965, pp. 415–432. Springer, Heidelberg (2008)
12. Dingledine, R., Mathewson, N., Syverson, P.F.: Tor: The second-generation onion router. In: USENIX Security Symposium, pp. 303–320. USENIX (2004)
13. Fuchsbauer, G., Pointcheval, D.: Anonymous proxy signatures. In: Ostrovsky, R., De Prisco, R., Visconti, I. (eds.) SCN 2008. LNCS, vol. 5229, pp. 201–217. Springer, Heidelberg (2008)
14. Feldman, P.: A practical scheme for non-interactive verifiable secret sharing. In: FOCS, pp. 427–437. IEEE Computer Society (1987)
15. National Institute of Standards and Technology: Secure hash standard (SHS). Technical Report FIPS 180-4 (2011)

Preserving Privacy in Production

Moritz Christian Müller

Fraunhofer IAO
Competence Team Identity Management
Nobelstraße 12
70569 Stuttgart
Germany
moritz.cm@gmail.com

Abstract. In modern manufacturing environments, new technologies are introduced that bring machines, analytics and people closer together. As a consequence, a rise in productivity, flexibility and efficiency is expected. However, these technologies raise new privacy concerns as well. We look at AssiEff, a tool to reduce the energy consumption of production systems, analyse its privacy issues and requirements regarding authentication and propose two approaches in order to address these issues. The first approach is based on anonymous credentials; the second follows an organisational approach. Both approaches are evaluated in regards to security-, privacy- and economic-aspects. In the end, we draw the conclusion that although anonymous credentials fulfil all security and privacy requirements, the organisational approach is the more appropriate solution in most scenarios. Costs are low and the privacy of the employees is protected sufficiently.

Keywords: Authentication, Anonymous Credentials, Industrie 4.0, Privacy.

1   Introduction

The rising trend of the Industrial Internet[1] and Industrie 4.0[2] is promising among others to bring machines, analytics and people closer together in manufacturing environments. This is achieved by connecting machines with sensors and software applications, by connecting people, for example with the help of mobile devices like tablet computers and by connecting both through advanced analytics. Thereby people get a better insight in the production process, are able to react faster to changing requirements and are able to communicate with co-workers, suppliers and customers more efficient. A rise in productivity, flexibility and efficiency is expected [1].

Several research projects have the goal to increase flexibility or to increase the energy efficiency in production [2].

Among those is the project AssiEff, which is focusing on the energy consumption of production systems in small and medium enterprises (SME). A study by [3] is

---

[1] www.ge.com/mindsandmachines
[2] www.bmbf.de/de/19955.php

M. Hansen et al. (Eds.): Privacy and Identity 2014, IFIP AICT 421, pp. 177–187, 2014.

stating that energy consumption in production can still be decreased up to 50 %. AssiEff is analysing especially components of production systems. A back-end service is automatically looking at the utilization of each component and is checking if the component still fits the needs of the production process. By turning components off or by exchanging them with components which are more efficient, energy and therefore money can be saved. The operators of the production systems, who are responsible for the production system on the shop floor get notified about ways to reduce the energy consumption on a tablet-computer and are able to act based on this information. For example, a recommendation can be sent out to turn off a component for the next hour. A machine operator has the possibility to follow this recommendation, which is then confirmed to the AssiEff back-end services [4].

Most applications, which are developed as part of the *Industrial Internet* and *Industrie 4.0*, have in common that they gather a lot of data about machines but also about people, who are interacting with them. With the help of this data, detailed profiles of each employee could be created. This raises privacy concerns. In the last years, several incidents made the news, where employees unduly have been recorded by hidden video cameras or their behaviour has been monitored [5,6]. Industrie 4.0 technologies could increase the range of surveillance further.

Although some of these measurements might be legal, they can affect the relationship between the employee and the employer. Studies have shown that some employees, who are monitored by their employer may feel that "they are denied the self-respect that comes with being trusted to do their jobs correctly on their own" [7].

For these developments to be successful, it is necessary to bare these privacy concerns in mind and to develop solutions that respect their concerns and provide privacy by design [8]. In case of the basic AssiEff-architecture, an employer has the possibility to examine which employee has followed how many recommendations and could use this data, to track the employees' behaviour, compare and rank them. It is very likely, that this functionality is not embraced by the employees and the staff council. Therefore, we want to look at solutions, which address with these concerns, fit into the existing AssiEff architecture and still provide the necessary security. The final version of AssiEff should then make use of the recommended solution.

In this research, we discuss the requirements of AssiEff from the view of an employee but also from the view of an employer, describe how the current authentication architecture is designed and how it could be extended in order to fulfil the requirements. Then we want to evaluate an approach, based on anonymous authentication and an approach which is based on pseudonym authentication. The proposed architectures are evaluated and compared by security, privacy and socio-economic standards. At the end of the research, we will recommend an approach, based on the evaluation and give a short summary.

2   Methodology

The introduced relevant privacy and security concerns for assistant systems in manufacturing are addressed by providing two IT artefacts. These two artefacts are developed and evaluated based on the Design Science approach as proposed by Hevner et al. [9]. The first artefact includes a novel authentication system based on anonymous credentials (ACs); the second includes an authentication system, following an organization approach. The technical principles, on which these approaches based, have been proven to fulfil high privacy and security requirements. The feasibility of these approaches is rigorously evaluated within the given environment. The environment includes the different stakeholders of the AssiEff system, processes within the system and the infrastructure. Business needs are derived from this environment. A knowledge base provides existing frameworks and techniques which will be applied on the development of the artefacts. From this knowledge base the requirements are derived as well. Furthermore, the business needs and the knowledge base are the foundation for the evaluation of these artefacts.

3   Related Work

We base our work on several studies discussing the effects of employee monitoring [10,7,11]. Similar to [12], we look at privacy issues in manufacturing environments, but contrary to this paper, we are examining the effects of monitoring the general behaviour of employees and how to minimize them. The environment we describe has been developed and introduced by [4].

One way to protect privacy of employees are ACs. The basic technique behind ACs was introduced by [13] and [14]. For evaluation, the acceptance of such a solution, the barriers, benefits and costs play an important role. These issues have already been discussed in [15] and [16].

4   Basic Architecture

The basic architecture of AssiEff includes two components: The AssiEff mobile application, which runs on a tablet-computer and the AssiEff-Server. The AssiEff server analyses production systems and production schedules and is looking for ways to reduce energy. If ways have been identified, it generates a recommendation, which notifies the user, how energy can be saved. On shop floor level, every employee is carrying a tablet-computer, which receives these recommendations.

Based on the username, employees can be identified at any time and any action can be linked. Also every user is a member of a role, which limits their actions in the AssiEff service. All user accounts are managed by the AssiEff-Server.

At the beginning of a work day, employees receive tablet-computers on which they sign in with their username and password. The AssiEff server verifies their accounts and grants them access to the AssiEff app, depending on the role they are assigned to. To keep users accountable for the tablet computer, the server also takes note, which tablet the employee is currently using. When they receive a recommendation on their tablet, they are able to follow the recommendation and confirm this action to the server. In the basic architecture, the server logs, which recommendation has been followed or declined by the user.

The following figure shows the structure of the current AssiEff architecture.

Fig. 1. Basic AssiEff architecture

5   Requirements

5.1   Basic Requirements

To restrict access to critical information and parameters, a role based user model is introduced, which allows the administrator of the system to define which kind of user has access to what kind of information [17]. Therefore, an authentication system must verify the users' role, when they want to sign in to the system [17].

Also, it must be possible to hold employees accountable for their actions. Thus employees have to log in to the authentication service with a unique identification.

These are the basic requirements of the AssiEff authentication system regarding authentication, authorization and accountability. They are already fulfilled by the existing AssiEff architecture. Also, it must be possible to hold employees accountable for their actions. Thus employees have to log in to the authentication service with a unique identification.

5.2   Extended Requirements

Additionally, not only security but also privacy and usability issues have to be addressed.

In AssiEff, employers could track how many recommendations an employee has followed. This data could influence decisions of personnel administration and may have negative effects for the employee. As stated earlier, it is very likely that this functionality is not embraced by the employees and may even be prohibited by the work council or labour courts. A closer analysis of this topic by legal experts is desirable but is not part of this paper. Therefore, solutions have to be found, which respect the privacy of the employees, but also guarantee secure authentication.

Furthermore, one has to bear in mind that AssiEff is focusing on small and medium enterprises (SME) with only a small number of manufacturing systems. Such enterprises may not have the money or expertise to set up and maintain elaborate IT-infrastructures. First unpublished measurements have shown that AssiEff might reduce the energy consumption of productions systems up to 40%. As an example, such a system might consist out of five small robots with a payload of 15kg. Each robot may consume 1.3kW energy on average and is run daily for 8 hours, 350 days per year [18]. In total all robots run 14,000 hours per year. This makes an energy consumption of 18,200 kWh. The energy costs for one kWh in typical companies in Germany are around 12 cent/kWh [19]. As a consequence the energy costs for these five robots are about €2184.00 for one year. Assuming, that the energy costs of these components can be reduced by 40% with the help of AssiEff, the energy costs can be reduced by €873.60.

Thus, the costs for expanding the basic architecture in order to achieve the aforementioned requirements must not exceed the amount of money, which can be saved with AssiEff.

Below, the requirements of the system are summarised.

- **Secure authentication:** Only valid users must be allowed to access the system.
- **Authorization:** Access-restrictions for specific areas must be possible.
- **Privacy protection:** Employer must not be able to trace the behaviour of its staff.
- **Accountability:** Administration must be able to hold users accountable for their actions with their tablet computer.
- **Economic aspects:** The cost for setting up and maintaining the authentication and authorization system should not exceed the amount of money that can be saved by AssiEff.

6   Extended Architecture

In order to fulfil the requirements, we want to propose and discuss two different approaches.

6.1   Anonymity

The first approach is based on ACs as first introduced by [20] and refined by [13].

ACs are based on the idea that a user can obtain a credential and then proves the possession of this credential to an organisation. The organisation does only know that the user possesses such a credential but does not know the identity of the user. Even if a user wants to demonstrate the possession of such a credential several times, the demonstrations cannot be linked.

The architecture of ACs consists out of three basic entities.

- **The User**, who wants to prove to an organisation, that she owns a certain attribute.
- **The Verifier**, which wants a proof from the user, that she owns a certain attribute.
- **The Issuer**, which can certify that the user owns a certain attribute.

Applying ACs to AssiEff, the user, which is in case of AssiEff the employee, wants to prove to the Verifier, which is in case of AssiEff the AssiEff-Server that she is a designated member of a certain role. This proof is provided by the Issuer, where the User has authenticated herself earlier. The verifier only knows that the user is a designated member of the role, but does not know who the user is. As a consequence, the user cannot be linked to her actions.

The following figure show, how such an infrastructure could look like.

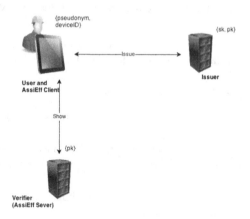

Fig. 2. AssiEff architecture with anonymous credentials

There are different entities who could act as an issuer. On the one hand the issuer can be hosted within the enterprise IT-infrastructure. There, the enterprise has full control over issued credentials and their revocation. On the other hand, third parties could also act as an issuer. For example, governments could support ACs and could issue credentials for their eIDs or eIDs could even implement an AC infrastructure itself as proposed by [21].

To hold users accountable in case of loss or damage of the tablet computer, the Issuer additionally has a table, where the device ID, the name of the user and the current date is stored. At the beginning of the work day, the user confirms to the Issuer, which device she has taken.

6.2   Pseudonymity

The second approach follows an organisational solution instead of a technical solution. Instead of full anonymity, it only provides pseudonymity for its users. In comparison to the first approach, transactions could still be linked to a unique user in case the real identity behind a pseudonym is being revealed.

Pseudonymity is achieved by separating authentication from the actual AssiEff server to an additional Authentication Server. There, the real name is mapped to a pseudonym. This Authentication Server is under control of an entity, which is trusted by the employees. The entity is the only instance, which has insight into the mapping of real-name to pseudonym and should not reveal this information to the employer.

Figure 3 shows the AssiEff architecture based on the pseudonym approach.

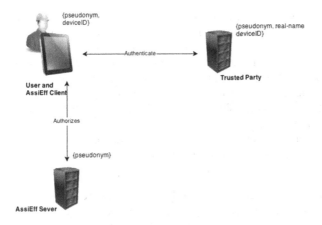

Fig. 3. AssiEff architecture based on pseudonym approach

At the beginning of a workday, users take a tablet computer and initiate the authentication process by using their user-name and password. The Trusted Party verifies the credentials. In case that the authentication was successful, the trusted-party sends a token with the pseudonym to the AssiEff client. It proves to the AssiEff server that the user is a designated member of a certain role. The client forwards this token to the AssiEff server which authorizes the user. The token does not include any information about the real identity of the user but a pseudonym. Only the Trusted Party knows the real identity of the user.

In order to prevent that the token can be forged, it must be encrypted with a pre-shared key. Thereby the use of an expensive PKI is avoided. Access to the authentication server must only be granted to the Trusted Party.

The role of the Trusted Party could be taken by the work council. Usually the work council is elected by the work force and enjoys the trust of the employees. The trust may vary from company to company and has to be built up over years [22].

7   Evaluation

Now it is examined, if the approaches fulfil the requirements for a secure authentication, support the described role-model and if they can be implemented within the limitations of the basic AssiEff architecture, in order to restrict access to the AssiEff services properly.

Second, it has to be evaluated, how the solutions fulfil the privacy concerns.

Because AssiEff is focusing on small and medium enterprises, the costs for planning, setting up and maintaining these authentication services play a crucial role and are being evaluated as well.

7.1   Evaluating Anonymous Approach

Security. First of all, the discussed solutions have to fulfil all requirements regarding a secure authentication of users at the AssiEff assistant as listed in 5.1.

The AssiEff back-end is based on Java and therefore an anonymous authentication implemented in Java is preferred. [14] proposes such an authentication framework called idemix. It provides all protocols, which are necessary to implement ACs in AssiEff. It has been proven that ACs are secure and therefore fulfil the requirement as mentioned earlier in 5.1. The required role model can be implemented seamlessly. The Issuer provides tokens to users, which proves that they are member of a certain role. Then, this token is being shown to the Verifier. The Verifies checks if the token is signed by the Issuer.

Because ACs are relying on a PKI, IT-administration have to guarantee, that the underlying public keys are distributed and the private keys are stored in a secure manner.

Privacy. Authentication based on ACs fulfils high standards of privacy and anonymity. Even if Verifier and Issuer are residing within the same organisation or pooling their data, as it is most likely the case in AssiEff, unlinkability between the provided credential and the real name is still guaranteed [14]. Even two successful logins, which were initiated by the same user, cannot be linked.

To make sure that anonymity of the users is fully guaranteed, the underlying communication channels must support anonymity [14].

It has to be taken in mind that AssiEff might be used by companies with only a small number of employees. Therefore it might be the case that only a few people are assigned to a certain role. By comparing shift schedules or attendance lists with the log of the Verifier, conclusions about the identity of the user could be drawn and unlinkability is not guaranteed anymore.

Pseudonyms can be implemented with ACs as well, if it is of interest of the company.

Economic. The focus of AssiEff on SMEs requires that the costs and efforts for applying an anonymous authentication system should be as low as possible.

However, the PKI which is necessary for ACs is costly. Costs for such an infrastructure include IT staff time, hardware, security measurements and facility [23]. [24] estimates the costs for an in-house PKI at \$157 (~€120[3]) per user and year. Although this estimation was made for 5000 users, similar costs for SMEs are expected. Thus a PKI environment with 10 users would cost €1200 per year. In comparison to the example as described in 5.2, this would exceed the costs by €326.40. This could put the willingness of the company at risk, to include AssiEff in their infrastructure. The costs can vary depending on the available hard- and software. Also a PKI might be used for other purposes, for example E-Mail signatures or log in for ordinary workstation computers. This reduces the total cost of ownership.

Besides the direct costs, there might be indirect costs caused by ACs as well. Issuing, showing and verifying credentials takes time. Measurements conducted with a prototype of idemix demonstrated that showing an AC can take up to 8.2 seconds [14]. The AssiEff client is running on low-powered tablet computers which are not designed for complex computations. This slows down the login process significantly and might lead to frustrated users. It is important that the acceptance is not reduced by bad usability.

---

[3] As at May 10, 2013.

7.2   Evaluating Organisational Approach

Security. The organisational approach relies on basic and approved security mechanisms. The authentication process can be secured with adequate cryptographic mechanisms without implementing sophisticated authentication mechanisms. The authentication server and the underlying communication channel must be properly secured. The required role model can be easily implemented.

Privacy. The achieved level of privacy depends on the Trusted Party. If it is assumed that the Trusted Party holds any information about the identity of the user confidential, then the employer is not able to track their behaviour. A work council could take over the role as a Trusted Party. However, 57.2% of all medium sized enterprises in Germany do not have a work council [25]. In these cases, it might be hard to find an entity, which is trusted enough by the employees. Also, as mentioned in 6.2, trust between the work-council and the work force depends on several influences and may vary from company to company.

Economic. The costs for this approach are relatively low. Besides an additional server for a Trusted Party, no additional hardware is necessary. It only must be guaranteed, that the server is protected from unauthorized access. Also it can be assumed that even untrained IT-personnel is able to set up and maintain such an infrastructure.

Even though the direct costs might be relatively low, this approach might cause indirect costs. These may occur due to an informational asymmetry between the employees and the Trusted Party. Because of the design of the organisational approach, employees cannot verify if the Trusted Party fulfils its task and holds the information confidential. Based on the Principal-Agent-Theory, the employee takes over the role of the principal and the Trusted Party takes the role of the agent.

In order to balance the informational asymmetry between principal and agent, the agent should take actions that make the principal easier to verify, if their information is handled with care. Actions may include the evaluation of the infrastructure by a third party, setting up logging mechanisms to track who accessed the server of the Trusted Party, or introducing harsh punishments if the trust between the user and the Trusted Party has been abused. These actions may cause agency costs and will raise the total costs of such an approach.

8   Discussion

Based on the evaluation in section 7, it has been shown that although ACs provide the best protection of the employees' privacy, the costs for implementing such an infrastructure exceed the cost saved by AssiEff by far. Thereby the main reason to use AssiEff is at risk and it will be hard to justify the implementation. This solution only makes sense, if an authentication system based on ACs is already available or companies are driven by ideological reasons.

Also, as described in [16], legal requirements might enforce a more strict protection of the employees' privacy which could be a reason for choosing this approach.

In most cases, the organisational approach is the more appropriate solution because costs are low and the employees' privacy is protected in a sufficiently manner.

9   Conclusion

In this paper, we have introduced the privacy challenges in the upcoming trend of highly interconnected machines, analytics-software and people. As an example, we have chosen AssiEff, an assistant to reduce the energy consumption of production systems. We have looked at its security requirements, privacy concerns and its basic architecture.

An anonymous authentication system, based on ACs and a pseudonym authentication system was proposed to address these issues. Both solutions have been evaluated based on security, privacy and economic aspects.

The anonymous approach guarantees full privacy of employee whereas the organisational approach can only provide pseudonymity. The main difference between these solutions is the costs of implementation. The anonymous approach relies on a PKI, which causes more costs than the organisational approach. We have come to the conclusion that addressing the privacy concerns is essential for the success of systems like AssiEff. The user's privacy is not protected in the basic architecture thus both solutions improve the privacy. Which solution will be chosen depends on several factors including the size of the company, the individual costs for the solution and the willingness of the company to protect the privacy of their employees. In our opinion the organisational approach is the more adequate solution for most companies.

References

1. Evans, P.C., Annunziata, M.: Industrial Internet: Pushing the Boundaries of Minds and Machines (November 26, 2012)
2. Gerlach, S.: »KAPAFLEXCY« Für die Industrie 4.0, IAO-News, no. Dezember 2012 / Januar 2013, p. 3 (2012)
3. Schmid, C.: Energieeffizienz in Unternehmen. vdf Hochschulverlag AG, Zürich (2004)
4. Laufs, U., Schneider, P., Zibuschka, J.: Design of a system for energy-efficient production in SMEs. In: ICPR 2011 - Conference Proceedings (2011)
5. Wilke, T.: Apple gewinnt Big Brother Award 2013 für, besonders dreiste Form von Videoüberwachung, GIZMODO (April 14, 2013)
6. Ziegler, P.-M.: Datenschutzverletzungen: Lidl fällt als Wiederholungstäter auf, heise online (March 26, 2008)
7. Ariss, S.S.: Computer monitoring: benefits and pitfalls facing management. Information and Management (2001)
8. Cavoukian, A.: Privacy by Design ...Take the Challenge. Information and Privacy Commissioner Ontario Canada (2009)
9. Hevner, A.R., March, S.T., Park, J., Ram, S.: Design Science in Information System Research. MIS Quarterly 28(1), 75–105 (2004)

10. Lasprogata, G., King, N.J., Pillay, S.: Regulation of Electronig Employee Monitoring: Identifying Fundamental Principles of Employee Privacy through a Comparative Study of Data Privacy Legislation in the European Union, United States and Canada, Standford Technology Law Review, vol. 4 (2004)
11. Alder, G.S., Noel, T.W., Ambrose, M.L.: Clarifying the effects of Internet monitoring on job attitudes: The mediating role of employee trust. Information and Management (2006)
12. Lucke, D., Westkämper, E., Eissele, M., Ertl., T., Siemoneit, O.: Privacy-Preserving Self-Localization Techniques in Next Generation Manufacturing. presented at the 10th Intl. Conf. on Control, Automation, Robotics and Vision, Hanoi, Vietnam (2008)
13. Camenisch, J., Lysyanskaya, A.: An Efficient System for Non-transferable Anonymous Credentials with Optional Anonymity Revocation (2001)
14. Camenisch, J., Herreweghen, E.V.: Design and Implementation of the idemix Anonymous Credential System. presented at the CCS, Washington, DC, USA (2002)
15. Roßnagel, H., Zibuschka, J., Hinz, O., Muntermann, J.: Users' Willingness to Pay for Web Identity Management Systems. European Journal of Information Systems (2014)
16. The European Commission, Ed., Study on the economic benefits of privacy - enhancing technologies (PETs) (July 2010)
17. Laufs, U., Zibuschka, J., Schneider, P.: Decision support for energy efficient produciton in SME, Mobility in a globalised world, pp. 135–144. University of Bamberg Press (2012)
18. Poonyapak, P., McDill, J.M.J., Hayes, M.J.D.: Improving Robot Efficiency to Reduce Energy Consumption (2007)
19. Bolay, S., Grajetzky, C., Hüwels, H., Andrea, K., Lechner, S.: Faktenpapier Strompreise in Deutschland (2012)
20. Chaum, D.: Security without identication: Transaction systems to make big brother obsolete. Communications of the ACM 28(10), 1030–1044 (1985)
21. Bichsel, P., Camenisch, J., Groß, T., Shoup, V.: Anonymous credentials on a standard java card. In: Proceedings of the 16th ACM Conference on Computer and Communications Security, Chicago, IL, USA, pp. 600–610 (2009)
22. Rami, U., Hunger, A.: Vertrauen als Legimitation für die Betriebsarbeit, Industrielle Beziehung, no. Jahrgang 18, Heft 3, 167–189 (2011)
23. Carayannis, E.G., Turner, E.: Innovation diffusion and technology acceptance: The case of PKI technology, vol. technovation (2005)
24. VeriSgin, Ed., White Paper: Total Costs of Ownership for Public Key Infrastructure (2005)
25. Hans-Böckler-Stiftung, Ed., Betriebsräte in mittelständischen Unternehmen weithin akzeptiert, Böcklerimpuls, no. 16/2007 (2007)

User Search with Knowledge Thresholds in Decentralized Online Social Networks

Benjamin Greschbach, Gunnar Kreitz, and Sonja Buchegger

KTH Royal Institute of Technology
School of Computer Science and Communication
Stockholm, Sweden
{bgre,gkreitz,buc}@csc.kth.se

Abstract. User search is one fundamental functionality of an Online Social Network (OSN). When building privacy-preserving Decentralized Online Social Networks (DOSNs), the challenge of protecting user data and making users findable at the same time has to be met. We propose a user-defined knowledge threshold ("find me if you know enough about me") to balance the two requirements. We present and discuss protocols for this purpose that do not make use of any centralized component. An evaluation using real world data suggests that there is a promising compromise with good user performance and high adversary costs.

Keywords: Decentralized Online Social Networks, Privacy, User Search.

1 Introduction

Popular Online Social Networks (OSNs) are logically centralized systems. The massive information aggregation at the central provider inherently threatens user-privacy. Data leakages, whether intentional (e. g., selling of user data to third parties) or unintentional (e. g., by attacks from outsiders), happen regularly[1]. Motivated by this insight, Decentralized Online Social Networks (DOSNs) have been proposed to mitigate the threats. When decentralizing a system, two challenges have to be met: to implement equal functionality without centralized components, and to provide user privacy under a significantly different threat model.

Here, we look at the functionality of user search, i. e., the lookup of a system-specific user identifier (e. g., a URI of a profile) based on information about the user (e. g., name, city, affiliation). The ability to search for users, in conjunction with other ways of traversing the social graph (e. g., friendlist of friends), is a basic building block of an OSN that allows users to find each other and thereby establish links.

---

[1] To name only two examples: Twitter leaking data from 250K users in February 2013 (http://blog.twitter.com/2013/02/keeping-our-users-secure.html), Facebook selling user data
(http://www.telegraph.co.uk/technology/facebook/8917836/
Facebook-faces-EU-curbs-on-selling-users-interests-to-advertisers.html).

M. Hansen et al. (Eds.): Privacy and Identity 2014, IFIP AICT 421, pp. 188–202, 2014.
© IFIP International Federation for Information Processing 2014

1.1   Our Contribution

We propose and evaluate protocols to support user search in a decentralized OSN that shield user data from parties who know less than a user-specified threshold amount of information about the target. To our knowledge, formalizing the use of this consideration is a novel application of knowledge-based access control. This type of restriction was inspired by an observation by Fong et al. [7] that being able to reach a user in an OSN is an integral part of access control in such systems.

We evaluate our protocols using real world data from the U.S. census to relate the performance for legitimate users to the costs of an adversary attempting to guess unknown information.

1.2   Related Work

To the best of our knowledge the privacy-findability tradeoff has not been formally investigated in this context. The closest example is user search in Skype. However, as far as we know, their protocol has not been described in detail, but only via external measurement studies, such as one by Baset and Schulzrinne [2].

Most user search functionalities, including ours, search for users within the global user database of the OSN, independently of who searches. In contrast, we note that recently, Facebook has debuted Graph search [5], which ties searching to the social graph, and where the goal is not only to find users, but also content. Several other approaches of personalized searching for content in an OSN have also be discussed, e. g., by Bai et al. [1] in a decentralized setting.

Although designed specifically to search for users in a DOSN, some challenges are shared with constructing a general purpose search in a peer-to-peer (P2P) setting. This has been studied by e. g., Li et al. [8], and Bender et al. [3]. There is also a commercial search engine using P2P, Faroo [6]. Two differences are our focus on access control and privacy, and the significantly smaller amount of information to be indexed in our setting. Similar to these proposals, we also build upon a Distributed Hash Table (DHT) as a core component to realize our functionality.

2   Decentralized User Search Protocol

As we design search protocols for a decentralized system, we cannot assume any trusted third party or central search provider to be available. Instead, we use a DHT to register and look up search terms, as it is a common component of DOSNs. As the DHT runs on nodes participating in the system, we must also protect the privacy of the participants against these nodes.

We propose two protocols, both designed to index and retrieve information in a DHT in a protected way. Our protocols provide two operations. A *register* operation, where users enter information that allows others to find them based on certain attributes, and a *search* operation that, given a set of search terms,

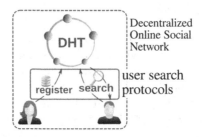

Fig. 1. System overview: The search protocols are one component of the DOSN and makes use of a DHT

returns the set of matching user identifiers. In a next step, out of the scope of the search protocols described here, these user identifiers can be used to view public profiles, and to send a message or friend request to the found user. Figure 1 illustrates the search functionality.

2.1 Protocol Specification

We consider a searcher, who wants to find a searchee. The searchee registers searchable information about herself in the DHT by choosing a number n of attribute labels l_i (e. g., lastname, firstname, city) and assigning each one[2] value v_i. This label-value pair (denoted as attribute a_i) is mapped to a user identifier uid of the searchee. Upon registration the searchee specifies a threshold number t of attributes which the searcher must know in order to obtain the user identifier.

2.2 Storing Values in the DHT

The DHT holds a mapping from user attributes to user identifiers, but this mapping must be protected, also against the nodes in the DHT. To this end, we propose a protocol that alters how values are added and retrieved from the DHT. The required property is to retain standard DHT functionality, while nodes in the DHT do not learn plaintexts of keys or values.

When storing a *key-value* pair the *key* is fed into a Key Derivation Function (KDF) together with a global salt *gSalt*, yielding the DHT-key for the put and get operations of the DHT. The *value* is encrypted using a secret that is derived from a random salt *salt* and the *key* (the attribute information, in our case). The *salt* is stored together with the ciphertext on the right hand side of the mapping. In short, the mapping of a *key-value* pair in the DHT looks like this:

$$\mathrm{KDF}(gSalt, key) \mapsto salt \| \mathrm{encrypt}_{\mathrm{KDF}(salt, key)}(value)$$

The *gSalt* has to be publicly available for all users to allow the lookup of any attributes. This invalidates the purpose of a salt, as pre-computing tables

---

[2] For simplicity we assume that each attribute can be assigned only exactly one value.

to reverse the left hand side becomes possible again. Nevertheless, we suggest to keep the *gSalt* as it at least requires the pre-computation attack to be targeted to each specific instance of our system and off-the-shelf pre-computed tables for the used KDF cannot be employed.

The *salt* is an individual random number different for every entry. Note that it in particular has to be different from *gSalt* as otherwise any DHT node could decrypt the *value* of items it stores, using the left hand side (without knowing the *key*).

2.3   Scheme 1: Storing All Allowed Attribute Combinations

We want a searcher to prove knowledge of a threshold number of attributes before obtaining the user identifier. One direct approach to achieve this is to map the user identifier only from attribute concatenations of the threshold length. If the searchee registered e. g., seven attributes and specified that at least four of them are necessary to find her *uid*, we would store the following $\binom{7}{4} = 35$ combinations:

$a_1||a_2||a_3||a_4 \mapsto uid$
$a_1||a_2||a_3||a_5 \mapsto uid$
...
$a_4||a_5||a_6||a_7 \mapsto uid$

where $a_i = (u_i, v_i)$, u_i attribute labels and v_i attribute values. We assume there is a canonical order of attributes (e. g., a lexicographic order of labels), and attributes are sorted by this order before concatenation.

Algorithm 1. Registration (Scheme 1)

1: $l_1, \ldots, l_n \leftarrow$ User.input("Choose searchable attribute labels (e. g., name,city,...)")
2: $v_1, \ldots, v_n \leftarrow$ User.input("Enter values (your name, your city,...)")
3: $a_i \leftarrow l_i||v_i$ // for $i = 1 \ldots n$
4: $t \leftarrow$ User.input("Enter threshold number of attributes necessary to find you.")
5: **for** all ordered sequences $a_p|| \ldots ||a_q$ of length t **do**
6:      $key \leftarrow a_p|| \ldots ||a_q$
7:      $dhtkey \leftarrow \text{KDF}(gSalt,key)$
8:      $salt \leftarrow \text{generateSalt}()$
9:      $value \leftarrow uid$
10:     $dhtvalue \leftarrow salt|| \text{encrypt}_{\text{KDF}(salt,key)}(value)$
11:     DHT.put($dhtkey,dhtvalue$)
12: **end for**

Algorithms 1 and 2 describe the protocol in more detail. For registration, all attribute combinations of length t are mapped to the user identifier and stored in the DHT according to the procedure described in Section 2.2. When searching, all provided search attributes are ordered and used to query the DHT (after the Section 2.2 transformation). If the result is empty or does not contain what the user was looking for, all subsets of the provided search attributes are subsequently tried, ordered by decreasing number of elements. The final result will contain the user identifier of the searchee (and possibly more hits from other users that registered the same attributes) if the number of attributes searched for is greater or equal than the threshold specified by the searchee.

Algorithm 2. Search (Scheme 1)

1: $l_1, \ldots, l_s \leftarrow$ User.input("Choose attribute labels to search for (e. g., name,city,...)")
2: $v_1, \ldots, v_s \leftarrow$ User.input("Enter attribute values (a name, a city,...)")
3: $a_i \leftarrow l_i || v_i$ // for $i = 1 \ldots s$
4: **for** $i \leftarrow s, \ldots, 1$ **do** // while result set is empty or the user requests more results
5:     **for** all ordered sequences $a_p || \ldots || a_q$ of length i **do**
6:         $key \leftarrow a_p || \ldots || a_q$
7:         $dhtkey \leftarrow$ KDF($gSalt,key$)
8:         **for** $salt, ciphertext$ in DHT.get($dhtkey$) **do**
9:             $uid \leftarrow$ decrypt$_{\text{KDF}(salt,key)}(ciphertext)$
10:             add uid to result set if decryption was successful
11:         **end for**
12:     **end for**
13: **end for**

One shortcoming of this scheme is that for sufficiently large numbers of n and t, the number of combinations might become infeasible for storage space constraints and KDF computation latencies during registration. Requiring e. g., 5 out of 20 registered attributes would yield 15504 combinations.

2.4   Scheme 2: Storing Each Attribute Individually

An alternative approach, overcoming the large number of combinations generated by Scheme 1, is to store each attribute individually. In order to require a threshold number of attributes to find the user identifier, a single attribute does not map directly to the uid but to an encrypted version. The key used for the encryption is based on a secret sharing scheme and one share is stored with each of the attributes. Instead of using the shared key directly, it is fed into a KDF together with an individual salt. This indirection allows us to independently tune the costs for requesting shares for one attribute (determined by the DHT latency and the KDF described in Section 2.2) and for trying to combine them (determined by the KDF used here). Furthermore, a bloom filter bf_i is attached to each share, to help finding the right shares to combine with, which is important for popular attributes with large response sets:

$a_1 \mapsto share_1 || bf_1 || salt_1 ||$ encrypt$_{\text{KDF}(salt_1,sk)}$(uid)

...

$a_n \mapsto share_n || bf_n || salt_n ||$ encrypt$_{\text{KDF}(salt_n,sk)}$(uid)

where sk can be recovered with t of the shares $share_1 \ldots share_n$.

The bloom filter that is stored with each share is created using all other $n-1$ shares belonging to the same key sk. To avoid the case in which two bloom filters for a related set of shares look similar, we introduce an individual salt for each bloom filter, which is used to modify elements before insertion. Thus, with each bloom filter bf_i, we store a salt $bfsalt_i$, and when adding or querying for an element (a share in our case) in bloom filter bf_i, we first hash the element together with the $bfsalt_i$. E. g. instead of $bf_i.\mathtt{add}(share)$, we do $bf_i.\mathtt{add}(\mathtt{hash}(bfsalt_i, share))$, where $\mathtt{hash}()$ is a cryptographically strong keyed hash function.

Algorithms 3 to 6 describe the protocol in more detail. When combining the shares in the search protocol, the bloom filter information is used to reduce the number of possible combinations. Note that for two sets of shares (and attached bloom filters) two reductions are possible: First a share in set one is fixed and its bloom filter is used to reduce set two. Then, for all remaining shares in set two, their bloom filters can be used to determine if they fit to the fixed share of set one. If not, they are removed from set two as well. This generalizes; for n sets, in expectancy the number of matches will be reduced by a factor of $\exp(bloomfactor, \sum_{i \in 1...n} 2(i-1))$, where $bloomfactor$ is the false positive probability of the bloom filter.

Algorithm 3. Registration (Scheme 2)

1: $l_1, \ldots, l_n \leftarrow$ User.input("Choose searchable attribute labels (e. g., name,city,...)")
2: $v_1, \ldots, v_n \leftarrow$ User.input("Enter values (your name, your city,...)")
3: $a_i \leftarrow l_i \| v_i$ // for $i = 1 \ldots n$
4: $t \leftarrow$ User.input("Enter minimum number of attributes necessary to find you.")
5: $sk \leftarrow$ generateKey()
6: $share_1, ..., share_n \leftarrow$ createShares(t,n,sk)
7: **for** $i \leftarrow 1, \ldots, n$ **do**
8:     $key \leftarrow a_i$
9:     $dhtkey \leftarrow$ KDF(gSalt,key)
10:    $bf \leftarrow$ createBloomFilter($\{share_j | j \neq i\}$) // using salted bloom filter (see text)
11:    $salt \leftarrow$ generateSalt()
12:    $k_E, k_S \leftarrow$ KDF($salt$,sk)   // derive keys to encrypt and sign
13:    $ciphertext \leftarrow$ encrypt$_{k_E}$(uid)
14:    $value \leftarrow share_i \| bf \| salt \| ciphertext \| \mathrm{MAC}_{k_S}(ciphertext)$
15:    $dhtsalt \leftarrow$ generateSalt()
16:    $dhtvalue \leftarrow dhtsalt \|$ encrypt$_{\mathrm{KDF}(dhtsalt,key)}$(value)
17:    DHT.put(dhtkey,dhtvalue)
18: **end for**

2.5 Extensions

Weighting of attributes. Some attributes might be easier to guess for an attacker than others because they have a lower entropy or represent more public information that is easy to research from system external sources. We therefore want

---

Algorithm 4. Search (Scheme 2)

1: $l_1, \ldots, l_s \leftarrow$ User.input("Choose attribute labels to search for (e. g., name,city,...)")
2: $v_1, \ldots, v_s \leftarrow$ User.input("Enter attribute values (a name, a city,...)")
3: $a_i \leftarrow l_i \| v_i$ // for $i = 1 \ldots s$
4: $setOfShareSets \leftarrow \emptyset$
5: **for** $i \leftarrow 1, \ldots, s$ **do**
6:     $key \leftarrow a_i$
7:     $dhtkey \leftarrow$ KDF(gSalt, key)
8:     $shareSet \leftarrow \emptyset$
9:     **for each** $(dhtSalt, dhtCiphertext) \in$ DHT.get(dhtkey) **do**   // > 1 res. possible
10:         $share \| bf \| salt \| uidCiphertext \| mac \leftarrow$ decrypt$_{\text{KDF}(dhtSalt, key)}(dhtCiphertext)$
11:         $shareSet$.add(($share, bf$))   // also remember $salt$, $uidCiphertext$ and mac
12:     **end for**
13:     $setOfShareSets$.add($shareSet$)
14: **end for**
15: $sk \leftarrow$ reduceAndCombineShares($setOfShareSets, \emptyset$)   // recovers sk iff $s \geq t$
16: $salt, uidCiphertext, mac \leftarrow$ lookup values for successful shares   // see line 11
17: $k_E, k_S \leftarrow$ KDF($salt, sk$)
18: $uid \leftarrow$ decrypt$_{k_E}(uidCiphertext)$ // and validate mac using k_S

Algorithm 5. reduceAndCombineShares (Scheme 2)

Input: $setOfShareSets, chosenShares$
Output: sk

1: **if** $|setOfShareSets| = 0$ **then**   // base case: try to recombine candidate shares
2:     $sk \leftarrow$ useShares($chosenShares$)
3:     **if** sk valid **then**
4:         **return** sk // for simplicity, return only the first valid key
5:     **end if**
6:     **return** $None$
7: **else**   // otherwise recurse
8:     $S \leftarrow setOfShareSets[0]$
9:     $SRest \leftarrow setOfShareSets \setminus S$
10:     **for** $(share, bf) \in S$ **do**
11:         $SRestReduced \leftarrow$ reduceShareSets($share, bf, SRest$)
12:         $result \leftarrow$ reduceAndCombineShares($SRestReduced, chosenShares \| share$)
13:         **if** $result \neq None$ **then**
14:             **return** $result$
15:         **end if**
16:     **end for**
17:     // if nothing was returned yet, try not to pick any share from the current set
18:     **return** reduceAndCombineShares($SRest, chosenShares$)
19: **end if**

Algorithm 6. reduceShareSets (Scheme 2)

Input: $share, bf, setOfShareSets$
Output: $reducedShareSets$

```
 1: reducedShareSets ← ∅
 2: for S ∈ setOfShareSets do
 3:     for share', bf' ∈ S do
 4:         if not checkBloomFilter(share', bf) then
 5:             S.remove(s')
 6:         end if
 7:         if not checkBloomFilter(share, bf') then
 8:             S.remove(share')
 9:         end if
10:     end for
11:     reducedShareSets.append(S)
12: end for
13: return reducedShareSets
```

to give the users the ability to weight attributes, that is, differentiating their contribution for reaching the threshold number t. In Scheme 1, this is straightforward to implement: instead of registering all attribute combinations with a certain number of attributes, we only register combinations whose weighted sum meets the threshold.[3] For Scheme 2, more work has to be done, to implement this functionality. A possible approach is, to first pick a granularity number g for the weighting factor (the number of discrete values the weighting factor can take). Instead of storing only one share with each attribute, 1 to g shares will be stored with each attribute depending on the weight for this attribute. The threshold number will be adjusted accordingly (e. g., multiplied by g). To hide the weight of an attribute, all attributes with less than maximum weight will store dummy shares. Following a convention to first store the real shares and than append dummy shares, the additional work (for legitimate users as well as adversaries) – when trying combinations of share values – is guessing this split-point between real and dummy shares for each attribute (e. g., for $g = 10$ and 4 shares, a factor of 10000).

Dummy-attributes for Plausible Deniability. Introducing plausible deniability for leaked personal information can mitigate the consequences of privacy breaches. This can be accomplished by adding random dummy-attributes along with the real attributes. Thus, the adversary cannot be sure if an attribute that she found to be related to a user is a real one or a generated fake entry. Dummy-attributes come, however, with the trade-off of increasing false positive matches for legitimate users. Furthermore, they can be debunked by adversaries with background knowledge. Finally, they might make brute-force attacks easier, as

---

[3] More precisely: only those combinations where the weighted sum is greater or equal the threshold and the removal of any included attribute would yield a weighted sum less than the threshold.

dummy-attributes increase the total number of attributes but not the threshold number of required attributes.

3   Threat Model

All information that the user gives away or generates while interacting with the system has to be considered as possibly sensitive. This comprises general administrative information (existence in system, date of registration, user-identifiers), entered information during registration (attributes, i. e., label-value pairs), search query data (who searches for whom, which previously unknown attributes are used to specify search-target) and behavioural data (online times, frequency of searching/registering/updating information).

3.1   Adversaries and Their Capabilities

All agents in the system can possibly act in malicious ways. This comprises nodes involved in the DHT storage, passive traffic observers and active adversaries, i. e., malicious users that can perform search and register operations. Their capabilities range from sniffing traffic and performing traffic analysis (e. g., analyzing query sizes), crawling the DHT (performing massive search operations) or analyzing data they might store, to actively inserting data into the DHT.

Example instances of these adversary models are curious users of the system, targeted attacks from parties with background knowledge about the target user (e. g., testing specific attributes of this user, also learning from negative results), or crawling attacks that aim to harvest information for e. g., spammers, targeted advertisement or insurance companies. We cannot perform a comprehensive security and privacy analysis of the protocols, taking into account all mentioned user assets and adversary capabilities. Instead, we will focus on several specific attacks and present one of them in more detail.

3.2   Subset Crawling Attack Scenario

The proposed protocols are trying to balance findability and privacy. Thus, they cannot provide perfect protection. In the worst-case of a targeted attack, an adversary with profound background knowledge about the target user will likely succeed. For example protecting the user identifier cannot be accomplished if the adversary knows as many attributes about the target user as legitimate users do. At the same time we assume that both schemes protect the users fairly well from large-scale crawling attacks as the search space of all possible attribute combinations is too large to brute-force and the protocols transform the registered user data in a way that inferences from the publicly stored data are infeasible. If an adversary chooses to constrain her effort to only crawl the data of a specified subset of the user-base, her chances might be better. We therefore focus on what we call a Subset Crawling Attack. In this scenario, the adversary chooses a number of sensitive attributes and tries to identify all users of the system that registered that attributes. For example, the adversary could try to identify all users working at a specific company by fixing the attribute "workplace" and then brute-forcing a set of identifying attributes such as "name", "firstname" and "city".

4 Privacy Evaluation

In the following we will evaluate the costs for an adversary to perform a Subset Crawling Attack and compare this to the search costs of legitimate users. We assume that a person's first name, last name, and the city the person is located at are identifying attributes and at the same time among the most popular search attributes. These attributes might be rather public information or easy to research, so we assume that users combine them with other, less public attributes. According to the Subset Crawling Attack scenario we assume that the adversary fixes at least one of the other attributes and tries to brute-force the identifying attributes.

4.1 Data Sources

To get evaluation results reflecting realistic distributions of values for identifying attributes, data from the U.S. census was used as input for the following calculations.

Distributions of U.S. *last names* were taken from [4, Table 1]. The data shows that there are 4 Million last names in total. 7 last names occur more than 1 Million times in the U.S. population. The top 3012 last names are shared by 55% of the population, the top 1 Million names are shared by 98.5%. The last name frequencies roughly resemble a power law distribution. Frequencies of U.S. *first names* were taken from [9]. The data is split into "male" and "female" first names. For our calculations we merged them assuming an equal distribution of the two categories. For U.S. *cities*, we used a dataset listing the population of all cities with more than 50000 inhabitants [10]. The data closely resembles a Zipf distribution. For the remaining population, we made a worst-case assumption of being distributed equally to cities with 50000 inhabitants (worst-case in the sense of getting less diversity for this attribute).

The validity of the evaluation results is therefore based on the assumption that the system's user base is a representative subsample of the U.S. population. In the following calculations we furthermore assume that all users registered all three attributes. A source of errors in our evaluation is that we treat these attributes as independent, because we were not able to find any statistics on joint distributions.

4.2 Brute-Force Probabilities Scheme 1

We investigate the success probability of an adversary, when trying to guess identifying attributes by brute-force, i.e., searching the whole value space. We assume the adversary will try most likely values (those registered by most users according to the value distribution in the population) first. Figure 2 shows the number of combinations to test in order to cover a certain percentage of the user population. This corresponds to the costs of an adversary, as in Scheme 1, to try one combination, one KDF operation plus one DHT `get` operation are necessary. For single attributes between 180 and 3000 combinations are enough to find a target with 50% success probability (4600 to 60 Million combinations for 100%). When the combination of two attributes has to be guessed, this increases to around 10^7 combinations for 50% success probability and up to 10^{15} combinations to search the whole value space.

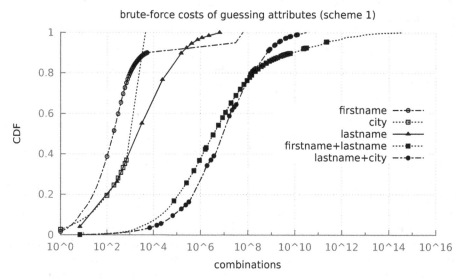

Fig. 2. CDF of brute-force success after trying a certain number of combinations (most likely ones first) for different attributes

4.3   Brute-Force Probabilities Scheme 2

In Scheme 2, bruteforcing works slightly differently. We assume, that the adversary knows some attributes (the fixed attributes that specify the subset to crawl, e. g., "workplace") and tries to guess other attributes (the identifying attributes). For each known attribute the adversary can issue a query and gets back a set of shares, each share having one bloom filter attached. Each share stems from a user who registered this specific attribute, i. e., a label-value combination (e. g., "workplace":"KTH") – several shares occur if several users registered the same combination (e. g., one from each user that registered their workplace as "KTH"). For an unknown attribute, the adversary will enumerate all possible values of the label-value combination (e. g., all possible lastname values for the attribute "lastname") and issue one DHT query each (after having performed a KDF operation to compute the DHT-key). This will result in one set of shares for each of the queries, again each share having one bloom filter attached. To know which share in each set should be picked, the bloom filters can be used to reduce the possible combinations. To test one combination, a second KDF operation (that might be tuned differently) has to be performed.

Figure 3 shows the work to be done for a legitimate user searching for three attributes and an adversary, who knows one attribute and tries to guess two unknown attributes. Additionally, the ratio of the legitimate user's cost to the adversary's cost is plotted, distinguishing two strategies of the adversary to search the value space: Either less popular values are tested first ("ratio") or more popular values first ("ratio biggest first").

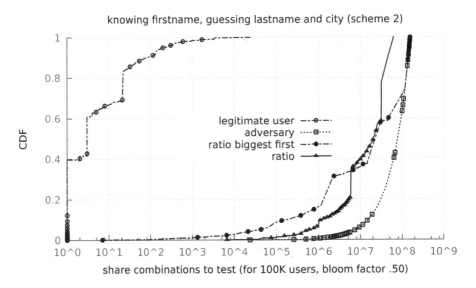

Fig. 3. Legitimate user searching for 3 attributes vs. adversary guessing 2 of them. Ratios depending on the adversaries strategy to search the value space.

4.4 Other Attacks

Existence Testing i.e., finding out if a user is registered in the system or not (without knowing enough attributes) is not possible in Scheme 1 and actively prevented in Scheme 2: Encrypting the user identifier under different keys (due to different salts) yields different ciphertexts and the bloom filters are salted differently. This is important as otherwise, searching e.g., for a certain firstname-lastname combination and getting the same ciphertext on the right hand side or similar bloom filters, reveals that there is a person with that firstname-lastname combination registered in the system, even if the person specified that more than two attributes are necessary to find her.

Search Query Data can give away information about the searcher (e. g., whom she is interested in) as well as previously unknown information about the searchee. A worst case example for the latter would be search queries that contain more information about the searchee than the searchee herself registered in the system. An adversary observing these queries can at least probabilistically learn more information about the searchee.

This attack does, however, require the adversary to reverse the KDF operation that transformed the plaintext attribute combination (denoted *key* in the pseudocode) into a derived *dhtkey*. For Scheme 1, the search protocol tries longer combinations first, which are harder to reverse. For successful search operations, this prevents the searcher from issuing queries with a lower number of attributes than specified by the searchee as threshold. Unsuccessful search operations will, however, issue eventually queries with only one attribute in the *key*. For Scheme 2, every DHT-query is derived from only one attribute, so successfully reversing the KDF might be more likely in this case. One mitigation would be to obfuscate the query origin (e. g., by using a different Tor circuit for each query), but time-correlation attacks could still be successful.

Replaying an observed search query does not help an adversary if she is not able to reverse the KDF operation (transforming a *dhtkey* value back in a *key* value), because without the *key* value, she cannot decrypt the result of the search query.

Impersonation is not prevented by our protocols as they do not try to solve the general authentication problem. Although the *uid* should be signed by the searchee and its signature validated by the searcher after it was found (not described by our protocols), this does not keep an adversary from setting up a fake profile for John Doe and register the attributes "firstname:john", "lastname:doe" into the DHT, mapping it to the *uid* of the fake profile.

5   Discussion

The results presented in the previous section describe the gap between the search effort of a legitimate user and the cost of an adversary trying to find user identifiers despite knowing fewer attributes than required. For Scheme 1, the former is constant in terms of DHT operations, the latter depends on the number and kind of unknown attributes, as shown in Figure 2. The adversary's costs for only one attribute are rather low, as expected. They can be tuned by KDF parameters but this will also affect the performance for legitimate users. The gap increases, however, combinatorially with the number of attributes the adversary has to guess. Already for two unknown attributes this might frustrate an attack: When tuning the KDF operations to take one second (delay for a legitimate user), an adversary with the same computational power as the user would need about 6 weeks to find the correct combination with 50% probability. The gap is not a global system parameter but can be tuned by each user individually (by choosing an individual threshold t for the registered information) but also depends on the adversary's knowledge about a target user. Scheme 2 can be tuned to achieve adversary costs comparable to that of Scheme 1, at the cost of slightly more work for legitimate users.

Apart from that, Scheme 1 has several advantages, compared to Scheme 2. It does not leak partial negative results, while Scheme 2, independently of any user thresholds, can reveal that a certain attribute combination is not registered in the system. For example, when searching for a certain lastname and workplace, and none of the shares of the two result sets are compatible according to the bloom filters, one learns that no user with this lastname registered this workplace. Furthermore, in Scheme 1 the adversary cannot make use of knowledge about other attributes of the user to decrease the search space for the identifying attributes. In Scheme 2, each additional attribute the adversary knows about the user, provides additional bloom filters to reduce the size of the result sets for the identifying attributes. Moreover, in Scheme 1 the user can specify even more fine-grained restrictions than only a minimum number of attributes. This makes weighting of attributes straightforward (see Section 2.5), but can even be used to explicitly exclude certain attribute combinations that the user does not want to be found by.

The advantage of Scheme 2 is the lower number of items to store in the DHT for each user. In Scheme 1, besides the higher storage load for the DHT, this is mainly a problem for registering a user, as for each of the attribute combinations also one KDF has to be computed. While this could be solved by accepting a longer delay for the registration operation and let it run in the background, the higher number of combinations might, however, also incur problems for search queries in certain cases. When over-specifying the search target in Scheme 1 (i. e., providing a number of attributes that is greater than the searchee's threshold t), successively all subsets of the attributes have to be queried while in Scheme 2 the number of DHT queries is always equal to the number of specified search attributes.

6   Conclusion and Future Work

We presented two approaches to realize a targeted user search in a DOSN. The search protocols implement a knowledge threshold, allowing the users to protect their user identifier from adversaries that do not possess enough information about them while legitimate users, who know enough about the searchee, are able to find her. We described the protocols in detail, sketched a threat model, and evaluated selected properties using real world data. The evaluation yielded insights into the brute-force costs of an adversary, which depend on the user defined knowledge threshold and the knowledge of the adversary about the target user. The results suggest that for a subset crawling attack, the proposed protocols offer promising protection against an adversary that tries to brute-force at least two or three identifying attributes.

One open problem to be investigated in future work is the possibility of combining the two presented approaches. Building on Scheme 2, several attributes that have a rather small value space could be combined in the way it is done in Scheme 1, thus avoiding the high number of combinations while still leveraging the advantages of Scheme 1.

Acknowledgements. Oleksandr Bodriagov and Guillermo Rodríguez Cano contributed to joint discussions of the ideas in Section 2. Some of the ideas were also discussed with Thomas Paul.

References

1. Bai, X., Bertier, M., Guerraoui, R., Kermarrec, A.M., Leroy, V.: Gossiping personalized queries. In: Manolescu, I., Spaccapietra, S., Teubner, J., Kitsuregawa, M., Léger, A., Naumann, F., Ailamaki, A., Özcan, F. (eds.) EDBT. ACM International Conference Proceeding Series, vol. 426, pp. 87–98. ACM (2010)
2. Baset, S., Schulzrinne, H.: An analysis of the Skype peer-to-peer internet telephony protocol. CoRR abs/cs/0412017 (2004)
3. Bender, M., Michel, S., Triantafillou, P., Weikum, G., Zimmer, C.: Minerva: Collaborative P2P search. In: Böhm, K., Jensen, C.S., Haas, L.M., Kersten, M.L., Larson, P.Å., Ooi, B.C. (eds.) VLDB, pp. 1263–1266. ACM (2005)
4. Word, D.L., Coleman, C.D., Kominski, R.N.: Demographic aspects of surnames from census 2000 (2000),
   http://www.census.gov/genealogy/www/surnames.pdf
5. Facebook: Introducing graph search (2013),
   https://www.facebook.com/about/graphsearch
6. Faroo: P2P search (2013), http://www.faroo.com/hp/p2p/p2p.html
7. Fong, P.W.L., Anwar, M.M., Zhao, Z.: A privacy preservation model for Facebook-style social network systems. In: Backes, M., Ning, P. (eds.) ESORICS 2009. LNCS, vol. 5789, pp. 303–320. Springer, Heidelberg (2009)
8. Li, J., Loo, B.T., Hellerstein, J.M., Kaashoek, M.F., Karger, D.R., Morris, R.: On the feasibility of peer-to-peer web indexing and search. In: Kaashoek, M.F., Stoica, I. (eds.) IPTPS 2003. LNCS, vol. 2735, pp. 207–215. Springer, Heidelberg (2003)
9. U.S. Census Bureau, P.D.: Genealogy data: Frequently occurring surnames from census 1990 (1990),
   http://www.census.gov/genealogy/www/data/1990surnames/names_files.html
10. U.S. Census Bureau, P.D.: Table 1. annual estimates of the resident population for incorporated places over 50,000, ranked by july 1, 2011 population: April 1, 2010 to July 1, 2011 (sub-est2011-01) (2012), http://www.census.gov/popest/data/cities/totals/2011/tables/SUB-EST2011-01.csv

An Explorative Mapping of the Belgian Social Media Marketing Value Network and Its Usage of Personal Identifiable Information

Rob Heyman and Jo Pierson

iMinds-SMIT, Vrije Universiteit, Brussel, Belgium
rob.heyman@vub.ac.be

Abstract. Research has shown an increase in both disclosure of personal data and means to gather this data on social media such as Facebook. Little research has been done to analyze what happens with this data and how it circulates between different actors. The aim of this research is to map a subset of the Belgian social media marketing companies as a value network and how these actors use social media users' data for marketing campaigns. The answer to this research question was obtained through expert interviews with experts from sector organizations and social media marketing companies. The consulted experts confirmed it was possible to use a myriad of personal information but their actual use was limited to age, gender, location and language. The main reasons are the unreliability of the data, legal insecurity and fear of scaring potential customers with privacy invasive questions.

Keywords: Social media, value network, privacy, targeted advertising.

1 Introduction

Previous research has shown an increase in both disclosure of personal data [1] and means to gather this data [2] on social media such as Facebook. On the other hand data gathering and profiling have been conceptualized as black boxes for users in a legal way [3] but also in users' understanding of targeted advertising [4] or their manipulation of privacy settings [5, 6] and authorization dialogs [7].

The aim of this research is to map how a subset of Belgian social media marketing companies are organized as a value network and secondly how they use social media users' data for marketing campaigns. This is motivated by the current opaqueness of these processes illustrated in previous research. But it is also necessary to inform current policy and legislation, which aims to regulate these practices. Lastly, this knowledge should also be used to illuminate how commercial entities influence algorithms, which are our gatekeepers in online and social communication [8, 9].

The answer to this research question was obtained through expert interviews with experts from sector organizations and social media marketing companies. The consulted experts affirmed the fact that it is possible to use a myriad of personal information although the actual use was limited to age, gender, location and language. The

M. Hansen et al. (Eds.): Privacy and Identity 2014, IFIP AICT 421, pp. 203–213, 2014.

main reasons are the unreliability of the data, legal insecurity and fear of repelling potential customers with privacy invasive questions.

The structure of this research paper is as follows. It first elaborates on the needed key concepts, which are social media, Personal Identifiable Information and value networks. After that the Belgian marketing sector is contextualized. The research outline of our expert interviews is described next. This is followed by the results, the conclusion and limitations of this research.

2   Concepts

The scope of companies that we research is limited to companies that market on behalf of advertisers in Belgium. Social media must therefore be an integrated part of their marketing products. For this we need to define the two ways social media can be used for marketing purposes. The most obvious way to use social media is to create an advertisement and use the provided targeting options, which are based on profile information submitted by the user. The targetable criteria for Facebook as example are country, town or city, age, gender, interests and connections (with other users or pages on Facebook) [10]. LinkedIn uses similar data, also derived from profile information and activities on the service [11].

Fig. 1. Facebook's advertising interface

The second mode to use social media for marketing purposes is by obtaining data from users by connecting to their API [2]. Facebook, LinkedIn and Twitter offer this possibility through applications and websites. The owner of a website or application can ask basic credentials for the registration or more elaborate information through extra permissions. The protocol used to authenticate these applications and websites is called OAuth[1].

---

[1]   For further reading visit http://oauth.net/about/.

2.1   Social Media

We define social media as 'a group of Internet-based applications that build on the ideological and technological foundations of Web 2.0, and that allow the creation and exchange of User Generated Content.' [12] Social network sites (SNS) [13] or online social network services (OSN) are a special instance of social media that focus on the creation of a network and a user profile. Social media is broader and therefore incorporates the micro blogging service, Twitter, which does not require these networks.

2.2   Personal Identifiable Information

Personal information is here defined as Personal Identifiable Information (PII), which originated in the K-anonymity approach [14, 15]. Sweeney [15] introduced K-anonymity to prove that anonymized databases are not anonymous if they contain unique records that may be linked to other databases with names and overlapping information. An IP-address is unique although this is not considered nonymous it may identify people when combined with other data. Sweeney proved this by combining an anonymized medical database with the voter registration of Massachusetts. We need this concept to show that the dichotomy of anonymous and its counterpart, identifiable information will not be made when looking at data in our research. This is motivated by the fact that anonymous information may still uniquely identify a user. In this case K, representing the smallest number of records sharing the same characteristics, is one. If $K = 1$, each user is uniquely identifiable. If $K > 1$, the data are aggregated in such a way that users are no longer uniquely identifiable.

2.3   Value Networks

Value network analysis [16–18] is an approach to evaluate business models within an environment of other businesses. It is used in a normative way to evaluate, which configuration of companies and underlying relations begets a perfect fit. A perfect fit is a situation where the configuration of roles, actors and relations is fair and viable on the long term. This research uses the value network perspective in a descriptive way to map the use of data within the social media marketing sector.

"A role is a distinct value-adding activity within the value network, which potentially can exist as a commercial entity in the marketplace, with its own cost and revenue balance" [16]. Actors are the commercial entities that function within a market by integrating one or more roles. Relationships are the interactions between roles or actors and are usually shown as arrows in diagrams which depict a monetary transaction, service or a tradable good [16]. In this paper, these arrows will represent the flow of PII.

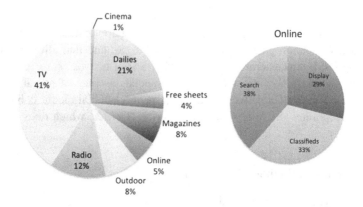

Fig. 2. Belgian Advertising Spending overview 2011. Source Adex Benchmark 2011 and UBA Jaarverslag

3   Situating the Belgian Value Network of Social Media Marketing

To situate the Belgian value network within the other advertising venues, the Belgian Union of Advertisers[2] annual report [19] was consulted. IAB[3] Europe's Adex Benchmark 2011 [20] presents a backdrop to compare the Belgian situation within Europe. UBA reported on online display advertising, which incorporates social media spending. Online spending normally also includes classifieds and search. Online spending was 183 million € for 2011, which is 5,1 % of the total measured advertising expenditure for Belgium in 2011. The global Belgian advertising expenditure rose with 2,9 % while online increased with 8,9 % when compared with the previous year. According to IAB classifieds and search were responsible for two thirds of total online advertising expenditure, which implied that online would represent 17,1 % of the total media spend in Belgium. Belgian online ad expenditure is on the lower end with the UK and the Netherlands leading with respectively 35,9 % and 27,9 % and Austria as the lowest with 13,0 % within Western Europe.

4   Research Outline

The results were obtained through expert interviews [21], which were conducted in two waves. The first wave consisted of interviews with directors of sector organizations that represented firms which are part of the social media marketing value chain.

---

[2] Unie der Belgische Adverteerders (UBA), for more information visit
http://www.ubabelgium.be/
[3] Interactive Advertising Bureau (IAB) for more information visit
http://www.iab-belgium.be/

These organizations are BDMA, IAB, UBA and ACC[4]. All interviews were performed in the summer of 2012[5]. The second wave consisted of interviews with actors within the value network.

We have found two distinct definitions of experts in two disciplines: international business studies [22, 23] refer to 'elites' while Pfadenhauer [21] situates 'experts' in the qualitative interview methodology. Both terms were kept as they point out different aspects important to our sampling strategy.

'Elites' are defined as: "an informant {...} who occupies a senior or middle management position; has functional responsibility in an area which enjoys high status in accordance with corporate values; has considerable industry experience and frequently also long tenure with the company; possesses a broad network of personal relationships; and has considerable international exposure." [23] As they use their knowledge, they reshape their environment: "By becoming practically relevant, the experts' knowledge structures the practical conditions of other actors in their professional field in a substantial way." [22] Although elite and expert were used, they both referred to a professional who does not only have expert knowledge but is also participating within his field of expert knowledge. We will refer to this kind of expert as participating expert.

Pfadenhauer on the other hand conceptualizes the 'expert' as a meta-specialist, who "knows what the (respective) specialists know in their fields of knowledge - and how what they know relates to each other" [21]. The expert is here defined as an observer or even an outsider who does not partake as an actor within the value network. These experts will be referred to as observing experts.

We have identified the following sector organizations as observing experts who were contacted to situate the value network but also to refer us to participating experts: BDMA, IAB, UBA and ACC. We have omitted sector organizations that did not have a direct link with online advertising[6].

The selected organizations share more or less the same goals: they wish to defend their profession from overregulation and they achieve this by lobbying and self-regulation on a national and international level. They wish to promote their profession through education, networking and research [19, 24–26].

These sector organizations were chosen because of their general expert knowledge about the sector, but also because they were able to introduce us to the other experts we were interested in. These are the CEOs or employees responsible for social media marketing. The introduction or referral from known authorities increases the likelihood of a positive reply [23]. Below is a representation of the actual course of inter-

---

[4] Belgian Direct Mail Association (BDMA) for more information visit http://www.bdma.be/ and the Association of Communication Companies.

[5] The exact dates can be found in the annex of this paper.

[6] Belgian Union of Daily Publishers (BVDU), the Federation of Belgian Magazines, Union of Publishers of Periodical Print (UPP), Association of Billboard Owners (AEA), Belgian Union of Audiovisual Media (BVAM). BVDU www.fleetproject.be, the Federation of Belgian Magazines www.theppress.be, UPP www.upp.be, AEA (has no online presence), BVAM www.abma-bvam.be.

views. The second wave experts were also asked to refer to experts, which sometimes created a longer chain of interviews.

- Jo Caudron, DearMedia founder and President IAB
  - Patrick Marck, General Manager IAB
- Greet Dekocker, Director BDMA
  - Philippe Arnauts, Marketing Manager WDM Belgium
- Erik Tamboryn, President of Comité van toezicht BDMA
- Chris Van Roey, CEO UBA
  - Nathalie Hublet, Media Manager UBA
- Luc De Leersnyder, CEO ACC
  - Rob van Alphen, Social Business Consultant
  - Bart De Waele, CEO Wijs
  - Anthony Bosschem, CEO and Founder of Darwin and former Talking Heads employee

The interviews were semi-structured. Questions were prepared according to the expert the researcher was facing. All guides were grounded on the same research questions to guarantee uniformity. The questions mapped the value network, how they used PII in general and on social media, how they used social media and lastly how they incorporated privacy in their products. A topic guide can be found in the annex of this paper.

The interviews took at least one hour or to one hour and a half depending on the expert's need to ask for more clarification or elaborate further on the main research questions. All interviewees agreed to be recorded. The interviews were summarized and grouped per distinct role and research question.

5   Results

Before discussing the results figure 3 should be explained because it represents the results in a value network diagram. Light grey boxes were used to identify actors. These actors have white boxes, which contain the roles they perform. Dark grey boxes were used to refer to companies that were important to the interviewed actors either as a starting point or endpoint of the service. We will discuss the most important roles within this value network. These roles are strategy, concept, coaching, build & launch, operate and evaluation. Afterwards we elaborate on the consulted experts' practices with regard to PII, which are targeting, evaluation and CRM[7].

The arrows between actors and roles symbolize the flow of PII. The arrows drawn on figure 3 are dotted if the transaction of PII is aggregated (K > 1). The full lines refer tot transactions involving PII that can uniquely identify a user (K = 1).

---

[7] Customer Relationship Management (CRM) is the model companies use to build and maintain a relation with their current and future customers.

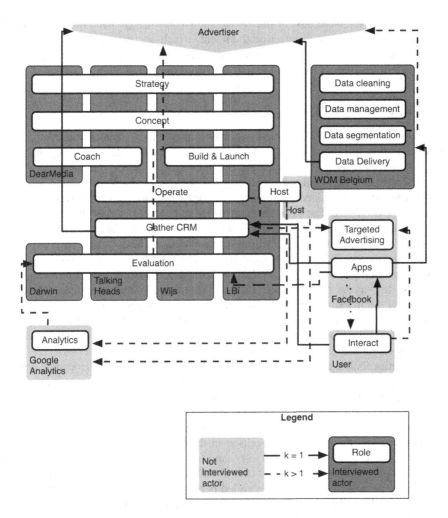

Fig. 3. Belgian Social Media Marketing Value Network

Four out of the six consulted actors plan the strategy of a company that wishes to advertise. They assess the advertiser's position and then evaluate whether a social media marketing approach is adequate. Wijs and LBi provide other online channels as well. In the concept phase and role, the strategy is further operationalized in concrete measurable steps, which are evaluated during the evaluation role.

The following roles contain the actual building and execution of the proposed concept: coach, build, launch and operation. This is when websites are built, advertisements are made and other social media actions such as creating and maintaining social media presence are executed.

Social media is not only used for its advertising purposes, it is also used to talk with consumers or to provide the content related to their brand. When advertising is used, it is always targeted as we will explain in section 5.1. The consulted experts were reluctant to try more than the basic advertising format shown on the right hand pane. Sponsored stories, updates that contain advertorial content, which are shown in the News Feed were used sparingly. Participating experts were unsure about these advertising products due to their obtrusiveness but also because they were shown too often[8].

5.1   Roles Requiring PII

When a medium is chosen or when an advertisement for a social media platform is made, an audience is targeted. The criteria for this audience are defined during the strategy and concept phase of the campaign. Broad categories that fit the advertiser's goal were preferred and they contained the following criteria: gender, age, location and education. The experts refrained from using categories such as likes or interests because these were less reliable. For example many different product pages of the same product exist and users may also like objects like a Ferrari without ever having the intention to buy one. Another reason to refrain from using more specific targeting criteria is Belgium's small market. Too much segmentation would exclude too many users.

A campaign's performance is evaluated through a funnel. A funnel is a technical and strategic way to evaluate performance. Measuring points are implemented on each step of the marketing process. Each number of users per step is compared to the number of the previous step in order to see how many users exited the funnel before they completed the marketing goal. Darwin offers this role as its only value proposition; to measure and report on the various social ads or social media platforms. This feedback information is required to increase the budget of high-performing actions and remedy the low-performing actions. The data required for evaluation purposes is aggregated ($K > 1$) and there is no need to uniquely identify a person.

This aggregated data of the evaluation process is very important because it is used to evaluate the efficiency of the marketing campaign. This is not only used to convince advertisers, the same data is reused in the operation phase to target the most efficient audience. The data are also important for attribution. Each publisher needs to report how many visitors saw the ad (this is called reach) and how many people interacted with the advertisement (this is called performance). Without these metrics it is impossible to bill advertisers because payments are based on reach or performance per number of users.

Lastly, WDM Belgium, LBi and Wijs gathered uniquely identifiable PII such as name and address for CRM purposes. This is the only instance where PII is gathered and kept identifiable. Otherwise the data is stripped from directly identifiable categories in order to render it anonymous (according to the consulted experts). In the case of CRM all interviewed experts were reluctant to ask for too much information because this could repel users from taking the next step in the marketing funnel. As little uniquely identifiable data as possible is gathered for three other reasons as well: to remain within legal boundaries. Because it is hard to foresee what information would be useful in future occasions[9] and lastly advertisers lack the necessary infrastructure to store data.

---

[8] Rob van Alphen, interviewed by Rob Heyman 2012, July 4.
[9] Jo Caudron, interviewed by Rob Heyman 2012, July 11.

PII is either gathered on Facebook through a dialog box, which authenticates third parties' access to social media APIs. WDM Belgium, LBi and Wijs preferred to ask data through forms on an external website. This happens for two reasons, Facebook does not allow application owners to store this data permanently. Secondly, these companies prefer to display their privacy statement on their own websites where a clear opt-in is guaranteed. Data most often required for CRM oriented campaigns, are preferences directly related to the advertiser's product categories and contact information[10].

It was already mentioned that most advertisers were lacking the proper means or knowhow to store PII for CRM purposes[11]. This is the main reason why companies such as WDM Belgium exist. Next to the previously stated roles, this company also implements data management systems for CRM. It also provides data cleaning and segmentation services. This is the only company we interviewed that sold data mining services. Social media was being tested to deduce extra information but it was deemed unreliable compared to other CRM data because users are less prone to use their real identity. This in turn illustrates why Facebook and Google implement a real name policy.

6   Conclusion

This research leads us to conclude that what is technologically possible in social media marketing is not necessary implemented by this subset of Belgian actors. Targeted advertising was limited to very broad target audiences and data gathering was also limited. The motivation to limit the use of these privacy intrusive tools was economic. None of the interviewed companies could afford to lose users (or clients) due to legal problems or being too intrusive towards users. Privacy was thus seen as a means to obtain something else and not a value an sich.

PII had to be uniquely identifying in two cases. First PII are used to count individual actions of users, but these are saved aggregated because they only need to be reported in total number of users for billing, evaluation and efficiency purposes. Secondly, PII is kept as $K = 1$ if and only if an advertiser specifically requests to keep this data for further CRM campaigns.

7   Limitations

The examples in this research and during the interviews were biased towards Facebook. This is due to its popularity but also the fact that Twitter for example cannot be contacted for advertising purposes in Belgium.

---

[10] Rob van Alphen, interviewed by Rob Heyman 2012, July 4.

[11] Erik Tamboryn, interviewed by Rob Heyman 2012, July 6. Greet Dekocker, interviewed by Rob Heyman 2012, July 10. Philippe Arnauts, interviewed by Rob Heyman 2012, September 5.

The researcher's focus was biased towards advertising instead of marketing before the advent of the interviews. The experts have pointed out that social media can also be used to create content and attract users without paying social media.

Lastly, more Belgian actors need to be interviewed within two categories that were under represented in this sampling; app developers and cross-media agencies.

References

1. Stutzman, F., Gross, R., Acquisti, A.: Silent Listeners: The evolution of privacy and disclosure on Facebook. Journal of Privacy and Confidentiality 4, 7–41 (2012)
2. Wang, N., Xu, H., Grossklags, J.: Third-party apps on Facebook: privacy and the illusion of control. In: Proceedings of the 5th ACM Symposium on Computer Human Interaction for Management of Information Technology, p. 4 (2011)
3. Gutwirth, S., Hildebrandt, M.: Some Caveats on Profiling. In: Gutwirth, S., Poullet, Y., De Hert, P. (eds.) Data Protection in a Profiled World, pp. 31–41. Springer Netherlands, Heidelberg (2010)
4. Ur, B., Leon, P.G., Cranor, L.F., Shay, R., Wang, Y.: Smart, useful, scary, creepy: perceptions of online behavioral advertising. In: Proceedings of the Eighth Symposium on Usable Privacy and Security, p. 4 (2012)
5. Heyman, R., De Wolf, R., Pierson, J.: Not all privacy settings are created equal - evaluating social media privacy settings for personal and advertising purposes. Presented at the IAMCR 2012, University of KwaZulu-Natal, Howard College Campus (July 15, 2012)
6. Liu, Y., Gummadi, K.P., Krishnamurthy, B., Mislove, A.: Analyzing Facebook Privacy Settings: User Expectations vs. Reality. Presented at the IMC 2011, Berlin (November 2, 2011)
7. Wang, N., Grossklags, J., Xu, H.: An online experiment of privacy authorization dialogues for social applications. In: Proceedings of the 2013 Conference on Computer Supported Cooperative Work, pp. 261–272 (2013)
8. Beer, D.: Power through the algorithm? Participatory web cultures and the technological unconscious. New Media & Society 11, 985–1002 (2009)
9. Pariser, E.: The filter bubble: what the Internet is hiding from you. Penguin Press, New York (2011)
10. Korolova, A.: Privacy violations using microtargeted ads: A case study. In: 2010 IEEE International Conference on Data Mining Workshops (ICDMW), pp. 474–482 (2010)
11. Heyman, R., Pierson, J.: Social media use and corporate dataveillance: exploring and assessing digital Personal Identifiable Information (PII) collection tools. In: Presented at the IAMCR 2011, Istanbul (July 13, 2011)
12. Kaplan, A.M., Haenlein, M.: Users of the world, unite! The challenges and opportunities of Social Media. Business Horizons 53, 59–68 (2010)
13. Boyd, D.M., Ellison, N.B.: Social network sites: Definition, history, and scholarship. Journal of Computer-Mediated Communication 13, 210–230 (2008)
14. Ciriani, V., Capitani di Vimercati, S., Foresti, S., Samarati, P.: k-anonymity. Secure Data Management in Decentralized Systems, pp. 323–353 (2007)
15. Sweeney, L.: k-anonymity: A model for protecting privacy. International Journal of Uncertainty Fuzziness and Knowledge Based Systems 10, 557–570 (2002)
16. Ballon, P.: Business modelling revisited: the configuration of control and value. Info. 9, 6–19 (2007)

17. Bouwman, H., Haaker, T., de Vos, H.: Designing Business Models: a practical and holistic approach. Telematica Institute, Enschede (2005)
18. Allee, V.: Value-creating networks: organizational issues and challenges. The Learning Organization 16, 427–442 (2009)
19. UBA: Jaarverslag 2011. UBA, Strombeek-Bever (2012)
20. Knapp, D., Marouli, E.: Adex Benchmark 2011, European online advertising expenditure. IAB Europe (2012)
21. Pfadenhauer, M.: At eye level: The expert interview - a talk between expert and quasi-expert. In: Bogner, A., Littig, B., Menz, W. (eds.) Interviewing Experts, pp. 81–97. Palgrave Macmillan, Basingstoke (2009)
22. Bandara, W., Indulska, M., Chong, S., Sadiq, S.: Major issues in business process management: an expert perspective (2007)
23. Welch, C., Marschan-Piekkari, R., Penttinen, H., Tahvanainen, M.: Corporate elites as informants in qualitative international business research. International Business Review 11, 611–628 (2002)
24. ACC: Mission statement, http://www.accbelgium.be/Content/acc/whatisacc/missionstatement/index.html
25. Decocker, G.: Bdma in het kort (2009), http://www.bdma.be/index.php?id=359
26. IAB: IAB Belgium home, http://www.iab-belgium.be

A   Appendix: Interview Guide

Questions to map the value network

— What is the core business of the sector your organization represents?
— Could you sum up the services of these companies?
— Who are the most important clients? i.e. what kind of company?
— What are the most popular services?
— Are these companies dependent of other companies?
— What are the most important companies they rely on?

Questions about their use of personal data in services

— Where is personal data used (either anonymous or identifiable) in their services?
— What are the different uses of personal data?
— How is personal data obtained?

Questions related to social media use

— How is social media used in companies represented by your organization?
— What are the most used social media platforms?
— What services are used within Facebook and other named platforms?
— What approaches work in social media?
— What approaches do not work?
— Do you segment data in order to target?
— What are the most important types of data to perform targeting?

Privacy Issues in Cross-Border Identity Management Systems: Pan-European Case

Svetlana Sapelova[1,*] and Borka Jerman-Blažič[2]

[1] Jozef Stefan International Postgraduate School, Ljubljana Slovenia
svetka@e5.ijs.si
[2] Laboratory for Open Systems and Networks, Jozef Stefan Institute, Ljubljana Slovenia
borka@e5.ijs.si

Abstract. The paper presents a Pan-European Identity Management System that was developed through the concerted efforts of several European research initiatives, and identifies gaps in the privacy protection mechanisms, which occur because privacy is considered strictly from the EU Data Protection regulation perspective. Privacy protection problems are identified, and measures to eliminate them are outlined on the basis of an extended notion of privacy, which includes aspects of unlinkability, transparency, anonymity and pseudonymity.

Keywords: Identity Management System, pan-European environment, regulation of privacy in the European Union, electronic identification, eID, pan-European eServices.

1   Introduction

The function of a Pan-European IdMs is to enable cross-border recognition of electronic credentials (eID) between the Member States (MS) of the European Union (EU) and to provide an interoperability bridge authorities located in different MS. In this way, foreign eServices (electronic Services) could identify citizens using identity attributes stored directly on the eID (i.e. Electronic Identity Card, Digital Certificate, or other type of credentials, which keep identity attributes) or delivered by Identity Providers (IdP) and Attribute Providers (AP) from another Member State.

Driven by multiple directives and roadmaps numerous research projects have addressed this problem. Embarrassed by its complexity, in particular by the sophisticated and often controversial data protection laws in force in different MS, they focused on the development of architecture that would be consistent with all these laws, and thereby would enable legal transfer of citizens' identity data between MS. This approach considers the protection of privacy in terms of conformity with the Data Protection rules. However, this leaves a gap with respect to the ubiquitous comprehension of privacy. One of the most recent European research initiatives – the

---

* Corresponding author.

M. Hansen et al. (Eds.): Privacy and Identity 2014, IFIP AICT 421, pp. 214–223, 2014.

STORK European Project [22] has developed a system in order to demonstrate the feasibility of cross-border eID recognition. In this paper we review the system and argue it suffers from multiple privacy protection gaps.

The paper is organized as follows: objectives of the Pan-European IdMs and related EU initiatives are presented in Chapter 2, Data Protection laws and the extended notion of privacy we use to analyze the system are reviewed in Chapter 3, architecture of the Pan-European IdMs is presented in Chapter 4, and the privacy analysis of the system is in Chapter 5.

2   Towards a Pan-European IdMs

The need to build a Pan-European IdMs has been emphasized by the European Commission (EC) with an objective to facilitate interaction between EU MS. Numerous initiatives [9], [3], [5], [14], [19], [20] driven by EC directives and roadmaps [1], [3], [7] have contributed to research and development in this field. The original proposal focused on the promotion of the cross-border eID recognition for eGovernmental (eGov) services. That would allow citizens to use foreign eGov services with electronic credentials issued either by their home countries or any other EU Member States. For instance, a citizen from Spain would be able to pay electricity bills via Italian eGov service, that would recognize a Spanish eID. Services enabled for cross-border communication would send identity attribute requests to citizens' native countries via the Pan-European IdMs system. The system will contact appropriate IdPs and send back highly reliable identity information from governmental and non-governmental registers. Currently no operable solution exists. The only prototype has been built by the STORK research initiatives (Secure Identity Across Borders Linked) [19] based on studies conducted by IDABC (stands for Interoperable Delivery of European eGov Services to Public Administrations, Businesses and Citizens) [5], a program launched in 2004 to promote the building of the cross-border IdMs for eGov services. STORK, launched by the EC in 2010, embraces not only governmental but also other spheres of life (eUniversity portals, eLearning platforms, eBank, and other services). The system developed within the project scope has been tested by several pilots. STORK is now in its second phase named STORK2.0 [20] that pursue the goals to extend the number of services participating in the cross-border collaboration, increase the number of identity attributes recognized across borders, and involve private service providers to collaboration.

The following use case illustrates a functional scenario of the STORK Pan-European IdMs:

A student from Italy wants to apply for Erasmus exchange at a Spanish university (eUni). In order to get identified by the service as an eligible participant, the student should provide the name of his home university, year of study, and a proof of a student status. This data is managed by the IdMs of his home university in Italy (homeUni). To collect the data eUni redirects the student to his homeUni IdMs via STORK IdMs, where he is identified with his home credentials, collects necessary identity attributes from the homeUni database and sends them back to the eUni via STORK IdMs. Because Italian and Spanish IdM systems have enabled interoperability and established mutual trust in advance, Spanish eUni grants access based on the attributes received from the homeUni.

3   Privacy Regulations in the Pan-European Environment

3.1   Privacy Perspective

EU data protection rules are delivered in the form of directives manifesting the legal notion of privacy [11], which must be respected by all Member States. The main EU directive on Data Protection is Directive 95/46/EC, the Data Protection Directive (DPD) [8], which regulates the transfer of Personal Identifiable Information (PII) [16] within and beyond the EU. National data protection laws in all EU Member States were harmonized with the DPD [8]. Because the STORK system serves for the transfer of personal identity data, it becomes a subject to the DPD rules. The Data Protection principles laid down by the DPD:

1. Personal data is only processed once the citizen gives unambiguous consent.
2. The purpose of data transfer must be explicitly specified.
3. The amount of data released to the service should be minimal.
4. The transfer of National Identification Number (NIN) is a matter of special concern. It must be processed according to the national legislation.
5. Respect the right of an individual to access his/her personal data.
6. Ensure the appropriate technical and organizational measures to protect data from unauthorized access, disclosure and loss.
7. There should be at least one supervising authority monitoring the personal data handling within the MS.

Every MS interprets and applies instructions laid down by the DPD in its own way. Complying with all local data protection laws is particularly challenging due to their heterogeneity and incompatibility. Some of the most challenging issues are: controversial regulations about the transfer of NINs (some countries allow the cross-border transfer of NINs, while others do not [15]), different amount of NINs used for the identification of citizens (single or multiple, sector-specific [15]), different obligations for the personal data processing (e.g., Austrian Data Processing Register must be notified of each data transfer and application, while Denmark does not require any notification [15]), and different regulations about data sharing between public administrations (some countries explicitly allow data sharing, if it complies with a specific law, while other countries have special authorities authorized to issue the data sharing permissions [15]).

3.2 Extending the Notion of Privacy

Although the adherence to all data protection regulations ensures the legitimate handling of data by an information system, it is not sufficient to cover all implications of privacy [10]. That is, with respect to eID Identity Management, protection and management of electronic identity are not addressed by legal regulations, thereby leaving room for interpretation [4]. Unlinkability, transparency, anonymity and pseudonymity were assumed to be of great importance for privacy protection in Identity Management [4], [24]. They manifest user control over personal data by adding user-centricity aspect to the system design. The paper uses this extended notion of privacy to analyze the privacy protection implications within the Pan-European IdMs.

We also refer to the recent Data Protection Regulation Proposal [25] that will soon replace the current DPD. We recap new elements introduced by the Proposal and recognize their impact on the identified privacy issues.

4 Architecture of the Pan-European Identity Management System

The biggest challenge in the use-case implementation is to comply with all data protection principles mentioned in the previous section. It was assumed that the following functional requirements derived from the principles were the most relevant ones for the system in question:

1. Built-in citizens' consent is the core of every transfer process.
2. Manage adherence to the data minimization principles.
3. Clearly inform the user about the purpose of the data transfer and the name of the data receiver.
4. Perform the data transfer only if the transfer complies with the legal regulations in the MS owning the data.
5. Implement appropriate security measures to protect the transferred data against unauthorized disclosure, access, or eavesdropping.

Figure 1 illustrates the architecture of the Pan-European IdMs for eGov delivered by IDABC and approved by the European Commission [13]. It is based on proxy services (PEPS), which function as gateways between the national eID IdMs, mediating the flow of data between MS. Such approach adapts to the heterogeneity of local data protection laws by hiding details of data handling behind the national gateways. Each MS is free to decide what identity attributes can be released and what eID IdMs technology to deploy. Because the Pan-European IdMs is placed on the proxy position between MS, not all data protection principles are applicable. Table 1 shows the relation between the data protection principles and the two types of data handling (cross-border transfer and data collection from the local source before the cross-border transfer) with respect to the described architecture.

So far, the PEPS-based architecture of the Pan-European IdMs is the state-of-the-art in the field and STORK project use it to design the system.

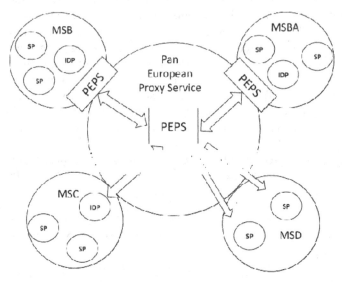

Fig. 1. Architecture of the Pan-European IdMs proposed by IDABC (Source: [13])

5   Privacy Issues in Cross-Border IdMs

This analyses privacy and identifies privacy breaches in the STORK Pan-European IdMs. It is impossible to perform an ubiquitous analysis of such a complex system based only on the scope of pilots; thus, we also review privacy with respect to the possible scenarios likely to occur once the system is pushed to its logical extreme.

5.1   The Loss of Control over Identity Data

The lack of control over the personal identity data in the eID IdMs has been identified as an issue long time ago [4], [21]. Some of the reasons were identified during the system review:

- The data handling mechanisms used by the system lack transparency
- In the light of emerging technologies the EU regulations get obsolete

The cross-border eID recognition catalyzes ubiquitous adoption of the eID identification and thereby creates a threat to privacy. The Pan-European IdMs amplifies problems of eID IdMs at the national level and propagates them to the cross-border context. Missing transparency masks data handling mechanisms and causes unawareness in legal regulations that apply to the system. Although the Pan-European IdMs obtains consent before it transfers identity data, it does not inform users about the legal aspects of the process, nor obliges the SPs to provide such information. It is necessary to inform users about the legal regulations in the MS that receives their identity data; having accepted these regulations, users should give their explicit consent.

Table 1. Relations between data protection principles and data handling types

	Cross-border data transfer	**Data collection within MS**
Unambiguous consent	PEPS obtains consent from users	Local IdMs infrastructure obtains consent
Purpose of data transfer	PEPS informs about the purpose of the data transfer	User is informed by the local IdMs infrastructure
Data minimization	X	Responsibility of the local eID IdMs
Process NINs according to the national laws	X	Responsibility of the local eID IdMs
Right of an individual to access his/her personal data	X (PEPS does not store any identity data)	Every MS implements it at the local level
Data protection	Protect data transferred between PEPSes	Protect data handled by the national eID IdMs
Supervising authority	X (no authority in cross-border contexts)	Every MS implements it at a local level

Further research is necessary to develop appropriate technical means to implement this procedure in the most convenient way. The issue has been recognized by the EC and addressed by the new Data Protection Regulation Proposal [25]. In particular, Articles 12, 13 and 14 of the Proposal emphasize the responsibility of data controllers in providing comprehensive information about the purpose of data transfer, the names of data recipients and the period   the recipient will store the data etc. By the decision of the STORK project Consortium, the roles of data controllers are assigned not only to the IdPs, but also to the SPs that receive identity data; in this way, the requirements laid down in the above-mentioned articles will be duly fulfilled by all parties, significantly increasing transparency of the cross-border identification procedure, and thereby easing the burden on the Pan-European infrastructure.

Another dimension of the problem emerges when identity data are put at the disposal of third parties; e.g., the cloud technologies. In the light of a growing interest for cloud storages, we can expect an increasing number of providers will use clouds to deploy their services and data storages. This poses a great risk potential for the privacy breaches [22]. For instance, third parties could monitor data stored on clouds [23], while the legal regulations that apply to the clouds and data handling mechanisms used by them are not clear. Another potential privacy threat is the lack of awareness of security measures employed by the cloud providers. The new Regulation does not explicitly address cloud computing, but refers to issues relevant to the technology such as data breach notification (Article 31), increased enforcement regime against controllers and processors (Article 79), assurance of proper security measures by data controllers and data processors (Article 30) etc. However, a lot of existing difficulties and problems with regards to cloud computing will still remain [26]; clearly, they will have to be carefully considered by all the involved parties when pushing the pan-European IdMs to the extreme.

5.2   Linkability by Default

The same NIN is used for identification purposes via the STORK Pan-European IdMs, leaving the possibility to link users' identities across different contexts. Furthermore, there is no data minimization compliance control in place. In order to tackle this issue, the STORK Consortium proposed the encryption of NINs before their cross-border transfer, and devised a NIN transformation scheme [18], however, the employment of the scheme is left to the discretion of every MS. Currently, every MS that legally allows cross-border transfer of simple NINs enables identity linkage by different parties. Multiple surveys identified this problem in the context of eID, and emphasized the necessity to adopt the "eID unlinkability" rule "as a must" [4][12], obliging eID IdMs to derive specific identification numbers for every context or service. This would reduce the risk of linkability through NINs, however, members states would have to invest significant efforts into the reorganization of their local eID IdMs. Clearly, the solution still has a long way to go.

Nevertheless, simple NIN proliferation prevention alone will not eliminate the problem of linkability. Identity linkage will still be feasible by comparing the sets of other identity attributes (sometimes referred to as the quasi-identifying attributes). For example, when a student provides a combination of his/her "fist name/last name/date of birth" to an eLearning service and sends the same data through an online application for Erasmus exchange, it is possible to claim with a certain degree of probability that the two sets of attributes belong to the same person. Adherence to the data minimization principle can help reduce the risk [10]. Raising user awareness regarding the linkability issues should encourage them to share only the minimum necessary information. It could be implemented as a feature of the pan-European IdMs that tracks the amount of identity data released by an individual user, alerting him/her about the risk of identity linkage before the transfer of data is launched.

With respect to the issue the new Data Protection Regulation Proposal brought several regulations that have a direct impact on the mitigating the risk of linkability. Thus, Article 23 of the Proposal sets obligations of the controller derived from "privacy by design" principles [2] that address different aspects of protecting Personally Identifiable Information (PII) such as follow the principles of data minimization, purpose binding, end-to-end security etc. Article 20 concerns the data subject's right not to be subject to a measure based on profiling. Profiling would be allowed only with a consent of users, when provided by law or when needed to pursue a contract. It must not lead to discrimination and should not be based on automated processing.

5.3   Anonymity and Pseudonymity

Because the STORK objective is to enable services to obtain highly trustworthy identity attributes from different MS, such problem statement left the consideration about the anonymous and pseudonymous participation out of the project's scope. However, with regards to the current efforts in providing means for a large number of heterogeneous services to use the STORK system [20] we can expect multiple STORK-enabled services will not require real data to identify users. The case a foreign service, which allow anonymous or pseudonymous participation, receives real identity data must be eliminated. Clearly, the step towards anonymous and pseudonymous participation must be taken by the MS. They have to enable these features in their local eID IdMs. Such approach would facilitate the adoption of anonymity and pseudonymity at the pan-European level. However, considering the current gap in the EU data protection regulations [4], the fastest way towards a solution is by means of the pan-European eID infrastructure that employ the anonymisation and pseudonymisation as additional PEPS functionalities.

6   Conclusion

However, STORK has demonstrated that interoperability by means of a pan-European IdMs is technically feasible, the system suffers from significant privacy protection gaps. Although the view of privacy as an implication of the Data Protection regulations is a prerequisite for a legitimate cross-border identity data transfer, it leaves a lot of privacy-related aspects out of scope. In our analysis, we identified privacy protection problems of the pan-European IdMs, using the extended notion of privacy that embraces transparency, linkability, anonymity and pseudonymity. We argued that the level of privacy protection provided by the pan-European IdMs depends not only on privacy protection mechanisms employed by the system itself, but also on the mechanisms provided by the local eID IdMS. The lack of such mechanisms is caused by insufficient EU Data Protection regulations, and inadequate attention to the problem from the MS. Clearly, the problem must be addressed from legal and technical perspectives. MS should join efforts to enhance technical means for privacy protection of their local eID IdMs and subsequently of the entire pan-European IdMs, while refining implication of privacy from the legal perspective. The recently proposed new Data protection Regulation is a first step with regards to the problem; it addresses important aspects of privacy like security, transparency, unlinkability and user centricity of local eID IdMs that consequently impact entire cross-border infrastructure. However, we' seen a lot of existing problems are out of the scope of the Regulation. This lays on an additional burden to researchers and requires them to undertake specific measures at the following stages of design and development of pan-European IdMs.

References

1. A Roadmap for a Pan-European eIDM Framework by 2010 (2010), http://ec.europa.eu/information_society/activities/ict_psp/documents/eidm_roadmap_paper.pdf
2. Cavoukian, A.: A Foundation Framework for a Privacy by Design – Privacy Impact Assessment (2011), http://privacybydesign.ca/content/uploads/2011/11/PbD-PIA-Foundational-Framework.pdf
3. Commission of the European Communities: i2010 eGovernment Action Plan, Brussels (2006), http://europa.eu/legislation_summaries/information_society/strategies/124226j_en.htm
4. de Andrade, N.N.G.: Towards a European eID Regulatory Framework, Challenges in Constructing a Legal Framework for the Protection and Management of Electronic Identities. In: Gutwirth, S., et al. (eds.) European Data Protection: In Good Health? (2002)
5. Document on IDABC - Interoperability Activities, http://ec.europa.eu/idabc/en/document/5319/5883.html
6. European Commission, How does the data protection reform strengthen citizens' rights? http://ec.europa.eu/justice/data-protection/document/review2012/factsheets/2_en.pdf
7. European Union (EU), Directive 2006/123/EC of the European Parliament and of the council on services in the internal market. Official Journal of European Communities of 23 November 1995, No L. 376, 36 (1995)
8. European Union (EU), Directive 95/46/EC of the European Parliament and of the Council on the Protection of Individuals with regard to the Processing of Personal Data and on the Free Movement of Such Data. Official Journal of the European Communities of 23 November 1995, No L. 281, 31 (1995)
9. FIDIS, Future of Identity in the Information Society, http://www.fidis.net/
10. Hansen, M.: Top 10 Mistakes in System Design from a Privacy Perspective and Privacy Protection Goals. In: Camenisch, J., Crispo, B., Fischer-Hübner, S., Leenes, R., Russello, G. (eds.) Privacy and Identity 2011. IFIP AICT, vol. 375, pp. 14–31. Springer, Heidelberg (2012)
11. Jori, A.: Data Protection Law – An Introduction. Privacy and privacy protection (2007), http://www.dataprotection.eu/pmwiki/pmwiki.php?n=Main.Privacy
12. Lusoli, W., Maghiros, I., Bacigalupo, M.: eID policy in a turbulent environment: is there a need for a new regulatory framework? European Commission Joint Research Centre (2009)
13. Majava, J., Graux, H.: Common specifications for eID interoperability in the eGovernment context, eID Interoperability for PEGS. Technical Report, IDABC eGovernment eServices (2007)
14. Modinis-IDM, https://www.cosic.esat.kuleuven.be/modinis-idm/twiki/bin/view.cgi
15. Otjacques, B., Hitzelberger, P., Feltz, F.: Identity Management and Data Sharing in the European Union. In: 39th Hawaii International Conference on System Sciences (2006)

16. Personal Identifiable Information, http://en.wikipedia.org/wiki/ Personally_identifiable_information
17. Stefanova, K., Kabakchieva, D., Nikolov, R.: Design Principles of Identity Management Architecture Development for Cross-Border eGovernment Services. Electronic Journal of e-Government 8(2), 189–202 (2010)
18. Stern, M.: D5.8.3d Security Principles and Best Practices. STORK Deliverable (2011)
19. STORK, Secure identity across borders linked, https://www.eid-stork.eu/
20. STORK2 – Secure identity across borders linked 2.0, https://www.eid-stork2.eu/
21. Strauß, S.: The Limits of Control – (Governmental) Identity Management from a Privacy Perspective. In: Fischer-Hübner, S., Duquenoy, P., Hansen, M., Leenes, R., Zhang, G. (eds.) Privacy and Identity Management for Life. IFIP AICT, vol. 352, pp. 206–218. Springer, Heidelberg (2011)
22. Svantesson, D., Clarke, R.: Privacy and consumer risks in cloud computing. Computer Law & Security Review, 391–397 (2010)
23. Whittaker, Z.: Yes, U.S. authorities can spy on EU cloud data. Here's how, http://www.zdnet.com/yes-u-s-authorities-can-spy-on-eu-cloud-data-heres-how-7000010653/
24. Zwingelberg, H., Hansen, M.: Privacy Protection Goals and Their Implications for eID Systems. In: Camenisch, J., Crispo, B., Fischer-Hübner, S., Leenes, R., Russello, G. (eds.) Privacy and Identity 2011. IFIP AICT, vol. 375, pp. 245–260. Springer, Heidelberg (2012)
25. European Commission, Proposal for a Regulation of the European Parlament and of the Council, on the protection of individuals with regards to the processing of personal data and on the free movement of such data (General Data Protection Regulation), Brussels (2012)
26. Marchini, R.: Cloud Computing Under The European Commission, Proposed Regulation To Revise The EU Data Protection Framework. In: World Data Protection Report, vol. 12, Bloomberg BNA (2012)

Constructing Security: Reflections on the Margins of a Case Study of the Use of Electronic Identification in ICT Platforms in Schools

Mariana S. Gustafsson

Department for Management and Engineering,
Political Science Unit, Linköping University, Sweden
mariana.s.gustafsson@liu.se

Abstract. This paper addresses how people construct meanings regarding "the concept of security", based upon the descriptions collected from participants in a case study of the use of electronic identification in ICT platforms in schools. The aim of the paper is to reflect on the concept of security by identifying and analyzing how people build their own understanding of security when using ICT platforms in schools. The analysis identifies three ontological instances of security: security as an ideal state of affairs, security as a value and information security. The analysis also clarifies the difference between the objective and subjective nature of security, as well as the differences between factual and perceived information security. As a result, I raise several research questions concerning "security", and identify common assumptions with regard to constructing the concept of security.

Keywords: security, ontological, epistemological, construction, meaning, empirical.

1   Introduction

Secure identification plays a crucial role in the relations between citizens and public authorities, and it becomes even more important as societies become more complex, integrated and globalized [1]. The process by which societies become increasingly technological and interconnected inherently involves multiple aspects of security [2] owing to the increased use of digital applications and tools [3-5]. The e-government environment is increasingly the forum for interaction between citizens and the state [6]. Identification through digital systems becomes a structural condition when societies build their electronic governments, as well as an issue affecting personal relations that govern daily practices [7-9]. The increasingly digital society within which e-government develops and becomes more integrated into citizens' daily practices raises the need for safe and trustworthy arrangements in relation to the use of ICT.

In a mature welfare state, where citizens express a high level of trust toward the state [10], there is also a high level of interaction between the state and its citizens. As a result, this type of state experiences increasing demands for more and

M. Hansen et al. (Eds.): Privacy and Identity 2014, IFIP AICT 421, pp. 224–236, 2014.

comprehensive public e-services and an increasing density of interactions between citizens and authorities. The context of the Scandinavian welfare state is interesting for the purpose of analyzing the construction of security in this sense, firstly because there is a high level of basic trust among citizens toward the state and secondly because there are clear policy ambitions to reach an almost complete coverage for e-government.

The use of ICT in education in Sweden has a long history and access to computers among teachers, pupils and parents is constantly increasing, approaching full population coverage, 94 percent in 2012, [11, 12]. A number of school reforms - and notably the new Education Act (2011) - demand increased and systematic reporting of pupils' school progression, which will lead to an increased use of ICT in education administration. In this context, systems for secure log-in and identification become essential and emerge as a commonly used platform within the local citizens - public authorities interaction. In this interaction, essential information, including sensitive information, is transferred among several user groups. The pupil's privacy, autonomy and integrity are ultimately at stake. Teachers, pupils and parents have to communicate on a variety of more or less sensitive issues including the study progression of the pupil, individual assessments and learning goal achievement. Teachers also have to report potentially sensitive data to head teachers, mentors and other administrative authorities. There is a general high demand on the teachers' professionalism and the standardization of pupil assessment tools and procedures in order to maintain a high quality of education and learning target achievement in schools. The use of ICT systems in teaching and in the administration of education is therefore developing rapidly and involving an array of security-related issues.

The aim of the paper is to reflect on the concept of security as the object of study by identifying and analyzing how people build their meaning regarding security when using ICT platforms in schools. In the following text, I present an account of 'security' from a constructivist perspective. I start with a clarification of the research design, where I present some analytical tools and assumptions within the constructivist approach and show how this case opens up to a reflective study. This is followed by a short presentation of the case study on use of ICT platforms in schools, which represents our empirical data source on the margins of which I build my reflections. Then, I engage in a reflective analysis to clarify the concept of security from ontological and epistemological perspectives. The reflective analysis is central in understanding the object of study, constructing further research questions and choosing frameworks for analysis and argumentation [13, 14]. Finally, I close with a few concluding remarks where I ask myself: what was the meaning of the argument, what can be learnt from it, and how can it be used in further research.

2 Research Design

As the title of this paper implies, this is a reflective account on the margins of a qualitative case study on the use of ICT platforms and secure log-in. 'On the margins' means that I engage in reflections on 'the concept of security', dialoguing with the empirical material from the case study, rather than using it to explain the theory [15]. 'On the margins' also means that I oscillate in my reflective constructions [15] between the theoretical realm and the empirical realm, viewing them as connected to each other. In my reflections, I use different names for the same things depending on whether I use them in the abstract, theoretical sense or in the empirical, practice-related sense. For example, I use in my analysis 'FRONTER-ICT platforms-platforms-technical artifacts' and 'teachers-participants-users-people' interchangeably depending on the level of reflection (i.e. closer to the theory or closer to the empirical material).

A methodological implication of this approach (experienced during the process of analysis) is that, when the analysis lies close to the theoretical realm, it is difficult to pinpoint specific quotes in the interviews and focus groups (as it is required in the conventional qualitative data analysis [16, 17] and expected by the reader). This is due to the fact that there are several complex layers of analysis and interpretation between what was actually said and my reflections on it. To a certain extent, the references used below will not be extracted directly from the raw interview transcripts, but those constructed in the process of dialogue with the empirical data. Reference is then made to the entire interview or focus group. The resulting critique is that the participant and the personal character of the qualitative data disappear when the reflections become more abstract. Apart from that, the analysis is based on a primary and classical structuring and systematization of data in categories (in this case: participants' use of notions, assumptions, functions, attitudes, beliefs and actions on security) and patterns (in this case recurring themes on security), followed by a 'dialogue' with the data using analytical tools from the constructivist approach and the distinction between ontological and epistemological stances. The questions that guide my dialogue with the empirical material are thus: how do people perceive 'security' in the context of their work in school; what is security believed to be, what are the assumptions, the attitudes and the actions involved.

For a more detailed account on the methodology of the empirical case study itself, I am compelled to refer the reader to two other papers that focus to a larger extent on the empirical level [18, 19].

2.1 Short Presentation of the Case Study

The qualitative case study on the use of ICT platforms and secure log-in was conducted in the Linköping municipality (150 000 inhabitants) in the framework of the nationally-funded project 'Future Safe Electronic Identification'[1]. We focused both on the municipality administration, which is responsible for education and schooling, and on the platform use at 5 schools. The sample choice was based on a preliminary mapping of the 'history of use' of ICT platforms by all 56 schools in the municipality, the inclusion of both public and private schools and the inclusion of large (more than 300 pupils) and small (less than 300 pupils) schools. All five schools were at compulsory and upper secondary level, one of the schools was a 'free school' publicly-funded but

[1] Project financed by the Swedish Civil Contingencies Agency

run by a private organization. Seven interviews and 9 focus groups, involving forty-four participants (school principals (4), teachers (17), schools' platform administrators (2), pupils (13)[2] and municipality officials - users of platforms (8)) were the main sources of primary data[3]. The research design strived to reach key participants who could report to us about the school organization and their experience with using the platforms FRONTER, DEXTER, SKOLA 24 and other ICT systems in their work and studies. In addition, local policy documents were analyzed in order to learn about the background of the processes and policy statements made both regarding these specific systems and the municipal e-government in general.

2.2   The ICT Platforms

In the analysis of the constructions of meaning on 'security', we draw on the empirical findings regarding the use of ICT platforms in schools. The two widely used ICT Platforms in schools are DEXTER and FRONTER, and SKOLA 24, which is used in the free school in our sample. Alternative platforms are not offered by the municipality. The municipality statistics show a constant increase in the use of the platforms, from 338 active users in September 2005 to 6865 active users in September 2012 [18]. The primary schools use the attendance function and the grading function offered by DEXTER. FRONTER is used both as a learning-teaching platform and as an administrative tool for managing work-tasks like pupil documentation (pupils' individual development plans (IUPs) and individual assessment (SOs), goals, portfolio and attendance records), administration and planning. All three platforms provide similar functions in the administration of education. The schools differ in their frequency and range of use of the platforms. FRONTER and SKOLA 24 have been used primarily as learning and teaching tools. They are now being considered for their administrative functionality in schools. As these platforms will be increasingly used in the administration of education, secure log-in solutions to access them are currently being considered. eID is presently considered as the most secure identification tool that can be used to log-in to the platforms.

3   A Constructivist Perspective and Analytical Tools

In my reflection on the concept of security, I borrow some analytical tools from Searle's theory on construction of social reality [20]. As a result, I embrace some of the assumptions that he makes concerning sense-making of reality, namely that there is a reality out there that is totally independent of people. According to this theory, people understand social reality – 'social facts' through their purpose for the human activity. For example, 'Cars are for driving, dollars for earning, spending and saving, bathtubs for taking a bath' [20]. The reality of everyday life is constantly interpreted

---

[2] Grade 9 in compulsory school and grade 1 in upper secondary school.

[3] In the accomplishing stage of this paper, some additional 11 interviews with parents have been carried out, but have not been included in the analysis.

by people and presents itself as meaningful to them. Berger and Luckmann differentiate between different spheres of reality, among which, one is chosen to be 'the reality of everyday life' - the reality that is most ordered and most meaningful to the consciousness of the person [21].

3.1   Assignment of Function, Objectivity, Institutional Facts

It lies in the human nature, or in our experience of the world, to assign functions to objects or phenomena, 'we do not experience things as material objects, much less as collections of molecules. Rather, we experience a world of chairs and tables, houses and cars, lecture halls, pictures, streets gardens, houses, and so forth' [20]. Sense-making and construction of social reality depends on our concept of objectivity and the difference between objective and subjective. Epistemologically speaking, 'objective' and 'subjective' are primarily predicates of judgment [20]. In the ontological sense, 'objective' and 'subjective' are predicates of entities and types of entities and they ascribe modes of existence [20]. Searle distinguishes between brute and institutional facts. Brute facts exist independently of any human institution, including language. Institutional facts require special human institutions for their existence. Language is one such institution, but there is a whole set of other institutions. I will not focus on the institution of language in this paper. 'Institutional facts' are dependent on collective human agreement or acceptance in contrast to 'brute facts' [20]. It is in these terms that I am interested to study the concept of security and its meaning in the 'reality of everyday life' of people. I proceed to do this by analyzing and interpreting people's understanding of security in connection to their use of the platforms. The concept of security can thus be considered as built on institutional meaning [21] or 'institutional facts' [22], as it is a result of institutional arrangements among people.

3.2   Actual and Perceived Security

Concurrently, I make use of Oscarson's [23] concepts of actual and perceived information security in order to clarify the distinction itself and generate further reflections on the construction of security as an institutional fact. Actual information security is a factual, objective state of information security in a system, including all aspects of security arrangements [23]. Perceived information security is a subjective interpretation made by a single individual in his or her context and based on personal knowledge and experience. There is always a difference between actual and perceived information security, since people never can reach a complete knowledge about the degree of actual information security at a specific point in time. The perceptions of information security can differ among different subjects who act in the same organization, as these are influenced by the nature of their work, the knowledge they possess, experience, own analysis and judgment. Even events outside one's organization or fields can influence one's perception, for example media representations, rumors, incidents in other organizations [23].

4   An Ontologic and Epistemologic Account on Security

The ontology of 'security' in this study is inevitably colored by the people, the schools' organizational set-up, and their actual use of a number of specific ICT platforms in their work. These people are active in the education system, which is within the authority of the state, and have specific roles as pupils, teachers, principals, coordinators, etc. This fact presents both the context and the active environment where, through their work and use of ICT platforms, they form and categorize their perceptions of security based upon their assumptions, beliefs and attitudes with regard to security and technologies in general.

4.1   Security in Terms of Categories Used

Security appears to be a current and relevant issue in the overall workings of the school system, specifically in the public administration of education as a whole. Two aspects appear to be central in the participants' systems of categories, beliefs, assumptions and actions: a) the nature of work in the school that continuously produces a large amount of information about the pupil; and b) the increasing use of electronic platforms for teaching, learning and the administration of pupil data. The security of pupil-related information thus emerges as a central concept in the interviews. Protecting sensitive data about the pupils and ultimately protecting the child is defined as an essential role assumed by the interviewees.

Due to successive reforms in the Swedish school sector, reflected also in the Education Act (2001), teachers are required to document and follow up each pupil in every subject. These legal requirements impose a change in work methods in schools so as to provide SOs for the pupils and thoroughly informed IUPs. Due to the thoroughness and systematic character of the process, the nature of this information is becoming increasingly sensitive, as more and more specific data about the pupil will be documented. Consequently, increasing administrative burden induces the use of ICT in the administration of education in schools. Thus, security implications lie in the potentially sensitive nature of pupil-related information per se and are further complicated by the digitalization of this information through the use of ICT platforms. While the fact that pupil-related information produced in schools is potentially sensitive, being often a gray area, and may lend itself to subjective evaluation is a serious issue, the confusion among the teachers concerning whether SOs and IUPs are subject to the principle of public access to official records is a fundamental problem.

The participants' perceptions of 'security' seem to be rooted in the two aspects described above. This fact explains the categories, the assumptions and the attitudes they have about security in connection to the use of and log-in to the ICT platforms. I intentionally chose to approach 'security' openly and not limit it to 'information security', or 'operational security' or 'individual's security', and thus followed openly the ways in which people expressed their thoughts, attitudes and assumptions by sharing and discussing their experience of using ICT platforms in schools. Based on my interpretation of- and dialogue with the participants' categories, assumptions and attitudes,

I identified three ontological instances of 'security': security as a desired state of affairs, security as a value and information security. Each of these are explained below.

Security as a state of affairs and an aim to be reached

On a very basic level, security is perceived as a state of affairs or a position that people desire and want to achieve in their organizations [24-27]. Security is in this respect an ideal situation that is intentionally sought and it seems to imply protection of the group and stability in the organization. Analytically, it appeared more relevant to refer to the systems of categories used, the logic of argument and the participants' assumptions rather than specific words, quotations, or categories that they used in the interviews. I observed intentionality in the individuals' understanding of security. This was expressed in their perceptions of what should be done to ensure security, in their emphasis on assuming a careful attitude in handling sensitive information and in their worries regarding negative effects in the eventuality of insecurity within the platform [28-31]. 'If more personal information will be stored there (ed. FRONTER), then it should be made more secure' [25]. 'There are always (ed. security) shortages with everything that is stored on the internet. Things that are too sensitive, that others shouldn't get access to, should not be stored there... Things get more secure apparently, but it is safest outside internet, outside the computer... You wouldn't even notice the intrusion.' [32]. At this fundamental level it is difficult to see any differences between the participants, and the citations presented above show just a glimpse of the entire picture that emerged from the interviews. Intentionality lies in the assumptions of participants, where it is implied that security is something desirable and necessary.

Security as a value

Again, on a fundamental level, security seems to be a value that is inherent to human activity. The value of protection of the person's integrity, autonomy and privacy seem to be fundamentally connected to the (assumed) virtues of democratic forms of organization. It was expressed, for example, in a focus group with pupils that: 'If the SOs will be more specific, then one needs to have more secure channels to store them... But if somebody gets access to your password and all your stored information, then it is not good' [25]. 'If somebody got access to my logbook (in the platform), then I would be hated in my class' [32]. In the same context, a school principal stated: 'From a security point of view, it feels really good to not need to e-mail things (ed. sensitive information) among us' [28]. A fact that is specific to the organizations in this study is that the subjects of these security concerns are children, who are considered vulnerable per definition and whose protection and security is seen to be at the center of their activity, next to education and socialization. A teacher in an interview described the situation: 'I create a room on FRONTER for the pre-school class where I want to show what we have done in different contexts. I must ask the parents to approve my use of the pictures. Then I have to make sure that those children whose parents didn't approve do not appear there. It's a lot like this today, if we shall film or not the Lucia parade. Unfortunately, we live in a society today where we have to be careful with these things' [30]. Another teacher specified a related aspect: 'Another question of pupil integrity is when parents get the opportunity to control the child through their access to the school platform, for example when you have honour-related conflicts in the family'. In this sense, security was often perceived in terms of the need to protect children as vulnerable persons, the need to protect and handle carefully sensitive data that could affect a child's integrity, autonomy or privacy. A common assumption that is observed here is that a person's integrity, autonomy and privacy are secured through democratic institutions, where these are part of fundamental human rights.

The category 'sensitive information' was central at this level. Sensitive, but also longitudinal and systematic information about the pupil, as well as work-related assessments on sensitive cases provide critical information that can tragically affect the respective pupil autonomy, integrity and privacy in case of criminal intent and unauthorized use. The participants' experience shows that the area is gray and that there are no clear legal regulations or policies to address this new type of sensitive data produced in schools [26, 29, 30, 33]. The teachers agreed that: 'We are forced to write down a lot of things about the pupils that you assume will not come out. But if an interested person comes and requests that information... She has the right to get them. Just make a copy and take with you' [26] . A school principal pointed that: 'We produce public records that we give to the pupil who can lose them on the bus or store them in a digital system where it can go astray. But this is a public record and we can't write sensitive information in a public record' [29]. Awareness of this gray area and actions to address potential dilemmas also emerged as issues of concern among the participants. Another important issue that emerged from the study, was the participants' increased concern with the potential negative effects of excessive emphasis on security as a value in the e-democracy and electronic public administration, namely, with its tendency to result in overprotection and intrusion into personal privacy that could lead to control and surveillance of individuals [30, 34, 35].

Information security
This is not a fundamental perception that is placed at the level of the two presented above. It is however obvious in our case that both the users and the schools are affected by the use of technical artifacts, in this case ICT platforms. Our participants need to use technical artifacts to manage their work and studies. They regard the platforms as tools to be used to achieve their primary goals of education and socialization. A school principal (backed by another principal in a different interview) emphasized that 'There is a tendency in the data system to impose requirements on how one should work. If it appears that FRONTER does not have the needed adaptability and presents too many demands to change the way we work, we will not use it or will use it sparely. We want a tool that fits our work and not vice-versa' [33]. They are also aware of the security risks involved with using electronic artifacts [26, 27, 30, 31, 33, 35]. The vocabulary and arguments used in this sense are more specific and have a clear message. At this level, there are plenty of concerns regarding operational security, secure log-in and advanced identification tools such as eID, privacy, unauthorized information access and differentiated information display, operability of the platforms, security risks, ownership of information, etc. These concerns are expressed specifically by the camp comprised of IT coordinators, municipality officials and

municipality system administrators, and even some FRONTER administrators in schools [24, 26, 27, 29, 31, 33-36].

As for the camp that represents the school system – principals and teachers, I observed a distance from the technicalities connected with security aspects of the ICT platforms that they use. It is either assumed among the principals that the platforms administered by the municipality meet the security requirements: 'I don't have that background and knowledge, I must rely on those who we buy the service from that they will take care of security' [28], or it is argued that the specific platform supposed to store and manage pupils IUPs and SOs, FRONTER, is not secure enough to contain sensitive information. Security risks and the reliability of the artifact belong to this discussion [24, 26, 27, 29, 31, 33-36]. As more and more sensitive information (pupil profiling) will be administered through more and more advanced ICT platforms, increasingly high demands will be placed both on the technical artifact itself and on the users of the artifact, i.e. teachers, pupils and parents. The platforms will have to meet high security requirements and will, at the same time, have to be simple and lend themselves to intuitive use, as expressed by the users: 'As more systematic and specific information will be shared at all levels..., it is important that sensitive information stays on the right side of the threshold... It will require the system to manage different types of information and at the same time be easy and functional for the different and frequent users' [27]. The users who will get administrative rights to change the content of the platform and even develop it through use will have a high burden of responsibility to manage sensitive pupil data accordingly. 'Responsibility' was thus another central category that fueled the participants' perceptions and assumptions with regard to achieving security through the use of ICT platforms in schools [28-31, 33, 37].

4.2   How Do People Construct Security?

Once I de-construct 'security' and conclude that at the fundamental level security is an ideal state of affairs that people intentionally strive to achieve and to which people assign a fundamental value, I proceed to reconstruct the concept of security based on the participants' categories, attitudes, actions and rules pertaining to their use of ICT platforms in schools. The analysis below engages in ontological and epistemological rationalizations regarding the concept of security based primarily on some of J. R. Searle's concepts and analytical tools pertaining to the process of constructing social reality. Clarifying the ontological and epistemological stances in approaching 'security' as the object of study is an important platform, upon which interesting, non-evident research questions can be constructed or theories built [13, 15]. While doing this, I try to keep the focus on- and correlate between the three ontological instances of security, i.e. security as an ideal state of affairs, security as a value and information security.

As discussed above, security exists at least in three different instances and the first question to ask is what kind of entity is security – is it something that is 'out there' independent of human perception, something like the rocks or the sun or is it something that exists only because we have created it and once the last human perishes it disappears from existence. That is to ask whether security has an objective or a subjective existence in the first place. It seems that security is both, based on an important distinction between ontological and epistemological stances that Searle helps clarify [22]. In the ontological sense, i.e. as a form of existence, security at the most fundamental level seems to be an entity dependent on the fact that people feel it, desire it and need it. That means that without people, security does not exist. In contrast, without people the sun or the rocks would exist; that makes them ontologically objective entities or facts. Therefore in ontological terms security is always subjective.

An interesting thing happens when I take the epistemological stance. That is, to judge whether security is a subjective or an objective fact. Through sense-making and judgment people make true or false statements about security. The truth and falsity of the judgments on security appear to depend on the attitudes, beliefs, and assumptions of the same or other people. Thus, from the epistemological point of view, security is subjective, but only *to a certain degree* [22]. Namely, if the same subjective judgment on security is made by a large part or an entire group of people, then this subjective judgment will objectivize the object of judgment, which is security in this case. From the epistemological perspective, I can thus say that security as an ideal state of affairs and security as a value presents objective judgments or objective facts (using Searle's terms) that are independent of individual attitudes, beliefs and feelings. The objectivized judgment about security (that needs further reflection) will thus be that regardless of individual culture, organizations, religions or beliefs, security in terms of protection and stability (i.e. security as a state of affairs and a value) is something that people need in order to live.

4.3   Perceived and Factual Security

What about information security, i.e. the third ontological instance identified in this case? Also from an epistemological perspective, I concentrate on the factual security and perceived security suggested by Oscarson [23] in his analysis of security of information systems. Factual security in this sense is the totality of people's judgments on whether an information system is secure, thus making it an objective fact. However, what I find in our case, when it comes to ICT platforms, people consider themselves as not having enough technical knowledge of FRONTER or other platforms in order to judge how secure they actually are [26, 29, 34, 35, 37]. There is thus a variety of judgments on the security of the platforms based mainly on the participants' actual use of these platforms in school, i.e. based on how they function, as well as on their beliefs and attitudes toward information technology in general.

The perceived security of the platforms is thus based on the people's experience and knowledge of them though practical use. And their experience as users shows clearly that the platforms are perceived as not secure [26, 29, 30, 33, 35, 37]. An epistemological question arises regarding what kind of knowledge and how much knowledge is needed so that a judgment on the security of an information system is objectivized? Lack of technical knowledge among the users of the platforms (all our participants are users of the platforms) appears, in our case, to be substituted with reliance on the authorities' (i.e. the municipality) knowledge and responsibility to ensure the security of ICT platforms. 'The municipality is considering a tool for digitalizing sensitive information. Then I assume that they have taken the responsibility to ensure that there is a sufficient level of security in it. This means some form of two-step log-in [29]', a school principal said. This substitution of knowledge seems to be enough for at least some of the users in order to assume that the platforms are secure [26, 29, 30, 33, 35, 37]. This substitution also implies trust in the authorities and their role in ensuring the security of the platforms.

However, this substitution does not seem to be sufficient to provide a base for all the users to judge the platforms as secure, since there are grounds to question whether the authorities indeed have the knowledge or take the responsibility to ensure the security of the platforms. This is also the case in our empirical study [29, 30, 37]. The question is then: when there is a perceived lack of technical knowledge about the platforms among the users, can they objectivize their judgments on the security of the platforms through mere use of the platform? The assumption would be that, if people use the platform long enough to see it function securely, they will eventually objectivize their judgment about it and perceive it as secure, i.e. achieve factual security. However, testing this assumption appears problematic as the ICT platforms' lives (and existence) are short, which means that in practice there will never be enough time to gather enough knowledge and experience enough use in order to objectivize a judgment on their security.

The next interesting question is then: can people, through their practical use of different technical artifacts, over time objectivize their judgments – and thus arrive at (construct) objective facts – regarding the security of these technical artifacts? Or, considering the fact (and this seems indeed to be an objectivized judgment) that all the information technology in the internet age involves security risks of different natures (and existences), security through technical artifacts is not possible in the epistemological sense. Furthermore, I may continue this thought and argue that through the perceived and actual security risks that are connected to technology, there is a possibility that information technologies can endanger the first two ontological (and fundamental) instances of security - i.e. security as a value and security as an ideal state of affairs.

5   Concluding Remarks and Further Research

What can then be concluded from these arguable accounts on security? Where and how can I use them? Where did they bring me? Have I brought you anywhere? Looking back at them, these are reflections on the nature of security driven by curiosity to learn about- and understand 'security' as object of research. I oscillate between different levels of abstraction and keep my case study in one hand (and Searle's book in the other), in order to keep me on the ground.

Making a difference between ontological and epistemological natures of objects is fundamental in understanding what I am studying. Through these accounts I have clarified some basic questions that need to be asked before building more meaning and argument about them through academic endeavors. The study presents some value for the information systems research by reflecting on the difference between factual and perceived security using the ontological and epistemological stances, opening thus further questions, such as - what kind of knowledge and how much knowledge is needed so that a judgment on security of an information system is objectivized; can people through their practical use of different technical artifacts over time objectivize their judgments in order to arrive to (construct) objective facts of security, is security possible to achieve through use of technical artifacts. The study presents also a contribution to the e-government research in terms of approaching security as an issue of e-government developing and integrating into citizens' daily lives. The study opens for further reflection on institutional arrangements, such as eID, that are currently created in the context of e-government.

References

1. Giddens, A.: The consequences of modernity. Polity in association with Blackwell, Cambridge (1990)
2. Beck, U., Ritter, M.: Risk society: towards a new modernity. Theory, culture & society. Sage, London (1992); 99–948605
3. Castells, M.: The information age: economy, society and culture. The rise of the network society, vol. 1. Blackwell, Malden (1996)
4. Castells, M.: The information age: economy, society and culture. The power of identity, vol. 2. Blackwell, Malden (1997)
5. Castells, M.: Communication power. Oxford Univ. Press, Oxford (2011)
6. Heeks, R., Bailur, S.: Analyzing e-government research: Perspectives, philosophies, theories, methods, and practice. Government Information Quarterly 24(2), 243–265 (2007)
7. Axelsson, K., Melin, U., Lindgren, I.: Public e-services for agency efficiency and citizen benefit-Findings from a stakeholder centered analysis. Government Information Quarterly 30(1), 10–22 (2013)
8. Melin, U., Axelsson, K., Söderström, F.: Managing the Development of Secure Identification – Investigating a National e-ID Initiative within a Public e-service Context. In: ECIS 2013. European Conference on Information Systems, Utrecht (2013)
9. Wihlborg, E.: eID (electronic identification) as an Innovation in the Interface of Politics and Technology, U. Symposium, Editor (2012)
10. Rothstein, B.: Creating Political Legitimacy: Electoral Democracy Versus Quality of Government. American Behavioral Scientist 53(3), 311–330 (2009)
11. Skolverket, IT-användning och it-kompetens i skolan, Skolverket, Editor. Stockholm, Skolverket (2013)
12. Sweden, S.: Use of computers and the Internet by private persons in 2012, Stockholm (2013)
13. Alvesson, M., Sandberg, J.: Constructing research questions: doing interesting research. SAGE, London (2013)
14. Alvesson, M., Sandberg, J.: Generating Research Questions Through Problematization. Academy of Management Review 36(2), 247–271 (2011)
15. Alvesson, M., Kärreman, D.: Qualitative research and theory development: mystery as method. Sage Publications, Thousand Oaks (2011)
16. Bryman, A.: Social research methods, 4th edn. Oxford University Press, Oxford (2012)

17. Creswell, J.W., Creswell, J.W.: Qualitative inquiry and research design: choosing among five approaches, 3rd edn. SAGE Publications, Thousand Oaks (2013)
18. Gustafsson, M., Wihlborg, E.: Organizing safe on-line interaction and trust in governmental services. A case study of identification channels for public e-services in schools. Je-DEM. The eJournal of eDemocracy and Open Government (2013)
19. Wihlborg, E., Gustafsson, M.: Electronic identification in practice – a case study of the use and organization of eID in public e-services in schools. In: SWEG 2013. 10th Scandinavian Workshop on E-government, Oslo (2013)
20. Searle, J.R.: The construction of social reality. Penguin, London (1996)
21. Berger, P.L., Luckmann, T.: The social construction of reality: a treatise in the sociology of knowledge. Doubleday, Garden City (1966)
22. Searle, J.R.: The construction of social reality. Free Press, New York (1995)
23. Oscarson, P.: Actual and perceived information systems security. Linköping studies in arts and science, pp. 0282–9800. Department of Management and Engineering, Linköping University, Linköping (2007)
24. FG_10.23_LK, FUSe - Framtidens säkra elektroniska identifiering – framväxt och användning av e-legitimationer. L. Universitet, Editor (2012)
25. FG_11.27_eBR, FUSe - Framtidens säkra elektroniska identifiering – framväxt och användning av e-legitimationer. L. universitet, Editor (2012)
26. FG_11.27_lBR, FUSe - Framtidens säkra elektroniska identifiering – framväxt och användning av e-legitimationer. L. universitet, Editor (2012)
27. I_10.22_LK, FUSe - Framtidens säkra elektroniska identifiering – framväxt och användning av e-legitimationer. L. Universitet, Editor (2012)
28. I_11.14_rBJ, FUSe - Framtidens säkra elektroniska identifiering – framväxt och användning av e-legitimationer. L. universitet, Editor (2012)
29. I_11.27_rBR, FUSe - Framtidens säkra elektroniska identifiering – framväxt och användning av e-legitimationer. L. universitet, Editor (2012)
30. I_12.04_FFK, FUSe - Framtidens säkra elektroniska identifiering – framväxt och användning av e-legitimationer. L. universitet, Editor (2012)
31. I_12.05_rFK, FUSe - Framtidens säkra elektroniska identifiering – framväxt och användning av e-legitimationer. L. universitet, Editor (2012)
32. FG_12.04_eFK, FUSe - Framtidens säkra elektroniska identifiering – framväxt och användning av e-legitimationer. L. universitet, Editor (2012)
33. I_11.06_rAT, FUSe - Framtidens säkra elektroniska identifiering – framväxt och användning av e-legitimationer. L. universitet, Editor (2012)
34. FG_11.14_lBJ, FUSe - Framtidens säkra elektroniska identifiering – framväxt och användning av e-legitimationer. L. universitet, Editor (2012)
35. FG_12.04_lFK, FUSe - Framtidens säkra elektroniska identifiering – framväxt och användning av e-legitimationer. L. universitet, Editor (2012)
36. I_11.12_LK, FUSe - Framtidens säkra elektroniska identifiering – framväxt och användning av e-legitimationer. L. universitet, Editor (2012)
37. FG_11.05_lAT, FUSe - Framtidens säkra elektroniska identifiering – framväxt och användning av e-legitimationer. L. universitet, Editor (2012)

Mobile Devices to the Identity Rescue

Gergely Alpár[1,2,*] and Maarten H. Everts[2,**]

[1] Institute for Computing and Information Sciences
Radboud University Nijmegen, The Netherlands
gergely@cs.ru.nl
[2] TNO, The Netherlands
maarten.everts@tno.nl

Abstract. Identity management is defined as the set of processes related to identity and access information for the whole identity life cycle in a system. In the open internet users need new methods for identity management that supply reliable authentication and sufficient user control. Currently applied methods often lack a proper level of security (*e.g.*, passwords) and privacy (*e.g.*, diverse processing of personal data).

A personal smart card and a personal smart phone can communicate using near-field communication (NFC). This allows users to apply their smart phone as a personal semi-trusted smart-card reader. For applications such as authentication, this `Trusted Couple` can then be used in a secure and intuitive way, like a remote card reader. As attribute-based credentials (ABCs) can efficiently be implemented on tamper-resistant smart cards with the current technology, we can achieve a more privacy-friendly and more flexible way of not only authentication but also role-based access control or management of personal information. In this paper we describe how a `Trusted Couple` can solve security, privacy, and usability problems in identity management.

Keywords: attribute-based credential, smart card, NFC, mobile phone, identity management.

1 Introduction

Identity management in our digital society is non-trivial. The traditional way of organisations to provision and manage identities is mostly not applicable across multiple domains and on the internet. There is currently no clear solution for users to manage their identities when carrying out transactions with different entities in a secure, privacy-friendly, and user-friendly manner [13,14,2]. As a result, typically service providers themselves manage all personal data about their customers now; however, this may not be desirable. The current practice of identity silos raises several problems for the data controller (i.e., the service provider, in this case):

* Partly supported by the research program Sentinels as project 'Mobile IDM' (10522). Sentinels is being financed by Technology Foundation STW, the Netherlands Organisation for Scientific Research (NWO), and the Dutch Ministry of Economic Affairs.
** Supported by the THeCS project as part of the Dutch national program COMMIT.

M. Hansen et al. (Eds.): Privacy and Identity 2014, IFIP AICT 421, pp. 237–247, 2014.

- Liability: in terms of data protection regulation;
- Economic: in terms of costs of authentication, authorisation, and keeping data up-to-date;
- Security: in terms of technical and procedural data protection, and prevention of phishing;

as well as for the users:

- Usability: in terms of the management of appropriate passwords and the use of many different authentication methods at various service providers;
- Privacy: in relation to the fact that personal data is processed by different companies in an opaque manner.

Practical solutions, with increasing adoption, exist in the form of network-based (centralised) identity management (e.g., SAML, OpenID). In such systems verifiers acquire identity information about users directly from the identity providers. Thus, this requires identity providers to be constantly online, resulting in security and privacy risk.

In contrast, attribute-based credentials (ABCs) [3,6,7,8,9] solve many of the identity-management problems without the need for the identity provider to be online at all times as it is not involved when a user interacts with a service provider. However, despite the promising properties of ABCs, building a practical system based on ABCs poses additional challenges in finding the appropriate trust models together with practical and intuitive user interaction.

Technological advances can support a transition towards user centricity in identity management [4]. The number of people owning NFC-enabled (see Section 2.3) smart phones[1] with internet access is increasing. Having a trusted smart card with a contactless communication interface, users can use their mobile phones as a smart-card reader to facilitate communication between the card and potentially remote verifiers (service providers). In this paper we argue that two personal devices, a tamper-resistant smart card that holds ABCs and an NFC-enabled smart phone, can constitute the proper user-controlled platform for authentication, for exchange of user attributes between identity providers and verifiers, and for managing personal digital information.

Our contribution is threefold. First, in Section 2 we describe a mechanism that enables a mobile phone to establish a channel with a web server that facilitates communication between a smart card and an authentication service. The process is simple and intuitive, moreover, it requires a user's explicit control over data release. Second, as this mechanism can host attribute-based credential technology, constituting a Trusted Couple, we study its possible, diverse applications. It supports not only secure and privacy-friendly authentication, but also personal attribute management and credential issuance. Third, recognising the strength of the setup, we show how ABCs and the Trusted Couple

---

[1] Smart phone brands that deliver NFC-enabled devices include Acer, Asus, Black-Berry, HTC, LG, Motorola, Nokia, Samsung, Sony, Vertu. http://www.nfcworld.com/nfc-phones-list/, accessed on March 14th, 2013.

can solve general identity management problems. These contributions bridge the gap between cryptography (theory, implementation) and deployment.

The rest of the paper is organised as follows. First, in Section 2 we give conceptual and technical background for attributes, ABCs, and the required wireless technologies. Second, having these tools, we can define a `Trusted Couple` in Section 3.1 and describe applications in Section 3.2; this includes authentication through a channel that enables remote card reading. Next, Section 4 gives an account of solutions for identity management problems. Finally, Section 5 concludes the paper with technical alternatives for the `Trusted Couple` and possible further research directions.

2   Preliminaries

Attribute-based credentials can be stored and deployed using mobile devices, and they motivate the introduction of a `Trusted Couple`. In this section the necessary underlying concepts and technologies (attributes, ABCs, NFC, and QR-codes) are discussed.

2.1   Attributes

An *attribute* in the context of this paper is a property or a qualification that holds for an individual. An *identity* of an individual within a scope can be considered as a set of his attributes. An attribute can be *identifying* or *non-identifying*. A name, a social security number, or a bank account number is identifying and, in fact, they are often used as identifiers. Non-identifying attributes can be the name of a city of residence or the boolean variable 'over 18', though in some specific scopes these attributes may be identifying.

A simple identity management model comprises three participants: an identity provider (or issuer), a service provider (or verifier), and a user. Although on an abstract level general identity management and ABC systems can be explained similarly (see Figure 1–(1)), the message flow in the latter case is quite different. Unlike in other conventional identity management in which the identity provider has a central position, the user is in the centre of the communication. A user can receive (a) certified attributes from issuers, and later show (b) the relevant ones to service providers (SPs) in order to authenticate—and eventually, to access some service or resource. The SP has to rely on the IdP that the attributes are true for the user; this trust assumption is the relation denoted by (c). We note that in conventional identity management the identity provider takes part of the actual authentication/authorisation process and it exchanges data with the service provider on channel (c).

2.2   Attribute-Based Credentials

An attribute-based credential [6,7,9] (ABC) is a cryptographic container of some attributes signed by an issuer who is entrusted with the task of attesting to and signing the credential. A name, a gender, and a date of birth are examples of attributes in an 'identity' credential, possibly issued by a governmental organisation. Further examples include (1) a 'loyalty' credential issued by an airline company consisting of a customer identifier, the current number of loyalty points, and a loyalty level attribute, or (2) an 'employee' credential consisting of a photo, an employee code, and some access right attributes issued by an employer.

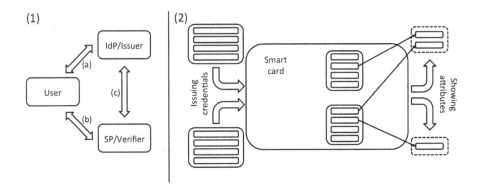

Fig. 1. (1) The general model of identity management. (2) An abstract view of attribute-based credentials on a smart card and selective disclosure of attributes.

Within the IRMA project[2] a secure ABC belonging to an individual is bound to a smart card which is, in turn, bound to its owner. Therefore, a credential or an attribute cannot be modified or transferred to a different user. Also, unlike in the physical world, attributes in a particular credential can be shown independently of each other using a so-called *selective disclosure* protocol; see Figure 1–(2). The processes of issuing credentials and showing attributes can be separated not only in time and place, but also in terms of cryptographic protocols: Issuer unlinkability and multi-show unlinkability make issuing and showing instances computationally unrelated by the underlying cryptographic techniques. The user-controlled communication operates as follows. After appropriate authentication and data verification (which may include attributes from the card), an issuer can issue a credential to a user's smart card. Later the card owner can show attributes from credentials on her card for authentication purposes to a service provider. Only relevant attributes (determined by some policy mechanism) needs to be revealed in this process.

---

[2] The IRMA technology is a pilot project and a proof of concept employing an efficient card implementation of Idemix attribute-based credentials [20]. IRMA stands for 'I Reveal My Attributes'; further information can be found on its web site: https://www.irmacard.org/. The current study is also based on the experiences in the IRMA project.

2.3   NFC and QR Codes

Two additional technologies are required to create a `Trusted Couple` from a phone and a smart card: NFC and QR codes.

Near-field-communication (NFC) is an extension of radio-frequency identification (RFID) and it provides a broader range of functionalities; see technical details and references in [1]. Applications using NFC in mobile devices include data exchange and payment. Several recent research projects propose to use NFC-enabled phones as card readers. While Alpár et al. [1] already consider the use of cards with ABCs, their primary focus is online banking. Morgner et al. [15] use an NFC-enabled mobile phone as a traditional card reader connecting it to a PC by a USB cable. Both papers argue that these devices are increasingly available; this is also in line with recent forecasts[3].

A QR code is a two-dimensional barcode that encodes text in a way that is easily scanned by machines; in particular using a camera included in most mobile phones. QR codes can be efficiently generated, making them available in applications with for instance ad hoc URLs. We note that unlike most of the technologies enabling communication between devices, scanning a QR code requires an intentional action from the user. This is particularly important in a world where wireless networks are ubiquitous. Furthermore, as shown in Section 3.2, a QR code enables easy connection from a browser session on a PC to a smart card (using a mobile phone) without problems related to firewall protection or mobile device discovery.

3   The `Trusted Couple`

We state that by combining a smart card and a mobile phone (`Trusted Couple`), the use of ABCs can become practical. To illustrate this, we describe three applications. But first, we specify what this `Trusted Couple` entails.

3.1   A Smart Card and a Mobile Phone

A `Trusted Couple` is defined as the combination of a smart card and a mobile phone that meet the following requirements.

– *Contactless smart card.* A smart card is assumed to be tamper resistant, so it cannot be cloned and secret values cannot be extracted from it. Furthermore, a smart card carries a working implementation of attribute-based credentials. It is possible to issue ABCs on the card and selectively disclose attributes from these credentials. A card holder is required to enter her PIN during a credential verification protocol. Finally, a card has a contactless interface that enables it to communicate with the phone.

---

[3] According to NFC World and API Research, 400 million NFC-enabled mobile devices are predicted to be delivered in 2013 and nearly 2 billion such devices are expected to be shipped in 2017. [21]

– *NFC-enabled mobile phone.* Using its NFC-interface, a phone can communicate with the smart card. In most applications, the phone is also required to have internet access to communicate with a remote server and to have a camera to scan QR codes. (In fact, this device does not need to be a phone, it can also be for example a tablet with Wi-Fi internet connection.) A phone is semi-trusted: it is assumed not to leak the PIN and attribute information. Note, however, that even if this information leaks, it does not enable a potential attacker to produce proofs about the attributes. In particular, an attacker needs a smart card to perform a full-fledged attack, which renders large-scale and remote attacks infeasible.

In summary, a phone acts here as a semi-trusted reader for the trusted smart card that helps in communicating both with the card owner and other entities (verifiers, issuers) in the identity management scope.

3.2   Running the Trusted Couple in Practice

Assuming the security and privacy properties of the attribute-based credential technology and their proper implementation (*e.g.*, [16,19,20]), we can design new applications using the Trusted Couple.

Authentication. Depending on the set of attributes that is disclosed in a verification protocol, we can distinguish two types. On the one hand, an identifying set of attributes provides a new, secure, and user-friendly way of authentication. For instance, a social network site or a governmental administration webpage can use the method as an alternative to logging in using a username and a password. On the other hand, non-identifying sets of attributes basically generalise the notion of role-based access control in a privacy-friendly manner. Attributes can carry general and specific information about the identity of a user and the relation between a user and her context.

Figure 2 shows an overview of such an authentication process, in which an NFC-enabled mobile phone becomes a *remote card reader* that is trusted by the user. The user visits (1) a webpage of a service provider (SP) that requires authentication. The SP's webpage presents a QR code (2). The user scans it (3) using her mobile phone. The QR code contains a URL that binds the browser's session to the phone. The mobile phone sends a request to that URL (4) to start a selective disclosure protocol and subsequently, receives the commands from the SP (5) to be sent to the smart card. The mobile phone asks the user to enter her PIN on the phone, and sends the commands to the smart card (6) through NFC. The smart card evaluates the request and verifies the PIN. The responses (in essence a fresh zero-knowledge proof about the attribute(s)) of the smart card (7) to the commands are then sent back to the SP (8) by the phone. Based on these responses the SP can decide whether or not the user should be given access to the resource. This is finally relayed back to the browser session on the PC (9) and in case of a successful authentication, the user is allowed to proceed to the service.

The use of a QR-code in this process not only binds the browser's session to the phone, it also requires a deliberate user action. Together with the application of the smart card, these conducts give the user a sense of control.

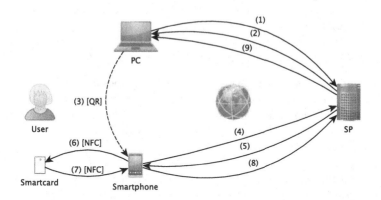

Fig. 2. Online authentication with the Trusted Couple

Credential Issuance. The verification process above can also be followed by a credential-issuing protocol in which case the SP is an issuer. We note that if the authentication is non-identifying, such a credential issuing process is in accord with the original notion of anonymous credentials [11,8].

To motivate anonymous use cases, we give an example. Consider the following privacy-friendly on-line shopping procedure. A user, already having an 'age' credential with the attribute 'over 16' and a 'student card' credential with the attribute 'university student', can buy an age-restricted 'festival ticket' credential with a student discount. Within the same secure session (not described, only assumed here), a verification procedure is extended with a subsequent issuance of a new credential. The resulting ticket credential may consist of the following attributes: serial number, beer coupon, start date, end date. The serial number makes sure that a ticket at the venue cannot be used more than once.

Card and Attribute Management. A smart card is trusted, but its content is usually not visible for its owner. However, because of the flexibility and variability of attribute-based identity management, it is desirable for a user to see what credentials she owns or when those credentials expire. Additionally, a user may also want to verify log entries on a smart card showing all credential issuance and verification events.

A Trusted Couple enables the owner to see the whole content of the card on the display of the phone. This application assists the management (*e.g.*, read, delete) of personal information and the possibility of checking a posteriori the use of a personal card.

4   To the Rescue in the Identity Crisis

According to [2], the current identity management practice, having a large number of unsolved problems, is an identity crisis. Similar concerns are presented in [10,13,12,14,18]. This section describes how a `Trusted Couple` can solve fundamental identity management problems.

By means of a `Trusted Couple`, attribute-based identity management is becoming practical which helps to realise the benefits of ABCs.

- First of all, the verification process of attributes does not *include the identity provider*; thus, security and privacy functionalities improve because (1) the IdP is not a *single point of failure*; (2) the IdP does not *know all user transactions*. As a result, no *surveillance* can be conducted based on such data records.
- Secondly, *phishing*, a major problem in online security in which users reveal secret authentication information to malicious parties, can efficiently be prevented. As authentication in our system relies on zero-knowledge proofs about secret keys and attributes residing on a tamper-resistant smart card, there is no efficient large-scale phishing possible. Also, as cards are assumed to be unclonable, *card owners have control over activities* of their cards. This also means that *identity fraud* becomes much harder.
- Thirdly, ABCs provide un*linkability across scopes*. In particular, showing credentials cannot be linked to their issuance protocols or other showing instances. This prevents tracing users, turning a system into *mass surveillance*, or construct combined profiles about them.
- Next, selective disclosure, a major functionality of ABCs, allows for revealing a minimally required amount of personal information during transactions. Furthermore, the attribute management is mainly carried out at the user's device, which is the lowest level and the most direct way in an identity system. Therefore, we achieve *proportionality* and *subsidiarity*. This is also in accordance with the European principle of data minimisation (Directive 1995/46/EC).
- Lastly, as attributes can express not only identifiers and roles but also such abstract concepts as *membership* and *ownership*, attribute-based identity management can achieve the new *paradigm of "is (s)he entitled?" to access a resource instead of "who?" accesses it*.

Not only do the benefits of attribute-based credentials become available, but also an important principle can be fulfilled. Having the `Trusted Couple`, the system achieves the law of *location independence*, defined in [2] as

> The identity system must allow a user to create, manage, and use his identity independently of his current location and current device in use.

First, users are not bound to one specific, static computer when they access different services. Even a potentially untrusted public PC can be suitable for users to log in to a system using their `Trusted Couple` as the authentication process does not require the transfer of secret information. Moreover, such a PC does not need any special hardware or software components, or additional drivers. In particular, smartcard readers are still not very common. Second, users do not have to involve their identity providers or any special infrastructure thereof when signing in to services.

In summary, ABCs provide security for verifiers and privacy for the card owner while the `Trusted Couple` provides independence for users from particular computers, systems, or identity providers.

5   Conclusion

In this paper we described how a `Trusted Couple` (a trusted smart card and a semi-trusted mobile phone) can help solving challenges in the current identity crisis. As smart cards become increasingly powerful, ABCs are expected to be available in many more applications. At the same time, more and more mobile phones are equipped with NFC chips. The ubiquity of these technologies makes the described setup and the applications truly practical and user friendly. As a result, processing of personal data and authorisation on the internet and in a broader context may become more secure and more privacy friendly.

Technological Variations. We briefly enumerate some possible alternatives and extensions to a `Trusted Couple`. (1) A *card reader* is an obvious alternative to a phone. However, it provides only a limited set of functionalities compared to a smart phone [15] and it entails an additional tool for users to carry. (2) As an improvement, the relation between the card and the phone can be reinforced by *binding* the devices within a `Trusted Couple`. This requires an additional shared secret key between the phone and the card. (3) Mobile devices are expected to provide *trusted states* in the near future; see ARM's TrustZone[4] and Intel's TXT[5]. Mobile phones in such a trusted state, being verifiably malware-free, can be used as a reliable PIN pad. (4) Besides a mobile phone's trusted state, phones may provide *reliable functionalities for storage and cryptographic operations*. Thus, they can act like a smart card. However, two problems then arise: (a) What can create the link between the phone's trusted and untrusted states? (b) How does the trust assumption change if the `Trusted Couple` merges into one device? Bichsel et al. [5] propose two protocols in this setup but in a different model: In their proposal, the local PC is more trusted and both directions of the zero-knowledge proofs are conveyed by QR codes. (5) Another trend is that *smart cards may be soon equipped with a display and a keyboard*[6]. Since smart cards are not yet expected to have other communication interfaces (*e.g.*, camera, any internet access), it is not clear how they can be applied in online scenarios. And again, merging the device that carries ABCs and the device that provides user-interaction changes trust assumptions.

---

[4] http://www.arm.com/products/processors/technologies/trustzone.php
[5] http://software.intel.com/en-us/articles/
  intel-trusted-execution-technology
[6] http://www.nidsecurity.com/microsite/mastercard/

Further Research. Other directions in research and development include *more direct and user-friendly control* when personal information is exposed. A system of verifier certificates and a posteriori log monitoring are possible using the current IRMA technology [3,20], but an intuitive selection of revealed attributes in particular applications is not yet provided to the user. The IRMA technology provides ways to separate different personas (*e.g.*, citizen, social web, financial, academic, etc.) of the same user by arranging credentials in different sets on a card or by applying multiple cards. After a proper analysis, the question raised by [2] *"How many identities should a user have?"* could also be answered.

Finally, future research also can explore how trust assumptions modify the flow of procedures in applications. First, emerging technologies can *change the* `Trusted Couple` *model* as described above. Second, phones can *enforce and control policies* in a more powerful way than a card (of much more limited resources) can. Third, a mobile phone, communicating with its environment, could decide about *in what mode it operates depending on its context* (*e.g.*, it behaves differently in a bank or at home than in the street). Using this feature, a phone can act adaptively when assisting ABC verification proofs. The latter two questions closely relate to contextual integrity and thus, they can contribute to even further improve privacy [17].

References

1. Alpár, G., Batina, L., Verdult, R.: Using NFC Phones for Proving Credentials. In: Schmitt, J.B. (ed.) MMB & DFT 2012. LNCS, vol. 7201, pp. 317–330. Springer, Heidelberg (2012)
2. Alpár, G., Hoepman, J.-H., Siljee, J.: The Identity Crisis. Security, Privacy and Usability Issues in Identity Management. Journal of Information System Security 8(3) (2013)
3. Alpár, G., Jacobs, B.: Credential Design in Attribute-Based Identity Management. In: Leenes, R. (ed.) TILTing Perspectives (2013)
4. Bhargav-Spantzel, A., Camenisch, J., Gross, T., Sommer, D.: User centricity: a taxonomy and open issues. Journal of Computer Security 15(5), 493–527 (2007)
5. Bichsel, P., Camenisch, J., De Decker, B., Lapon, J., Naessens, V., Sommer, D.: Data-minimizing authentication goes mobile. In: De Decker, B., Chadwick, D.W. (eds.) CMS 2012. LNCS, vol. 7394, pp. 55–71. Springer, Heidelberg (2012)
6. Brands, S.A.: Rethinking Public Key Infrastructures and Digital Certificates: Building in Privacy. MIT Press, Cambridge (2000)
7. Camenisch, J., Krontiris, I., Lehmann, A., Neven, G., Paquin, C., Rannenberg, K., Zwingelberg, H.: D2.1 Architecture for Attribute-based Credential Technologies. Technical report, ABC4Trust (2011)
8. Camenisch, J.L., Lysyanskaya, A.: An Efficient System for Non-transferable Anonymous Credentials with Optional Anonymity Revocation. In: Pfitzmann, B. (ed.) EUROCRYPT 2001. LNCS, vol. 2045, pp. 93–118. Springer, Heidelberg (2001)
9. Camenisch, J.L., Lysyanskaya, A.: A Signature Scheme with Efficient Protocols. In: Cimato, S., Galdi, C., Persiano, G. (eds.) SCN 2002. LNCS, vol. 2576, pp. 268–289. Springer, Heidelberg (2003)
10. Cameron, K.: Laws of identity (May 2005), http://www.identityblog.com/stories/2004/12/09/thelaws.html

11. Chaum, D.: Security without identification: transaction systems to make big brother obsolete. Communications of the ACM 28, 1030–1044 (1985)
12. Dhamija, R., Dusseault, L.: The seven flaws of identity management: Usability and security challenges. IEEE Security & Privacy 6(2), 24–29 (2008)
13. Jøsang, A., Zomai, M.A., Suriadi, S.: Usability and privacy in identity management architectures. In: Proceedings of the Fifth Australasian Symposium on ACSW Frontiers, vol. 68, pp. 143–152. Australian Computer Society, Inc. (2007)
14. Maler, E., Reed, D.: The Venn of Identity: Options and Issues in Federated Identity Management. IEEE Security & Privacy 6(2), 16–23 (2008)
15. Morgner, F., Oepen, D., Müller, W., Redlich, J.-P.: Mobile Smart Card Reader Using NFC-Enabled Smartphones. In: Schmidt, A.U., Russello, G., Krontiris, I., Lian, S. (eds.) MobiSec 2012. LNICST, vol. 107, pp. 24–37. Springer, Heidelberg (2012)
16. Mostowski, W., Vullers, P.: Efficient U-Prove implementation for anonymous credentials on smart cards. In: Rajarajan, M., Piper, F., Wang, H., Kesidis, G. (eds.) SecureComm 2011. LNICST, vol. 96, pp. 243–260. Springer, Heidelberg (2012)
17. Nissenbaum, H.: Privacy as Contextual Integrity. Washington Law Review 79(1), 119–158 (2004)
18. Pfitzmann, A., Borcea-Pfitzmann, K.: Lifelong privacy: Privacy and identity management for life. In: Bezzi, M., Duquenoy, P., Fischer-Hübner, S., Hansen, M., Zhang, G. (eds.) Privacy and Identity. IFIP AICT, vol. 320, pp. 1–17. Springer, Heidelberg (2010)
19. IBM Research Zürich Security Team. Specification of the Identity Mixer cryptographic library, version 2.3.4. Technical report, IBM Research, Zürich (February 2012)
20. Vullers, P., Alpár, G.: Efficient Selective Disclosure on Smart Cards Using Idemix. In: Fischer-Hübner, S., de Leeuw, E., Mitchell, C. (eds.) IDMAN 2013. IFIP AICT, vol. 396, pp. 53–67. Springer, Heidelberg (2013)
21. NFC World. Forecast, http://www.nfcworld.com/technology/forecast/ (last accessed: September 10, 2013)

Author Index

Printed in the United States
By Bookmasters